Emotional Alchemy

Emotional Alchemy

How the Mind Can Heal the Heart

TARA BENNETT-GOLEMAN

Foreword by the Dalai Lama

HARMONY BOOKS  NEW YORK

Published by Harmony Books,
New York, New York.
Member of the Crown Publishing Group.

Random House, Inc.
New York, Toronto, London, Sydney, Auckland
www.randomhouse.com

HARMONY BOOKS is a registered trademark and the
Harmony Books colophon is a trademark of Random House, Inc.

Printed in the United States of America

Design by Barbara Sturman

Library of·Congress Cataloging-in-Publication Data
Bennett-Goleman, Tara.
Emotional alchemy : how the mind can heal the heart /
by Tara Bennett-Goleman.—1st ed.
1. Meditation. 2. Emotions. 3. Buddhism—Psychology. I. Title.
BF637.M4B46   2001
158.1'2—dc21   00-044847

ISBN 0-609-60752-9

10 9 8 7 6 5 4 3 2 1

First Edition

For the light of wisdom
within everyone

Contents

IV

Spiritual Alchemy

Foreword
by the Dalai Lama

We all desire happiness and do not want suffering. Because the very purpose of life is to be happy, it is important to discover what will bring about the greatest degree of happiness. Whether our experience is pleasant or miserable, it is either mental or physical. Generally, it is the mind that exerts the greatest influence on most of us. Therefore, it is extremely worthwhile to try to bring about mental peace.

Although material progress is important for human advancement, if we pay too much attention to external things and give too little importance to inner development, the imbalance will lead to problems. Inner peace is the key: if we have inner peace we will be able to deal with situations with calmness and reason. Without inner peace, no matter how comfortable our life is materially, we may still be worried, disturbed, or unhappy because of the circumstances.

When we have inner peace, we can be at peace with those around us. When our community is in a state of peace, it can share that peace with neighboring communities and so on. When we feel love and kindness toward others, it not only makes others feel loved and cared for but also helps us to develop inner happiness and peace.

As a Buddhist I have learned that what principally upsets our inner peace is what we call disturbing emotions. All those thoughts, emotions, and mental events that reflect a negative or uncompassionate state of mind inevitably undermine our experience of inner peace. All such negative thoughts and emotions as hatred, anger, pride, lust, greed, envy, and so on have the effect of disturbing our inner equilibrium. They also have a taxing effect on our physical health. In the Tibetan medical system, mental and emotional disturbances have long been considered causes of many constitutional diseases, including cancer. Scientists and health professionals in the West increasingly share this point of view, too.

Disturbing emotions are the very source of unethical conduct. They are also the basis of anxiety, depression, confusion, and stress, which are such a feature of our lives today. And yet, because we so often fail to recognize their destructive potential, we do not see the need to challenge them.

In this book, *Emotional Alchemy*, Tara Bennett-Goleman offers a method to calm the mind and free it from disturbing emotions: a practical application of mindfulness in the realm of emotion. Based on personal experience she has drawn together insights and methods from cognitive and brain science, from psychotherapy, and from Buddhist psychology and mindfulness practice. She shows people how they can use mindfulness to loosen the hold of mental and emotional habits that prevent them from being happy.

A great Tibetan teacher of mind training once remarked that one of the mind's most marvelous qualities is that it can be transformed. I offer my prayers that readers of this book who put the advice it contains into practice may indeed be able to transform their minds, overcome their disturbing emotions, and achieve a sense of inner peace. Not only will they then be happier in themselves, but they will undoubtedly contribute to greater peace and happiness in the world at large.

June 3, 2000

I

Emotional Alchemy

1

An Inner Alchemy

From the window of my London hotel room Big Ben displays itself, a prominent, elegant presence amid the vista of river, billowing clouds, and spreading jumble of skyline. Big Ben has a grandeur as a piece of architecture, but I find my eye drawn more to the broad, open expanse of sky and river. ● The panorama above and below Big Ben's rounded bluntness includes a resplendence of steeples and bridges that occupy the central view from my window. I notice how my mind, at first glance, takes in the spaciousness of the cloud-filled sky and the soothing expanse of the river below like a regal oil painting by some turn-of-the-century landscape artist, or like a postcard-perfect snapshot. ● But as I gaze more carefully, with a sustained attention, I notice that the still snapshot-like rendering of this scene dissolves into a whirl of constant motion, a continuing series of tiny movements that add up to a vastly altered picture. There are tiny successive changes in the shape of clouds as they glide across the sky, sometimes opening up patches of sky through which rays of sunlight spill along the landscape, illuminating shadows into patches of light. There's the translucent shine of buildings and roads and bright red buses as they momentarily bathe in the glow. The scene before me shimmers with kinetic energy. ● And so it is with our inner landscapes. This shift in my perception mirrors how the mind works: the tendency to assume it has got the whole picture on first glance, to rush on without a closer look, and the sometimes startling fact that if one continues to look more carefully, there is always more to be discovered beyond those initial assumptions. Too often we take our first impressions, the conclusions from a first hasty glance, as the lasting truth of the moment. ● But if we keep looking and noticing, we become aware of greater detail and nuance, of changes and second thoughts, and much more. We can see things more as they actually are, rather than as they appear to be. We can bring a more precise understanding to the moment.

If we sustain our gaze within, sometimes our probe may detect pain behind the masks we wear. But if we continue to look, we can see how the patterns of pain hold that very mask in place, and as we investigate further we see even these patterns shift and rearrange themselves. We see how our reactions to our emotions can keep us at a distance from ourselves. And if we sustain our focus, allowing ourselves to open more honestly, our awareness penetrates further, unraveling and dissolving, peeling away the layers as we look still further. We begin to connect with more genuine parts of ourselves, at first in glimpses. Then, as we sustain our gaze, we connect with a source that breathes awareness into every layer of our being.

This book is about seeing ourselves as we genuinely are, not as we seem on first glance as viewed through the filters of our habitual assumptions and emotional patterns. We will explore how through the practice of mindfulness—a method for training the mind to expand the scope of awareness while refining its precision—we can reach beyond the limiting ways we see ourselves. We will see how to disengage from the emotional habits that undermine our lives and our relationships. We will discover how a precise mindfulness can investigate these emotional habits, bringing an insightful clarity to distinguish between the seeming and the actual.

The Power of Mindfulness ● I've seen the power of this distinction in the lives of my clients. One client found herself obsessed by self-recrimination for not having done something well enough. Though highly successful in her career, she was her biggest critic. She told me, for example, "Last week I had to give a very important presentation—lots of people were going to be there whose opinions really matter to me. So I prepared more than usual and thought I had done a pretty good job. Afterward, several people complimented me. But one person said, 'You did a terrific job. It could have been a little shorter, though.' That was it. For the last several days that's all I can think about—how I went on too long. I wake up in the middle of the night worrying about it."

This was no isolated event. The feeling that she never did things quite well enough haunted her—in her work, in her marriage, in caring for her children, even in her cooking. It was a constant preoccupation, one that marred her closest relationships and made the smallest challenge an occasion for self-doubt or self-criticism.

A more systematic investigation led her to realize that at the root of this preoccupation was a hidden emotional pattern, the deep conviction that no matter how well she did something, it would never be quite up to her own impossibly high standards. This mistaken conviction distorted her perceptions, so she overlooked the evidence of how well she actually did accomplish things. And it led her to drive herself far too hard, so that she cheated herself of time for life's meaningful pleasures. Mindfulness helps us to identify such hidden emotional patterns, bringing them into the light of awareness so that we can begin to free ourselves from their hold.

One couple had fights that threatened their relationship. A mutual mindful awareness allowed them to detect the hidden patterns that caused them to have essentially the same argument over and over. Whenever she started to feel insecure about his affection for her, she would become needy. He would feel that she was controlling him and withdraw in anger. The result: a stormy fight. By looking closely at what had happened after they both calmed down, they were able to see how his angry withdrawal and her anxious clinging were both emotional reactions to an underlying symbolic reality.

Their constant battles, on closer investigation, had little to do with the situation at hand, and much to do with the symbolic meanings of what had happened: his fear of being controlled and her oversensitivity to signs of rejection because of a deep feeling that she was being emotionally deprived. Learning to identify these habitual emotional reactions as they began to take hold allowed the couple to avoid fights and to communicate more skillfully.

A dedicated meditator who had tried to relieve the distress of her lifelong feelings of disconnection by going on long retreats found herself obsessing even more about these very feelings while meditating at a retreat center. As she put it, "Your madness follows you on your spiritual path." But learning how to see these seemingly formidable emotional reactions as transparent and temporary allowed her to use them as fuel for her practice, deepening her compassion for herself as well as for others.

This transformation begins with refocusing the lenses of our conditioning to see things more clearly, as they actually are. You might wonder, Who am I, if I am not my usual pattern of assumptions and self-definitions? This question can be asked from both a psychological and a spiritual perspective—a process of inner discovery that I hope this book will inspire.

The Metaphor of Alchemy ● "Each thing has to transform itself into something better, and acquire a new destiny," Paulo Coelho writes in his novel *The Alchemist*. Coelho describes the world as only the visible aspect of God, with invisible spiritual forces at play that remain largely unknown to us. Alchemy occurs when the spiritual plane comes into contact with the material plane.

I was given Coelho's book by a client, who told me, "This reminds me of our work together." Indeed, alchemy offers an apt metaphor for the process I will be describing.

Alchemists, the tales go, sought to use a magical philosopher's stone to transmute lead into gold. But lead and gold, in the more philosophical school of alchemy, were metaphors for internal states: the alchemist's discipline was one of psychological and spiritual transformation. Alchemists realized that the mystery they sought to solve was not outside but in the psyche.

Some alchemical schools liken our ordinary state of mind to a lump of coal and compare clear awareness to a diamond. There would seem to be no greater contrast in the material world than that between coal and a diamond, and yet the two are but different arrangements of the identical molecules of carbon. Just as a diamond is coal transformed, so clear awareness can arise from our confusion.

What intrigues me about the metaphor of alchemy is not the gold—some grandiose goal—but rather the importance it places on the *process* of transformation. One client, an acupuncturist who has studied Chinese medicine, told me that the word "alchemy," better than any other word, describes the process of integrating mindfulness with emotional work: "Alchemy is accepting everything in the pot without trying to reject or correct it—seeing that even the negative is part of the learning and healing."

Mindfulness means seeing things as they are, without trying to change them. The point is to dissolve our *reactions* to disturbing emotions, being careful not to reject the emotion itself. Mindfulness can change how we relate to, and perceive, our emotional states; it doesn't necessarily eliminate them.

The warmth of sunlight dissolving the moisture of clouds—nature's alchemy—echoes the warm fire of mindfulness melting the emotional clouds covering our inner nature. The effects of such periods of insightful clarity may be fleeting and momentary, lasting only until the next emotional cloud forms. But rekindling this awareness again and again—bringing it to bear on these inner clouds, letting it penetrate and dissolve the haze in our minds—is the heart of practice, a practice we can learn to sustain.

I believe that, given the right awareness tools, we all have the potential to be inner alchemists, with the natural ability to turn our moments of confusion into insightful clarity. Gradually, as we practice doing this with our troubling feelings, we can gain an understanding of their causes.

For the most part these insights are psychological, especially at first. But if we continue this process we can gain insights into the workings of the mind itself that can be spiritually liberating. It's as though there are two levels of reality in our lives: one dominated by these deeply ingrained emotional patterns and another that is free from conditioned patterns. Mindfulness gives us breathing space from this conditioning.

Emotional alchemy allows for the possibility that our bewilderment and turmoil might blossom into insightful clarity. "In almost every bad situation," says Nyanaponika Thera, a Buddhist monk, "there is the possibility of a transformation by which the undesirable may be changed into the desirable."

There is a simple but ingenious judo in this emotional alchemy: to embrace all experiences as part of a transformative path by making them the focus of mindfulness. Instead of seeing disturbance and turmoil as a distraction realize that they too can become the target of a keen attention. "In that way," Nyanaponika notes, "enemies are turned into friends, because all these disturbances and antagonistic forces have become our teachers."

Refining Awareness ● Physics tells us what happens when moisture builds up and clouds develop into a density so thick that, at first, the light of the sun can't penetrate them to evaporate the moisture. Initially the light literally bounces off the droplets of water, each a little spherical mirror, scattering the light in all directions. But as the sun's steady presence warms the water droplets that make up the cloud, the moisture slowly starts to evaporate. Eventually the clouds dissipate.

This parallels emotional alchemy—a transformation from a confusing, dense emotional state to clarity and lightness of being. Mindfulness, a refined awareness, is the fire in this inner alchemy. Again, this doesn't mean that the mental fog will lift every time we become mindful of it. But what *can* shift is how we perceive and relate to the various mental states that we encounter.

Mindfulness is a meditative awareness that cultivates the capacity to see things just as they are from moment to moment. Ordinarily our attention swings rather wildly, carried here and there by random thoughts, fleeting memories, captivating fantasies, snatches of things seen, heard, or otherwise perceived. By contrast, mindfulness is a distraction-resistant, sustained attention to the movements of the mind itself. Instead of being swept away and captured by a thought or feeling, mindfulness steadily observes those thoughts and feelings as they come and go.

Essentially, mindfulness entails a new way of paying attention, a way to expand the scope of awareness while refining its precision. In this training of the mind we learn to let go of the thoughts and feelings that pull us out of the present moment, and to steady our awareness on our immediate experience. If distractedness breeds emotional turmoil, the ability to sustain our gaze, to keep looking, can bring greater clarity and insight.

Mindfulness has its roots in an ancient system of Buddhist psychology, little known in the West, that even today offers a sophisticated understanding of the painful emotions that sabotage our happiness. This psychology offers a scientific approach to inner work, a theory of mind that anyone, Buddhist or not, can draw insights and benefit from. When we apply this approach, the emphasis is not so much on the problems in our lives as on connecting with the clarity and health of mind itself. If we can do this, our problems become more workable, opportunities to learn rather than threats to avoid.

Buddhist psychology holds a refreshingly positive view of human nature: our emotional problems are seen as temporary and superficial. The emphasis is on what is *right* with us, an antidote to the fixation of Western psychology on what's wrong with us. Buddhist psychology acknowledges our disturbing emotions but sees them as covering our essential goodness like clouds covering the sun. In this sense, our darker moments and most upsetting feelings are an opportunity for uncovering our natural wisdom, if we choose to use them that way.

Mindful attention allows us to delve deeper into the moment, to perceive finer subtlety, than does ordinary attention. In this sense, mindfulness creates a "wise" attention, a space of clarity that emerges when we quiet the mind. It makes us more receptive to the whispers of our innate intuitive wisdom.

The Emotional Alchemy Synthesis ● Through my own inner work, as well as in my work as a psychotherapist and workshop leader, I have found that combining a mindful awareness with psychological investigation forges a powerful means to penetrate dense emotions. This meditative awareness, I've found, can bring us a remarkably subtle understanding of our emotional patterns and so help us find ways to unravel deep fixations and destructive habits.

This synthesis draws from many sources: from Buddhist psychology and the tradition of mindfulness meditation, from Tibetan Buddhism, from cognitive science and cognitive therapy, and from neuroscience. Key among the scientific discoveries behind emotional alchemy: that mindfulness shifts the brain from disturbing to positive emotions, and that the brain stays plastic throughout life, changing itself as we learn to challenge old habits. Neuroscience also reveals that we have a crucial choice point—a magic quartersecond—during which we can reject a self-defeating emotional impulse. I put all these findings to practical use.

In this work, I've found two methods to be especially potent for detecting and transforming emotional patterns: mindfulness meditation and a recent adaptation of cognitive therapy, called schema therapy, which focuses on repairing maladaptive emotional habits. Both of these methods—one ancient and one modern—bring awareness to destructive emotional habits, and that is the first step toward healing them.

Becoming aware of these emotional habits is the first step, because unless we can catch and challenge them as they are triggered by the events of our lives, they will dictate how we perceive and react. And the more they take us over, the more they'll keep coming back, complicating our relationships, our work, and the most basic ways in which we see ourselves.

Early in my work as a psychotherapist I trained with Dr. Jeffrey Young, the founder of the Cognitive Therapy Center of New York. He was then developing schema therapy, which focuses on healing maladaptive patterns, or schemas, like the sense of emotional deprivation, or relentless perfectionism. In working with my own therapy clients, I began to combine mindfulness with schema therapy, as they seemed to work together so naturally and powerfully.

Schema therapy gives us a clear map of destructive habits. It details the emotional contours of, say, the fear of abandonment, with its constant apprehension that a partner will leave us; or of feelings of vulnerability, such as the irrational fear that a minor setback at work means you will end up jobless and homeless.

There are ten such major schemas (and countless variations); most of us have one or two principal ones, though many of us have several others to some extent. Other common schemas include unlovability, the fear that people would reject us if they truly knew us; mistrust, the constant suspicion that those close to us will betray us; social exclusion, the feeling we don't belong; failure, the sense that we cannot succeed at what we do; subjugation, always giving in to other people's wants and demands;

and entitlement, the sense that one is somehow special, and so beyond ordinary rules and limits.

A first application of mindfulness is learning to recognize one or more of these patterns in ourselves—it's helpful simply to recognize how these patterns operate in our lives. And the very act of being mindful loosens their hold on us. Then the way is open for us to use the tools of schema therapy to further unravel these destructive fixations.

Mindfulness Applied ● Let me give an example of how mindfulness works as the catalyst in emotional alchemy. Early on in my practice one client, whom I'll call Maya (all client names herein have been changed), came to me for help in her battle with chronic ulcerative colitis. As a part of her therapy I introduced Maya to mindfulness, which she had already been interested in and now began to practice regularly. I had been practicing mindfulness myself since 1974, and using it in work with the dying. I had participated in an intensive hospital-based training program at the University of Massachusetts Medical School with Jon Kabat-Zinn, who developed an inspiring application of mindfulness to help patients heal stress-related symptoms.

My work with Maya extended beyond her health concerns to the arena of deeper emotional issues. As she observed her reactions with mindfulness, she started to notice that her attacks were associated with a particular emotional pattern: a relentless perfectionism, the sense that nothing she did was ever quite good enough—it had to be perfect. We then expanded the scope of our work together to include being mindful of these patterns. After several months the colitis symptoms faded.

By then Maya had cultivated the habit of being mindful during distressing moments throughout her day. One of the ways she applied mindfulness was in her struggle with overeating; her binges on rich foods did little to help her colitis. So Maya decided to use her very desire to eat as the focus of her mindfulness. Every time she felt an urge to munch, she restrained herself and instead became mindfully aware of all the sensations, thoughts, and feelings in her mind and body. She closely observed the discomfort in her body that accompanied the strong desire to satisfy her craving for food.

A habit like overeating can veil underlying emotional issues. One day as Maya was mindfully investigating this desire, she suddenly saw how, at its height, her craving for food was actually masking her need for emotional nurturance. As her mindful investigation of this craving became more precise, she realized the feelings actually were not about food at all but stemmed from an underlying longing to fill an emotional void within. Her sense of *emotional* deprivation—that she would never get enough love or caring—was a major issue for her. And it was driving her to crave food.

That insight alone was powerful. But Maya sustained her efforts. As she carefully experienced those thoughts and feelings—observing them without identifying with them or judging herself—she watched them fade and eventually dissolve. As these impulses faded, her desire to eat eventually faded, too. And as she went on to practice this consistently, whenever she felt an urge to overeat, she discovered a new strength in herself as her awareness became stronger than her craving. That freed her to find healthier ways to receive the nurturance she was truly craving.

The deep belief underlying Maya's problem was that she would never get enough caring or nurturance, that she would always be emotionally deprived. Such self-defeating beliefs about ourselves and the world are highly charged; whenever something triggers them our feelings flare and our perceptions become distorted. They trigger emotional overreactions such as out-of-control anger, intense self-criticism, emotional distancing, or, in Maya's case, bingeing. Such deep-seated patterns of thought, feeling, and habit are maladaptive schemas; I'll describe them in greater detail in Chapters 4 and 5. These emotional habits operate as powerful lenses on our reality, leading us to mistake how things seem for how they actually are.

The Path to Transforming Emotions ● When I suggested that Maya use a mindful awareness in dealing with colitis symptoms and compulsive eating, I was extending mindfulness beyond its traditional uses as a meditation on our usual experiences, into intentionally exploring the realm of emotional issues and maladaptive patterns. This and similar cases marked a turning point for me in my own therapy work: it illumined the power of mindfulness to help clients see the otherwise invisible emotional patterns at the root of their suffering.

It became clear to me that adding mindfulness to psychotherapy could greatly enhance its effectiveness. I was struck by how much the therapy process was accelerated when a client practiced mindfulness. Through working with my clients, I have found that combining a mindful awareness with psychological investigation forges a powerful tool for cultivating emotional wisdom on a practical, day-to-day level.

Much time in psychotherapy typically entails bringing the detailed anatomy of emotional habits into the light of awareness so they can be investigated, reflected on, and changed. But mindfulness can make *any* system of psychotherapy more precise and attuned, letting us bring our own wisdom to the psychological unfolding. Instead of seeing the therapy or even the therapist as the cure, we can shift our focus to the healing qualities of our own inner wisdom. This wake-up call need not be set apart from our lives; it needn't be something we do only in isolated hours in a therapist's office. It can be part of life moment-to-moment with the application of mindfulness.

Mindfulness is synergistic with virtually any psychotherapy approach, not just schema therapy. If you are in psychotherapy, mindfulness offers a way to cultivate a capacity for self-observation that you can bring to whatever confronts you during the day. Combining mindfulness with psychotherapy may help you use more fully the opportunity for inner exploration that your therapy offers.

Of course, you don't need to be in psychotherapy to apply mindfulness to your patterns of emotional reactivity. This approach is also an education in applying mindfulness with emotions, work I have taught for more than a decade to people in workshops. I've found that by practicing these methods people develop the capacity to be more aware, sensitive, and skillful in handling the emotional reactions that trouble them.

This book reflects the many dimensions and applications of mindfulness. Some readers may find inspiration in a shift of perspective, and so be drawn to seeing things in new ways. Others may be intrigued by the emerging integration of cognitive science and neuroscience with ancient principles of Buddhist psychology. Some people may be engaged by the psychological investigation of habitual emotional patterns, and with the work of changing these habits. Still others may be drawn to exploring the many applications of mindfulness, or the spiritual aspect of working with emotions.

We will explore a path that touches on each of these dimensions, a path that offers a gradual freedom from the hold of what Buddhism calls "afflictive" emotions. When it comes to the turbulent feelings that roil within us, it's not that we are able to wrap up our bewildering emotions in neat formulaic explanations but that we can use an ongoing inquiry to reach small epiphanies, insights that grow one on the other toward a greater clarity.

In a sense, our darker moments and most upsetting feelings are an opportunity for spiritual growth and uncovering our natural wisdom, for waking up—if we choose to use them that way. If so, our deepest insights can emerge from working directly—with awareness—with our own difficulties.

A strong emotional obsession or pattern is like the scene in *The Wizard of Oz* where Dorothy and her companions finally get to Oz. The Wizard is this powerful, looming presence that terrifies them—until the little dog Toto calmly goes over and pulls back the curtain to reveal an old man stooped over the controls, manipulating a huge Wizard image. Emotional fixations are like that—if you see them clearly, unflinchingly, for what they really are, you take the power away from them. They no longer control you.

Confusion dawns as clarity.

If You Want to Try a Moment of Mindfulness

Take a few moments right now to gather your attention by simply being fully present with your breath as it enters and leaves your body.

Notice the slight movements of your body with each breath. Pay attention to the rising and falling of your chest or abdomen as you breathe in and out.

Keep your attention there for several breaths, being aware of your breathing in a calm and effortless way, allowing its rhythms to unfold naturally, staying present with your awareness.

An Inner Alchemy

Should you work on your own or with a therapist? ● I've written this book so people can, for the most part, do this work on their own. But there is the possibility that this inner work may stir up emotions that are too overwhelming to face without some support. This does not happen for everyone, of course, but if you find yourself preoccupied with strong feelings that you can't drop, and if they keep you from doing what you need to do in the course of your day—in other words, if you find this work too disturbing—then either stop or find a psychotherapist to work with. ● And, of course, if you have serious psychological problems, you should work with a psychologist or psychiatrist on those problems before you attempt this emotional alchemy. This process—like this book—is in part an education about yourself, in part an approach to therapy. It works best for people who are functioning in their lives but who suffer from some self-defeating emotional habits. ● In general, because this inner work can be emotionally intense, I recommend that those of you who want to go through this emotional alchemy find a supportive person to talk about it with, someone you feel rapport with and whom you trust. It may be a trusted friend. As we'll see in Chapter 13, you can do schema work with a willing partner. Or a supportive group of people whom you feel connected with can be helpful, if that appeals to you. ● In any case, you may want to work with a psychotherapist. Psychotherapists whose training has been in any number of approaches may be well suited for giving you such guidance, if you feel that you have a good working relationship with them—that they understand you and can help you. If you are looking for a psychotherapist who has been specifically trained in schema therapy and who is particularly well qualified for this kind of inner work, see the Guide to Resources at the back of the book for more information. If you go that route, it may be up to you to bring mindfulness into the therapy process. ● If you do choose to work with a therapist, remember that the crucial learning is your own. Rather than seeing the therapist, or even therapy, as the source of the cure, I encourage people to trust more in their own insights, even if that insightful clarity is dimmed at first. We all have this ability to understand; we just need to cultivate it. Practicing mindfulness strengthens this capacity.

2

A Wise Compassion

The week before my grandmother died, I took a bouquet of lilies to her in the hospital. She was developing pneumonia, however, and her labored breath made it clear that the scent of the lilies was too strong for her. So I took them home and put them in a special place next to her picture. ● I'm familiar with the life cycle of lilies, since they're my favorite flower. These lilies surprised me, lasting much, much longer than usual. In a sense, it was as though I still had something of my grandmother's life with me—taking care of her flowers, which lived on even after her life had come to an end. ● The lilies had a place of honor in the sunroom, where I ate breakfast each morning. As each petal was transformed from soft pink into sienna, folding in its edges as its life came to a close, I watched the bouquet dwindle down to just the decorative greens, which also lasted several weeks beyond their typical life span. Two stems with shiny green leaves were still standing alert after five weeks. ● One morning when I came downstairs I looked for the last brave remnants of my grandmother's bouquet—and the vase was empty! A houseguest who didn't know about my quiet ritual had, understandably, thrown out the last two stems of greens as she was tidying up. ● I made breakfast as I absorbed the shock. "They're gone now. It's time to let go," a grown-up voice inside me soberly instructed me—as I almost poured coffee into my eggs. ● "I want my grandmother's flowers back!" a less grown-up inner voice protested. I was not ready for the vase to be empty, just as I wasn't prepared for my grandmother to be gone, even though she was ninety-one. ● "We were supposed to have more time together," the voice complained. I hadn't expected my grandmother to be absent from my life with such suddenness. I knew I should accept the loss, but something in me just couldn't. ● I could feel the inner tug-of-war between the rational voice that advised acceptance and the emotional voice that fought against it—the rational adult voice of reason telling me to let go now, and the voice of the vulnerable granddaughter who needed to adjust to this profound loss through her quiet ritual of decaying flowers.

As I quietly reflected on these abrupt losses, I felt a sense of compassion for my own denial. When someone we love is taken away from us so quickly, the shock seems too much to bear all at once. Too often we let our impatient, judgmental grown-up inner voices browbeat us about how we're *supposed* to feel. The vulnerable child inside understands that she will eventually have to adjust—but she needs more time.

As I watched each flower petal gradually wither as its life came to a close, I was reminded of the natural life cycle of a flower, of a human life, of my grandmother. Observing this process gave me time to adjust emotionally to this sudden and profound loss. There grew an understanding of things as they are naturally—the truth of impermanence symbolized by the absent flowers.

Grieving for the loss of a grandmother, of course, is a natural and healthy process. But with patterns of feeling that may be less healthy, we need to be just as compassionate with ourselves. As we enter the territory of our most difficult emotional habits, we need to bring to bear a tender empathy for ourselves as we let go of these old familiar ways of being. Before we can turn to a more rational view, we need to empathize with our emotional needs—before we can change, we need to accept and be loving to ourselves.

The Unfolding of Compassion ● As we unravel the webs of meaning woven into our emotional habits, a sense of compassion for ourselves can naturally emerge, along with the insights this work reveals. In one of my workshops, for instance, we had been discussing schemas, the life events that gave rise to them, and the intense feelings like anger or sadness connected with these patterns. And then we meditated on these feelings, not thinking about the feelings so much as allowing a mindful presence to listen, receptive to any insights or messages that are ready to come into awareness.

Afterward, a woman reported her insight into a lifelong pattern. "Whenever I feel depressed or just sad, I get this strong fear that I might die," she said. "I've had these feelings ever since I can remember, and it's always puzzled me. It's not as if I want my life to end. During the meditation, those feelings came to mind—the fear mingled with the sadness. As I sat with these feelings, I suddenly had a clarifying memory: being a toddler in my crib, crying and crying, with no one responding, sobbing so much I started to choke, and still no one came. I was terrified that I would die, and deeply sad about being left all alone."

Then, after a reflective pause, she continued: "I remember my mother telling me years ago that when I was little, she raised me according to a parenting manual that was popular in those days. It told her to feed me only every four hours, on a strict schedule, and not to console me no matter how much I cried—doing so would spoil me, ruin my character. I see now where this connection I've had between sadness and a fear of dying came from, and I know that I'm not going to die of sadness."

For this woman, unraveling the hidden meanings behind these recurring feelings of sadness and fear unleashed a strong empathy for herself. The qualities of insight and compassion illuminate the truth, as they melt inner barriers, letting us connect more genuinely with ourselves.

This empathy can also be extremely helpful when we are relating to such vulnerability in others. Even if we don't rationally agree with someone's emotional reactions, we can have compassionate thoughts such as "He seems to be overreacting, but given what I know about his past, I can understand how he might see things as threatening."

This stance does not condone how the person may be reacting. But seeing others through the lens of compassion like this gives us more information, letting us make sense of what would otherwise be perplexing reactions, and enables us to be more spacious in our own response. Compassion can make our difficulties feel more workable.

Wisdom and Compassion ● On this path wisdom and compassion work together; the insight of seeing things truly needs to be balanced with a compassionate acceptance of the way things are. My teacher Tulku Urgyen Rinpoche described it as the two wings of a bird: without either one of the wings, the bird is unable to fly.

As we engage in this emotional work we may start to see many things about ourselves and others with a new honesty as truths are laid bare. Here a compassionate attitude—the wish to be of help not just to ourselves but to others as well—becomes essential. Without that attitude, we may see those truths more harshly.

I remember returning from a few months of intensive meditation practice many years ago. The momentum of practice had become so strong that after I got home, everything but meditation seemed like a distraction. I felt I was seeing things about myself and other people very clearly, especially the ways we perpetuate our own suffering, driven by habitual impulses and patterns but oblivious to their root causes. I found it very disturbing, especially the ways all this happened with so little awareness.

Then, after some time, I realized there was a missing element: compassion. Once I realized this, I felt a deep wish to understand more clearly—and compassionately—these habitual cycles of conditioning that contribute to our suffering. The inner work, both spiritual and psychological, I undertook with that resolve eventually led to this book.

The important learning for me at that point was seeing so clearly the crucial role of compassion in this work, whether it be at the level of understanding psychological patterns that motivate us, or the wish that everyone be free from suffering.

Embodied Compassion ● I was sitting in a taxi on a bustling

street in New Delhi, waiting at what seemed an interminable stoplight. A beggar was taking the opportunity to make his alms rounds among the waiting cars. He was missing one arm and one leg, but somehow managed to glide gracefully from car to car.

There was something unusual about this beggar: he seemed to give something of himself as he approached each car. That something could not be measured by material standards; on that level he had only rags. It was something greater: a spirit of lightness and resilience. He didn't seem at all bothered by his physical condition. Nor did he seem to hold the slightest grudge against the people in cars who gave him nothing—he seemed to nod in understanding and gracefully hop to the next car.

As he reached my taxi I pulled out of my bag what turned out to be a large rupee note and handed it to him, smiling. In India, beggars are usually given just a few paisa, the almost worthless Indian coins, if anything.

He glided to the side of the road, seemingly to reflect on his good fortune. In the moments before the light turned green, he looked at me with an engaging warmth in his eyes and a smile so radiant it melted my heart.

That special quality in this beggar, I realized, was his compassionate presence and the gift of his spirit, which he freely gave to those he encountered—whether they gave back to him or not.

The quality of this man's being was the gift he offered. When we are free of self-concern or self-pity, free of inner preoccupations, compassion emerges as a spontaneous expression of our awareness. I've read that the Dalai Lama's first thought as he awakens each morning is a prayer of love and compassion. He dedicates all the coming actions of the day to the benefit of all living beings.

Forming this intention in the mind—to benefit other living beings—is a habit that can be cultivated as a practice. With persistence, it can become a habit so strong that it infuses our mind-stream as an automatic way of relating to others.

Watching the Dalai Lama interact with people offers proof of this possibility: he seems to have a knack for connecting with people in exactly the way they need in that moment. And he connects with everyone, without being bound by the arbitrary social conventions—time and again I've seen him notice the people in a situation who are so often overlooked: guards at the stage door of a theater, handicapped people in wheelchairs hidden in the crowd.

He seems to have a compassionate radar for people who are struggling in some way, reaching out to them in a crowd in the passing moments while he walks through a throng. He offers a living example of embodied compassion—something possible for each of us.

As the Dalai Lama often teaches, the ability to embody compassion can be developed through practices designed for that purpose. In one tradition of mindfulness meditation, each session ends with a short practice of *metta,* the word in the Pali language for loving-kindness. This prayer expresses the same compassionate wish for oneself, for one's loved ones, for people one has difficulties with, and finally for everyone.

That compassion should radiate in all directions, including toward oneself, is an idea that has gotten lost in the West, where we tend to think of compassion only as aimed toward others. The Dalai Lama emphasizes that the concept of compassion in Tibetan Buddhism explicitly includes oneself as well as others—a notion captured by the bodhisattva wish: "May I be liberated for the benefit of all beings."

That is a key point, one we will return to as we explore the path of emotional alchemy.

Equanimity ● While emotional alchemy involves empathy with our distorted thoughts, this is not the same as colluding with those skewed ways of seeing, nor does it mean believing in these irrational ways of thinking about ourselves or other people. It means understanding how we perceive and how our perceptions are colored and swayed by hidden meanings.

Equanimity is a profound quality of mindfulness that cultivates the ability to let go. With equanimity, we can acknowledge that things are as they are, even though we may wish otherwise. It allows us to accept things that we have no control over, and it allows us to have the courageousness of heart to stay open in the face of adversity. Equanimity can be used as a practice in itself, to help bring a mental ease to turbulent emotions like anxiety, worry and fear, frustration and anger.

Of course, equanimity does not imply indifference or that we should simply accept everything as it is—injustice, unfairness, and suffering all call for action to make what changes we can. But even as we do so, an inner state of equanimity will make us more effective. And when it comes to those problems in life over which we have no control—and to our emotional reactions—equanimity offers a great inner resource: a sense of nonreactivity, of patience and acceptance.

Courageousness of Heart ● My mother once told me about an

experience she had many years ago on the streets of New York City. She was walking alone at night, having left her purse and money at home, when a disheveled young man approached her. My mother, being naturally warm-hearted, immediately felt sorry for him.

As she expected, he asked her for money. As he was asking, she noticed, out of the corner of her eye, a bulge in his pocket pointing toward her—what might have been a weapon.

It was a potentially dangerous moment, but she remained in touch with her compassionate urge, responding with a heartfelt, "I'm so sorry—I wish I could help you, but I didn't bring any money with me."

The young man was clearly taken aback, disarmed by her unexpectedly caring response. Backing away, he said, "That's okay, lady," and walked on.

Of course, incidents like this can easily turn nasty; a wise option might have been to try to get away from such a risky situation, and I certainly feel relieved that no harm came to my mother. But many years later I still find myself reflecting on what might have been so disarming for that man on the street.

I wonder if my mother's genuine compassion could have played the crucial role. In Buddhist psychology, compassion is seen as a direct antidote to aggression. Or perhaps it was her equanimity as she calmly faced the potentially threatening situation.

I'll never know for sure, but one possible explanation might have to do with research showing that when the part of the brain that generates positive emotions becomes more active, the centers for disturbing emotions quiet down. Emotions are contagious: I wonder if my mother's genuine compassion might have played a role in shifting the man's brain response.

Similarly, a few years ago I was at a conference on peacemaking with the Dalai Lama and some social activists, including young people from the inner city. Some very practical concerns were raised by the teenagers: What can I do to get home safely from school? How can I be more confident in risky situations so I can deal better with tough kids?

Inspired by their discussions with the Dalai Lama about using meditation and compassion to deal with these issues, many of the youths came to see that tempering their own emotional reactions gave them a way to feel less helpless. And that actually might help them deal with tough situations more skillfully and with more equanimity.

Making Friends with Ourselves ● Equanimity and compassion are invaluable inner resources as we unravel the conditioning of our deep patterns, or grapple with our reactions as we confront challenging life situations.

If we don't move beyond our personal identification with our emotional pain or confusion, we can miss another opportunity. We need to be open to deeper insights that might redefine our limited sense of ourselves, or of others. If we get too caught up in grappling with our emotions, we might miss the chance to turn toward essential qualities within. We might miss significant messages from the very pain we have been resisting. Or we might begin to identify too much with our patterns rather than releasing them. Release would allow us to free up energy that had been trapped, letting us be more creative, more present, more available—or of greater service—to others.

Glimpses of these changes and openings along the way let us keep in mind what's possible. These glimpses can give us courage or inspiration to continue along the path of this inner work.

It takes great courage to face this unknown territory of our emotional habits, and sometimes we may lose heart, wanting to avoid facing painful truths or troubling feelings. It's only human to let our distractions shield us. Turning to compassion and equanimity can be a refuge at every stage of this work.

When people go on meditation retreats where they practice intensively, the first few days or hours are often a time of discomfort. We feel physically uncomfortable, we miss our habitual comforts and routines, and we start to quiet down enough to tune in to emotional struggles that have long gone unnoticed but that suddenly are there, on retreat, waiting to greet us. Then, depending on the practice we have come to do, we may try to escape or cover up the pain by practicing a soothing meditation.

But with the practice of mindfulness, everything becomes the focus of our meditation—including the pain, the discomfort, even the emotions that we would rather have left behind in some closet of the mind. And we find that not only are those emotions here, waiting for us, but other triggers lurk nearby as well, poised to set us off afresh. We did not leave the inner strife at home; we brought it right along with us—in our minds.

We don't need to go on a meditation retreat to do this work, but the experience of watching our minds on retreat does encapsulate what can happen when we observe our minds closely.

In an intensive mindfulness retreat there is a familiar progression. As we bring mindfulness to bear, we get to a point where we've observed our mind long enough to become more aware of its repetitive cycles, playing the same tapes over and over, in endless variations. We begin to recognize patterns as we learn what is actually going on. Sometimes we will gain psychological insight into the underlying causes, or into some other aspect, of these story lines. But as time goes on, there's typically a shift of focus from the story, from the specifics of the mind's contents, to the process of the mind's workings.

After a while, we start to relate to these emotional struggles as a part of settling into mindfulness practice, as we make friends with ourselves in a deeper way through bringing precise awareness to our experiences. As mindfulness deepens and we make more space within ourselves for all of our feelings, discomforts, and reactions, our relationship to them shifts. We bring more acceptance and openness to this inner turmoil.

As we practice staying with the course of a feeling until it comes to its natural end, but in doing so with the equanimity of mindfulness, we begin to see more clearly the arising and passing of the endless stream of thoughts and feelings that course through our mind and body. We become less compelled to act *on* those reactions or to react *to* our reactions; we just let them come and go. And with this loosening of our usual identifications, we become less defined by our reactions as we widen the scope of who we think we are. We can begin to rest more and more in our awareness, rather than being swept away by our experiences.

As we move on to the specifics of dealing with our disturbing emotional patterns, it's useful to keep this overview of the transformative path in mind as a larger perspective on this work.

If You Want to Cultivate
Equanimity and Compassion

Begin with the practice of loving-kindness combined with a reflection on equanimity.

There are two approaches, both involving short reflections. One begins the practice of loving-kindness with a reflection on equanimity. The other integrates the equanimity and loving-kindness practices into one.

Equanimity practice can be an inner resource to turn to whenever we face difficult moments. The practice of equanimity involves silently repeating to yourself a phrase while you reflect on its meaning. When your mind wanders, bring it back to the phrase, and to the feeling of equanimity it evokes. You can do this for just a few moments or for several minutes.

The phrases used in this practice have real power; all help cultivate an attitude of impartial equanimity toward all beings. Here are some examples (you can change and adapt these phrases to make them more relevant for you):

> *May I accept things as they are.*

> *I wish you happiness and well-being, but I cannot make your choices for you or control the way things are.*

Loving-kindness Practice

In this reflection, you repeat phrases that reflect this quality of loving-kindness. Whenever your mind wanders, reconnect again with a feeling of love or warmth toward people.

As with the equanimity practice, the specific wording of the phrases you use is up to you; change them so they have resonance or meaning for you.

In this practice, you repeat the same phrase, but direct it toward yourself, toward specific people, and finally to everyone. Others to whom you can direct loving-kindness include your benefactors, your loved ones, groups you feel neutral about, people you have particular difficulty with, and all beings in all directions throughout the universe.

There are several forms of the loving-kindness meditation. Here's one.

> *Just as I want to be free from suffering, may all beings be free from suffering.*

Another classic form:

> *May I be free from suffering and the cause of suffering.*
> *May I have ease of well-being.*
> *May I be protected and safe.*
> *May I be happy.*

Then express the same wish for others—your loved ones, difficult people, or whomever you choose. Finally extend these genuine wishes of compassion and love to all beings everywhere:

> *May all beings be free from suffering and the cause of suffering.*
> *May all beings be protected and safe.*
> *May all beings be happy.*

Here's a short form of the loving-kindness practice, expressed toward all beings:

> *May all beings be safe, happy, healthy, and free from suffering. May all beings be liberated.*

If that appeals to you, you can express those wishes first for yourself, then for the other groups, and finally for everyone.

You can also integrate equanimity practice with loving-kindness. A simple way is to come back to an equanimity phrase after reciting those for loving-kindness.

Equanimity balances compassion and loving-kindness. The Dalai Lama advises practicing equanimity before loving-kindness as a way to take the sting out of attachment to wanting things to be a certain way. This balance blends into a wise compassion.

3

The Healing Qualities of Mindfulness

The phrase "tea mind" refers to the Zen-like qualities of awareness inspired by the Japanese art of tea—harmony and simplicity, a mind alert but at rest, clear attention to the moment. During the tea ceremony, attention focuses on the present, as we savor the subtle details of the occasion: the taste of the tea, the aroma of the incense, the sound of the whisk as the host mixes the green tea powder into a frothy brew. ● We slow down to appreciate the gracefulness of the movements, the silent communication, the simplicity of the room, the beauty of each tea object. The mind grows empty, and each movement becomes more full. Nestled in timelessness, attention wraps itself intimately around each moment. ● In the tearoom no one wears a watch. You forget about time as you settle into the present moment. There's nothing to discuss except what pertains directly to the tea experience at hand. There is nowhere else to be but the present. ● You are just as present to the bare moment even when you are outside the tearoom, in the tea kitchen, where you prepare and clean up. No one sees you there, but you sustain a mindful awareness as though you were serving the bowl of tea to your guests in the tearoom. ● When this timeless presence is extended beyond the tearoom into life, it inspires more awareness. We are more present to our everyday experiences: being with a moment more fully, not rushing on to the next moment or lingering in the previous one, but simply being awake to the present. ● Some years ago as a tea student I experienced tea mind spilling over more often from the tearoom into my daily life, even in Manhattan, where I studied tea. Leaving the school, stepping mindfully down the city streets, I found that the city's collage of sounds, sights, smells, and sensations no longer pulled my mind in all directions at once. They became ways to engage my senses, one after the other, seeing each thing as it came and went, delighting in it all from a center within . . . then came the challenge of rush hour on the subway!

We needn't study the tea ceremony or the Japanese arts to become mindful, but these meditative arts do offer one model for bringing a more focused sensibility to our activities and inner life. If we cultivate a practice of mindfulness meditation, we can enhance any activity with an attentive presence. There's a vast difference between drinking a morning cup of tea with full attention and drinking it while preoccupied by our plans for the day.

This same awareness can be brought to how we relate to our emotions. Our emotional reactions often distract us from the present, filling our minds with relentless thoughts about another time and place, filling our bodies with turbulent feelings. The timeless presence of tea mind, a form of mindfulness, offers a direct antidote to this inner turmoil.

A Surrender to the Present ● The traditional Japanese arts, like tea and flower arranging, are an amalgam of art and philosophy, embracing spirituality, artistic enrichment, and personal enlightenment. Inspired by the Zen tradition, they have always meant more than a purely aesthetic appreciation, though that is sometimes emphasized more than the spiritual aspect of cultivating a refined awareness. My teachers have embodied both dimensions.

My first tea teacher was a colorful woman in her late seventies who had a playful spontaneity and depth. She had suffered a lot in her life, having outlived her husband and two sons, both of whom died tragically. She turned to Zen meditation and to tea as a refuge and a place to grieve silently and to channel her pain into creative and meditative practices.

She was a mentor for me in this way, a living example of transforming suffering. Though she never complained, I could sometimes sense her sadness. Her artistic expression seemed to include her feelings of loss, a woven tapestry of inquiry and meaning, of subtle adjustments and understanding, of wondering without needing answers. All that brought a quiet depth to her silence during tea.

On a tranquil afternoon in her tearoom, she offered to serve me a bowl of tea. As she whisked the green powdered tea, I noticed how her hands mirrored the etched lines of the antique tea bowl, casting new light on the weathered beauty of old age. The blue veins and brown spots on her porcelain skin revealed *wabi*, the well-defined character of something seasoned with age.

Bringing the tea to a close, she gracefully lifted the long bamboo dipper and refilled the urn with fresh cold water. As I listened to the water pouring into the silence, I heard her whisper, "We give back to the waters of life that which we have taken away."

This quality of being attuned to and surrendering to the mood of the present is invaluable when dealing with emotions. Some things in life can't be changed, but we can change our inner relationship to them. Accepting their presence mindfully helps us hold even roiling emotions with a depth of spirit, a soulful wisdom.

A Fight in a Tea Garden ● On our way to one of the serene Zen gardens of Kyoto, my husband and I are lost in a disagreement. He feels I have overreacted; I feel he has been insensitive. The matter unresolved, we arrive at the entrance gate, both of us still fuming.

How could he be so thoughtless? My mind is still caught in our disagreement as we pass through the gate, or *roji*. Then I think of its meaning: the *roji* symbolizes leaving behind the dust and troubles of the world.

As we pass from the ordinary to the extraordinary world, the harmonious placement of the stepping-stones on the path has a stilling effect on my mind: *Well, maybe he didn't realize what he was doing. . . .*

Glancing at a willow tree beside the path, my gaze rests on a delicately curved branch. Its graceful simplicity invites me to the present moment, softening the edges of my mind state. I notice the same sense of wonder in my husband's eyes.

The dust of the mind scatters with the gentle wind. A single leaf falls.

That moment in the Zen garden reminds me how delighting in the present can soften even the most hardened emotional attitudes, as this line from a Zen poem reflects: "Even the general took off his armor to gaze at the peonies."

The interweaving of aesthetic, philosophic, and emotional threads that the meditative arts cultivate exemplifies how we can bring a mindful presence into the daily workings of our emotional life.

The Space within the Clutter ● In Japanese flower arrangement, another mindful art form, the space *around* the flowers and branches is just as significant as the flowers themselves. When there is an empty space to define it, we can see the delicacy of the flowers more clearly, appre-

ciate more fully the natural grace of a winding branch. The flowers' fragile beauty is enhanced by the empty space that outlines them. The surrounding openness illuminates and crisply defines the lines of the flowers.

It's the same with our minds. When our minds are cluttered with thoughts and caught up in reactivity, we are pulled from the present, unable to see the open quality of our mind's natural state. The natural state of the mind is an open, clear, and luminous awareness, reflecting everything in our experience like a mirror. And like a mirror, the mind has the capacity to be undisturbed by the images that appear in it.

This natural awareness is like space—our thoughts and feelings, our perceptions and memories, arise within the openness of that space. The aim of training our minds in meditation is to awaken to this natural spacious awareness.

But the jumbled branches and flowers of our mental and emotional habits seem to fill up the space. Sometimes when we're trying to get more clarity about some issue in our lives, we end up cluttering our minds with a confusing proliferation of thoughts about it—interpretations, reactions to interpretations, second thoughts, and on and on. We fill our minds with concepts about our experience, but we end up more confused.

When our minds stop racing and quiet down a bit—whether through meditation practice, a retreat, or just taking a walk in nature—we can often see things more clearly, with a fresh perspective. Insights into the problem can more easily emerge as our mind becomes uncluttered. The emptiness and simplicity can reveal the natural quality of our awareness.

Again, this clarity is not something foreign to our minds, something that we have to work hard to build up; it reflects our natural state. What's temporary is the upset, the stormy buildup of emotion. The space of clarity that emerges when we quiet our mind makes us more receptive to the whispers of an innate intuitive wisdom.

Mindfulness offers a range of tools for doing this, each putting to use one or another of its many qualities. Just as quieting our tumultuous thoughts offers one such tool for sorting out the jumble in our mind, other qualities of mindfulness provide powerful means for exploring our emotional lives. Among them are spacious clarity, calmness and equanimity, freedom from self-judgment, confidence and courage, intuition and trust, freshness and flexibility. Perhaps most important for emotional alchemy is a sustained investigative awareness, the ability to inquire with openness into an emotion until its meaning is revealed (I'll be talking much more about essential quality). All of these qualities of mindfulness bring us closer to the truth of a moment, to seeing things more as they actually are.

A Space of Clarity Mindful awareness stands in sharp contrast to the halfhearted attention that so often dominates the mind. A closer look at the state of our stream of awareness reveals a rather motley mess. As the Buddhist scholar Nyanaponika points out, when we look into our minds, apart from the occasional purposeful thoughts, there is a disconcerting sight: we are "everywhere faced with a tangled mass of perceptions, thoughts, feelings, casual movements, etc., showing a disorderliness and confusion which we would not tolerate, for instance, in our living room. . . . Hundreds of crosscurrents flash through the mind, and everywhere there are bits and ends of unfinished thoughts, stifled emotions, and passing moods."

This mass of distraction, confusion, and disorder makes up much of our waking mental activity. The everyday state of distractedness creates a breeding ground for what Nyanaponika calls "our most dangerous enemies—powerful emotional forces like frustrated desires and suppressed resentments, upsurging passions like greed, hatred and anger, delusion."

The antidote to this distractedness is mindfulness. While ordinary attention swings rather wildly from focus to focus, carried here and there by distractions—random thoughts, fleeting memories, captivating fantasies, snatches of things seen, heard, or otherwise sensed—by contrast, mindfulness is distraction-resistant. A sustained attention, mindfulness keeps its beam of focus fully in the moment, and maintains that focus on to the next moment, then the next and the next—and on and on. If distractedness breeds emotional turmoil, the ability to sustain our gaze, to keep looking, is one essential quality of awareness in working with our emotions.

Two qualities are essential to mindfulness: even-hovering attention and tenacity. These qualities allow us to perceive finer subtlety than does ordinary awareness. In this sense, mindfulness creates a sustained attention that can pierce through initial impressions and shallow assumptions to see a fuller, more nuanced truth.

For instance, to avoid emotional pain we often distract ourselves from disturbing feelings and thoughts, tearing our attention away from pain and so cutting off the feeling prematurely. But when we fail to stay with a feeling long enough to allow it to run its natural course, we cut ourselves off from what we might otherwise be able to learn from it.

If we stay with it mindfully, we will notice that it moves through many changes, and that we can deconstruct it into its elements—such as pain, constriction, fear, pulsations of intensity, trains of thought and reactions—both the immediately obvious ones and their more subtle nuances. By keeping our attention on the feeling as it goes through these changes, we can investigate the emotion, culling a rich yield of insights into its causes and contours.

Seeing Afresh ● In the garden of his teahouse, Sen Rikyu, who founded the tea ceremony in the late sixteenth century, grew gorgeous morning glories, at the time a rare flower in Japan. Toyotomi Hideyoshi, the ruthless ruler of Japan in that era, sought an invitation from Rikyu so he could see these rare flowers. Arriving at the garden, Hideyoshi saw not a single morning glory; they had all been removed. Enraged, Hideyoshi stormed into the teahouse, the worst of manners in a tea guest.

Once inside, though, Hideyoshi's anger gave way to calm delight. For there, in the alcove of the teahouse, was a single, perfect morning glory, waiting for him to gaze upon it.

That morning glory symbolizes the aesthetic of tea, which has a way of recasting the ordinary in a fresh light. The Japanese use the term *mitate*, which translates as "reseeing," or seeing afresh. This quality of seeing things freshly, as though for the first time, lies at the heart of mindfulness.

Mindfulness is not bound by expectations, habits, or the weight of our past, and so lets us see what we are doing as though for the first time. In Zen, this is called beginner's mind, seeing the old and familiar as though it were new, even surprising. Beginner's mind keeps awareness fresh.

This fresh awareness has a neurological basis. Ordinarily when we see or hear something that is very familiar to us—like the tick of a clock in our bedroom, or the same old sights on our daily route to work—the brain registers it for a moment or two, then tunes it out, no longer responding to it. For the brain, it's just not worth putting that much energy into observing the same old familiar things.

But the brain gets energized whenever something new or unusual comes along, getting more active as it perks up to pay attention—something like a bored one-year-old who suddenly sees something exciting, like another baby or a dog. This quickening of brain activity occurs whenever we register something for the first time. It's called the orienting response—the neural equivalent of beginner's mind. This perked-up interest continues until the

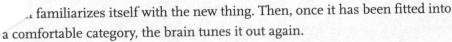

familiarizes itself with the new thing. Then, once it has been fitted into a comfortable category, the brain tunes it out again.

Boredom is a symptom of low levels of attention. When we are bored, as our interest wanes, our brain activity decreases accordingly. By contrast, one of the pleasures of change and novelty comes from the heightening of attention—and the rise in brain activity—it brings. In this neural excitation lies our delight in the new, whether it be a new outfit for the season, traveling to an exotic destination, or moving the furniture around in the living room.

But we don't have to change the environment to perk up the brain: we can do it simply through sharpening our attention to whatever is there. Full attention is the antidote to boredom. Mindfulness rouses the brain, jump-starting the orienting response. This was discovered in a classic study of seasoned Zen meditators. The meditators, all of whom were practicing a form of mindfulness, listened to the beat of a metronome-like device that tapped out the same sound over and over again.

When people who were not meditating heard the endlessly repetitive sound, their brain habituated to it by the tenth tap or so—their auditory cortex, which registers sound, literally did not respond. But the brains of the Zen meditators, especially the more experienced ones, registered the fortieth tap as strongly as the first! In other words, they were resting in perpetual beginner's mind; they had the capacity to take in each moment with freshness.

Mindfulness training, like most meditation practices, sharpens perception. Summarizing the research on the perceptual effects of meditation practice, psychiatrist Roger Walsh says, "Meditators report that perception becomes more sensitive, colors seem brighter, and the inner world becomes more available . . . perceptual processing can become more sensitive and rapid, empathy more accurate, and introspection and intuition more refined."

The first time we encounter something that intrigues us, the natural quality of our attention is open and fresh, our focus total. With mindfulness, we can *choose* to observe our own lives with the same alert, sustained attention. Mindfulness gives us the power to be with any moment as though for the first time.

A Calm within the Storm ● It was every mother's nightmare: Suzanna awoke to sirens and smoke at 2:00 A.M. The apartment down the hall was on fire. Gathering her children—ages three, five, and seven—she tried to stay calm, but was feeling an inner panic. A fireman outside was yelling something she couldn't understand; smoke was curling under the

door. Terrified that they would be trapped in her apartment, she crawled out into the hall to the stairway—only to see it filled with flames and smoke.

Even though she had heard it was the wrong thing to do, Suzanna went to the elevator—the only other exit she could think of—and, luckily, got herself and her children to safety. But a neighbor died in the fire.

Somehow Suzanna showed up at a workshop I was giving the next morning—clearly still in shock and close to tears. Understandably, all she could think about was the trauma of the night before. Like most people who have undergone trauma, she was obsessing about the details of her ordeal, and she found herself caught up in self-recriminations about how she had endangered her children by taking them down in an elevator. After telling her story to the group, she was so shaken she went to the ladies' room and cried.

When she returned during our break, a few members of the group went over to her, very empathic and supportive, calming her a little. But she was still shaken, her mind captive to the night before. Then we had our first meditation of the day. Gamely, she gave it a try.

She was fidgety when I started the instructions to let thoughts and feelings go, and pay attention to the natural rhythm of breathing, staying with the sensations of inhalation and exhalation—a classic calming practice that is the basis of mindfulness.

For several minutes she continued to fidget. But gradually her body became more peaceful, and by the end of the twenty-minute session she was sitting perfectly still.

Afterward, she was a different woman. She now had a peaceful look on her face, and said, "I think I'm okay now. I'm here now, not caught in what happened last night."

This dramatic shift in Suzanna's consciousness offers a testament to the calming power of mindfulness. In part this calm comes along with the mental focus mindfulness builds on. Staying in a mindful state requires that we let go of any and all thoughts as they come and go. This includes our most troubling thoughts: instead of getting caught up in them and swept away, and so feeding the feelings of distress that go with them, we let go of those thoughts—and of the feelings that go with them.

A Shift in the Brain ● The power of sustained awareness lies in its impact on our thoughts, moods, and emotions. When we face a jumble of emotion with mindfulness, our sustained attention quiets the inner disorder and confusion; as mindfulness gains a hold, it calms the turmoil.

This critical shift from turbulence to calm parallels what happens in the brain as we bring mindfulness to our upsetting emotions. Richard Davidson, a psychologist at the University of Wisconsin, does research on how emotions affect the brain. In some of his recent work he has explored how mindfulness shifts the brain into a different mode.

He says that in our normal state of awareness we have stronger emotional reactions than we do when we become mindful. As we shift into a mindful mode, the brain shifts, too. As he says, "We start to regulate an upsetting emotion the moment we become aware of it."

Davidson measured brain changes in people who were trained in mindfulness by teacher Jon Kabat-Zinn. The shifts were most remarkable in the activity of the left prefrontal area, the part of the brain just behind the forehead that generates positive feelings and dampens negative feelings. After just two months of mindfulness practice, these areas had become more active, not just while the people were meditating but also while they were simply sitting at rest.

The brain's executive center resides in the prefrontal area; the decisions we mull over and the actions we decide to take are determined for the most part in this area of the brain. When we experience an intensely disturbing feeling, there is a surge of messages from the amygdala, a center deep in the emotional brain that drives the prefrontal areas. At least, this is the case when we are "mindless," letting ourselves react unthinkingly and impulsively. If we simply let the emotion take us over, these restraining neurons give way to the force of the impulse, and the strength of the emotional response is at full force.

But if we can have the presence of mind to bring mindfulness to a moment when we are awash with anger or fear, for example, something begins to occur in the brain. The left prefrontal area contains a main array of neurons that tone down disturbing surges from the amygdala, something like the way a dam holds back all but a mild flow from an otherwise raging river. Mindfulness strengthens this dam, making these restraining neurons more active, so that they act as more powerful curbs to a distressing emotion.

These restraining cells strengthen their activity in direct proportion to our bringing our emotional impulses and reactions into the light of awareness, and through bringing reason to emotion. The more we do this, the stronger these circuits seem to become, just as more repetitions with a free weight make a muscle stronger. Of course, it's best to make these neural connections strong in childhood, but we can strengthen them through practice at any point in life. This seems to account for the discovery that mindfulness practice improved the ability of the meditators' brains to control their negative emotions.

Equanimity and Courage ● This enhanced control may be one

reason why mindfulness practice cultivates equanimity, a balance of mind that extends this calm into the rest of our lives, beyond the sessions when we are meditating. Cultivating this quality of mindful attention allows us to go through our days with the ability to notice any thoughts or feelings, no matter how initially disturbing, and be relatively unperturbed. This gives us the capacity to face distressing feelings, like fears, in a way that renders them less overwhelming.

By becoming mindful we can drop the compulsion to try to make disturbing thoughts go away, to agitate ourselves by worrying, or to try to make things better or in any way different. We can be with life just as it is, observing completely what happens, without immediately trying to change it. This is not a detached observation but an intimate connection with what we are experiencing inside. Simply being, without reacting, is in itself calming, and we can bring this inner attitude to whatever comes up in our lives.

Of course we should use our discriminating wisdom in deciding which of life's burdens we can change for the better and which we need simply to accept. But an inner stance of mindfulness allows us to face life's inevitable crises with more equanimity. This attitude of serene composure was embodied by an old friend, Mary McClelland, while she was dying from stomach cancer. One day I visited Mary, a devout Quaker who had learned to bear silent witness to life, a few weeks before she died. As I came into her room, she was calmly changing the dressing on an open sore on her abdomen. It was challenging to witness so graphically the decay of her body.

As she was finishing, she began to talk to me about dying. With her blue eyes reflecting a great serenity, she said, "Dear, there's nothing to fear in this process."

Acceptance, Patience, and Confidence ● Sometimes

people confuse the concept of letting go of a thought or feeling—noticing it arise in your awareness but not pursuing it—with pushing a painful feeling away by trying to suppress it. But suppression is not mindfulness. Mindfulness hides from nothing. It allows us to cut through the daze of denial and be straight with ourselves. Mindful attention lets us see the bare facts and not fall for our own cover stories.

When we look directly at intense or painful emotions, we develop a kind of courage and acceptance of how things are naturally unfolding in our experience. At such moments, we're not driven by hope or fear, not likely to repress the pain, to distract ourselves to avoid it, or to hope for something to happen so we won't have to feel what we fear. Instead, when we face the fear directly, we see that we're probably more afraid of our concept about how distressed we will be than of the actual experience of feeling it. Confidence and patience grow from this bold, challenging awareness.

If we can listen to our self-judgments and our self-critical inner voice with mindfulness, we can put them in perspective more easily. Mindfulness does not judge, blame, or condemn us for whatever emotions arise in the mind: our feelings come up on their own, unbidden. And that includes self-critical feelings. Mindfulness helps us see the distortion more clearly, as just another troubling emotion, not the voice of truth.

Sustained Awareness ● I remember S. N. Goenka, one of my

early meditation teachers in Bodh Gayā, India, instructing us on the fifth day of a ten-day course to meditate for one hour without moving a muscle. We were simply to observe closely, with sustained awareness, whatever physical sensations occurred.

And occur they did. After twenty or thirty minutes, virtually everyone in the room was fixated on some intense ache: in the back, neck, or a knee—somewhere. Urges to relieve discomfort and fulfill our desires go on at a subtle level every few moments, ordinarily outside of our awareness. At the physical level when we sit still, the body—largely without our awareness—continually shifts to adjust to discomfort, avoiding the buildup to these pains. But if we override that impulse to adjust our posture, muscle tension inevitably builds to the point where it crosses our pain threshold.

My pain was in my right knee, just above the kneecap. At first it was finely focused, a knot of excruciating intensity that built and built as the minutes ticked on. I wanted more than anything just to straighten my leg and end the pain. But instead I sharpened my resolve and continued to observe what was actually happening as the pain intensified. I resisted the seduction of strong thoughts that would occasionally blast through my resolve, thoughts pleading or threatening that if I didn't move, my knee would be ruined for life.

Then, when the agony seemed absolutely unbearable, something changed: what I had experienced as a rock-solid block of horrible pain melted into more fluid elements: heat, pressure, throbbing.

And then something astonishing happened: The pain disappeared altogether. There was just the heat, the pressure, the throbbing. No pain. No torrent of thoughts about how to end the pain.

The dread of the pain and the fixation of thoughts on doing something to end it just dissolved and were replaced by the open curiosity of mindfulness itself. Instead of wanting to escape the pain, I now found myself quietly fascinated by its constituents.

A sustained mindfulness allowed me to stay with the pain long enough to observe these changes. Staying with pain, or pleasure—or indifference, for that matter—until these attitudes of mind change offers us an insight into the impermanence of our experiences, whatever they may be.

Everything changes—an insight that can help free us from the pull of pleasure and the aversion to pain. And whenever we can observe the moment of intention that precedes our action—as with simply watching the urge to move come and go—we gain an insight into the chain of cause and effect at the root of all mental habit.

With an emotion like anger, sustaining our attention can bring us another crucial insight: if we can stay with the anger long enough, we will see it change into something else—hurt, sadness, some other feeling—or even dissolve. What had seemed so solid breaks down, is transformed. The key lies in staying with the experience through all its changes.

What's more, this sustained investigation lets us see that our assumptions about things being a certain way are just that: assumptions. "The opposite of investigation is assuming—assuming that we already know how things are," says Narayan Liebenson Grady, a mindfulness teacher. "Investigation is wanting to know clearly and directly for ourselves. If it's a painful experience, it's helpful to be able to stay with the pain long enough until we see it change. To be able to stay with pleasure until we see it change."

In doing so, she adds, "we can begin to see that what we thought to be inherently a certain way, isn't." The key is in sustaining mindfulness—our interest in how things actually are—which lets us experience more clearly what is happening.

Attunement to the Present ● When people begin meditation, they are typically surprised by how hard it is to keep their attention focused on what is going on in the present moment. The body may be in the perfect

meditation posture, completely still. Yet the mind is off and running some- where else: speeding through a frenzy of daydreams, reveries, drowsiness, agitation, random thoughts and plans, judgments about those thoughts and plans, reactions to those judgments . . . and if we happen to notice how our mind has wandered off, we can remember to come back to the present moment once again.

Mindfulness makes vividly clear the difference between being present and being distracted. This same realization can crop up in our daily lives: we may notice when we are not really present to what we do during the day, going through the motions of being present like an automaton, while our minds are off somewhere else. We realize how disconnected we can be from the activities of our lives, even the moments we most treasure, as the mind speeds on to something else.

One aim of mindfulness is to keep us attuned to the present. Mindful- ness is not thinking *about* what we experience, but a direct, bare attention to the experience itself. Distractedness is one sign that we are avoiding the truth of the moment.

A mindful inquiry—What is keeping me from being in the present?— can aid that subtle attunement. Sometimes the answer reveals the hidden influence of our most deeply ingrained emotional patterns, as we will see in Part Two of this book.

Often the very thing that makes us resist experiencing emotions is our habitual reaction to them. Because of fear or avoidance, we are unable to face the experience as it actually is with a neutral, centered awareness. It's the mental counterpart of shifting our posture to avoid the slightest discomfort.

The power to sustain our awareness with steadiness can cut through the mind's resistance to the reality of the moment. A steady investigation can bring a sense of equanimity to whatever happens. If it is pleasant, be aware without clinging. If it is unpleasant, be aware without resistance. If your response is indifference, precise awareness can prevent it from becoming boring.

That equanimity lets the investigating awareness stay with whatever comes up in the moment, without reverting to our normal state of distract- ing ourselves to avoid what we find unpleasant, or pursuing a mirage-like pleasure.

Flexibility, Buoyancy, and Challenging Preconceptions

● I remember being invited for a bowl of tea by an old Zen teacher at a monastery on the edge of Kyoto. I had been taking classes at one of Japan's main schools for tea ceremony, steeping myself in the precise formality of exactly how to serve tea. Every step in the tea procedure is precisely choreographed; there is a correct form for every detail, from how to fold the silk napkin to how to whisk the tea.

Being a proper tea student, I expected all the formalities and ritual order of serving tea. But this old master was a study in the informal spirit of Zen that originally informed the tea ceremony. He followed the general form for serving tea, but improvised in his own way. At the tea school we had learned the precise and graceful ways to fold the silk napkin before using it to wipe the teaspoon. This master, however, didn't have the requisite silk napkin, so he just reached for a box of Kleenex and casually wiped off the teaspoon.

At first I was taken aback; I thought, "But he forgot to . . ." Then, as I watched him, I noticed that he paid perfect attention to what he was doing, and broke the rules in the most natural way. It was an earthy contrast to the rarefied decorum of the tea school—a lesson in challenging preconceptions.

When our mind is on automatic, our thoughts following the same familiar ruts, our lives have a static, fixed quality. Flexibility can be useful in our daily lives. Rather than responding in our habitual ways, we can try doing something differently, whether it's putting the kids to bed or taking some moments for a quiet pause when we get home instead of rushing to open the mail.

When we run through the same old routines of thought and feeling, there is little likelihood that much will change. But since mindfulness sees things afresh, it can open up new possibilities, allowing the potential for change.

Concentration and Insight ● Mindfulness, like all forms of meditation, can be viewed as a systematic attempt to retrain attention. Two main approaches to attentional training in meditation are concentration and insight.

Concentration aims to strengthen the mind's ability to hold attention undistractedly on one point of focus, such as the breath. Whenever the mind wanders off—to a memory, to thoughts of things we need to do, or to a preoccupation, say—the meditator is supposed to drop the distraction and return her attention to her breath. The effect is to make the mind more focused and tranquil. Concentration cultivates the power of mind that allows it to stay focused on the object of attention, without being pulled away by distractions.

As one of my teachers, Sayadaw U Pandita describes it: "Without the eyeglasses of concentration, the world appears hazy, blurry, and indistinct. But when we put them on, all is bright and clear. It is not the objects that have changed; it is the acuity of our sight. When you look with the naked eye at a drop of water, you do not see much. If you put a sample under the microscope, however, you begin to see many things dancing and moving, fascinating to watch. If in meditation you put on your glasses of concentration, you will be surprised at the variety of changes taking place."

As this beam of attention "penetrates into the object of observation moment by moment, the mind gains the capacity to remain stable and undistracted, content," he adds. However, U Pandita points out something that is missing from concentration: "It simply cannot bring the understanding of truth."

That takes insight, a different attentional stance. Instead of considering everything other than one point of focus a distraction, with insight the meditator cultivates a strand of awareness that regards any and all parts of experience with an even, nonreactive awareness. It's a neutral witness to all that goes by—something like an apartment house doorman whose job is to notice everyone going in and out.

This witness awareness observes precisely while experiencing what goes on moment to moment in the mind. You try not to get lost in a thought or memory or anything else that enters the mind, but simply to note its coming and going. Mindfulness allows you to become more keenly aware of the processes at work in your mind—something to which we are often oblivious.

Concentration and mindfulness work hand in hand as mental training. The Tibetan term for concentration can be translated as "tranquillity," which Tulku Thondup explains as "the steadying of the mind, the clearing of muddy water into openness." Mindfulness, or insight, says Tulku Thondup, "is awareness and oneness with the openness itself." He adds that "the practice of tranquillity makes it easier, outside of meditation, to bring a relaxed mindfulness to whatever we do."

The meditation on loving-kindness at the end of the preceding chapter is calming, since compassion has the effect of quieting down our disturbing emotions. In this sense, compassion is a great tranquilizer.

Ajahn Nyanadhammo, a monk in the Thai Forest tradition, describes concentration as an inner peace: "the ability to let go of what is disturbing and go to a place in the mind which is less disturbing." The more we let go of disturbing thoughts, the more peaceful and tranquil the mind becomes. Tranquillity meditation paradoxically energizes the mind by giving it a place of rest. "When the mind comes out of that state," he adds, "we can put it to work."

The two practices, tranquillity and mindfulness, are synergistic. "Each person," he says, "will have his own balance of how much the mind needs to go into tranquillity, and how much the mind needs to work, to investigate and consider, in order to develop insight and understanding." In this fine-tuning, the two work together. In short, calming the mind down, when combined with insight, offers greater access to wisdom.

Sharpening Perception through Investigation ● One

of my clients was plagued by the thought that some minor medical problems she had been feeling—vague stomach pains, mostly—were symptoms of a terrible disease, possibly cancer. She was haunted by the specter of a dread disease, and found herself drawn again and again into frightening visions of being hospitalized, her family keeping a bedside vigil as she wasted away and died.

Then she went to a three-month intensive mindfulness retreat. There she practiced a form of mindfulness called *satipatthana,* a careful, precise attention to the senses—hearing, seeing, sensation, and so on. In this practice she learned to aim her attention heedfully, noting whatever was being observed, exploring the object of her attention with diligence.

The week after she came home, she went to see her doctor for a checkup. Before, she had been vague about her symptoms while reporting her fears at great length, but this time it was different. My client described the symptoms she had been having and launched into vivid detail about the exact nature of each one—exactly what she felt, how it changed over time, the nuances of her experience. But she did so calmly, without any mention of her old fears.

Her doctor was amazed, remarking, "You have such a precise way of observing your symptoms!"

Then, when she talked to me during a therapy session, she was able to give an equally detailed description of her fearful reactions and the nuances of their changes with time. And now she saw them clearly as blown out of all proportion.

That precision of awareness is one of the qualities of mindfulness that is of great use in working with our emotional habits. Like sustained awareness, it helps us distinguish between the thoughts that trigger an overreaction, the feelings that flood through us during the peak of the emotion, and our added reactions—such as irritation, impatience, fear, or resentment—to those feelings. This precision, as we will see, offers an extremely powerful method for tracking the psychological habits that most often trigger emotional turmoil in us.

Lightheartedness and Playfulness ● When we are mindful—free of preconception and judgment—we are automatically imbued with a lightheartedness. We can step far enough back from ourselves to make room for a sense of humor and playfulness. Richard Davidson's research on mindfulness meditators found that their brains shift in a way that fosters positive, upbeat moods rather than negative ones.

I remember a story told by one of my tea teachers. He always said that bringing tea mind into the world included having a deep peace in oneself that is unperturbed by small annoyances, and being flexible, capturing the lightness of the moment.

Once he hailed a cab in midtown Manhattan. As the cab stopped and he was about to go over to open the door, a woman dashed in front of him, taking the cab for herself. Maybe she thought it had stopped for her, or maybe she was just being rude.

But instead of getting mad and berating her, he simply opened the door for her—a gallant Japanese man in full kimono dress—and gave a dramatic, ceremonious bow as she rode off.

An Investigative Awareness ● Because mindfulness simply witnesses what's going on in the mind without reacting to it, this awareness allows us to experience things without judgment or interpretation, without clinging or resisting. This quality of investigative awareness goes beyond the level of just thinking about what's going on, to a deep inner listening that observes thoughts and feelings as they come and go.

If we see only through the lens of our assumptions—our thoughts and beliefs—we are not in touch with how those lenses distort the reality of the moment. In fact, being content with our assumptions can cut us off from this mindful investigation.

By bringing our thoughts and feelings under the purview of an observing awareness, we can see things as they actually are rather than how we *think* they are. In this mindful investigation we simply observe our reactions without identifying with them.

These are two different levels of reality: the raw experience, just as it is, and the overlay of mental reaction to it. If we separate the raw experience from the mental overlay we bring to it, we can clear a mental space. In that space there is room to examine whether we harbor distorted assumptions, ungrounded beliefs, or warped perceptions. We can see the ways our thoughts and feelings define us as they come and go—we can see our habitual lenses themselves.

So mindfulness lets us experience more directly, not through the clouded lens of assumptions and expectations but with an exploratory awareness. The investigative nature of mindfulness is one of its principal qualities.

A teacher asked a class of first graders what color apples are. Most of the children answered "Red," a few said "Green." But one child raised his hand with another answer: "White."

The teacher patiently explained that apples were red or green, and sometimes yellow, but never white.

But the youngster insisted. Finally he said, "Look inside."

"Perception without mindfulness keeps us on the surface of things," says Joseph Goldstein, who tells that story, "and we often miss other levels of reality."

In the ancient Pali language that Buddha spoke, the term for this mindful investigation is *vipassana,* which literally means "seeing things as they really are." The first step in this clear seeing comes when we pause and become mindful, interrupting the flow of our habitual thoughts, feelings, and reactions.

If You Are Interested in Learning Mindfulness

You can start now, on your own.

But if you do so, I still strongly urge you to go to a retreat at some point so you can ask a qualified teacher any questions you may have about meditation practice. Information on finding such retreats can be found in the Guide to Resources section at the back of this book.

To help you get started on your own, here are several basic instructions for the two main approaches, calming practice and mindfulness.

You can meditate for just a few minutes at first. But as a daily practice, do at least a ten- to twenty-minute session. If you can, work up to a half hour—or longer.

You can sit in a chair or, if you're used to it, on a cushion on the floor. Try to keep your back in a posture that is not too stiff but not so relaxed you will get drowsy. You can meditate with your eyes closed or open; if open, don't look around, but just let your gaze rest a few feet in front of you.

To begin each of these methods, first read through the instructions; then try the exercise on your own.

Mindfulness of the Breath

As long as we are alive, we are always breathing. Meditation on the breath means simply keeping our attention on the natural process of breathing, without trying to change it in any way.

Focus your attention on the place in your body where you experience your breath most clearly. It may be where you notice the rising and falling of your belly or chest with each breath; it may be at the nostrils, where you feel the movement of air as you inhale and exhale.

Whenever your attention wanders from your breath, remind yourself to reconnect with the natural rhythm and presence of your breathing. Begin fresh with each new breath, remaining fully aware as the breath appears and is known.

Remain aware throughout the whole sequence of inhaling, exhaling, and pausing between breaths. After the initial observation, sustain your awareness. . . . The continuation of attention strengthens mindfulness.

Stay with your breath in its own natural movement, as each breath reveals itself in its own unique way, feeling the sensations of each breath accurately and precisely. Sometimes a breath may be longer, sometimes shorter, sometimes rapid, sometimes deep. Let your attention stay with these natural changes, noticing the nuances of shifting sensations as they arise and disappear.

Relax into each breath, being with it just as it is, without trying to alter it in any way, renewing your awareness with each breath.

Focus your attention on the beginning of the breath, and sustain your attention throughout that entire breath, one breath at a time, connecting and sustaining your attention with each new breath, being aware of how it is from moment to moment, connecting with the beginning of the breath as it arises in your awareness. Sustain your awareness until the next breath begins.

Use the breath as an anchor for your attention, a place to come home to whenever your mind wanders. When you realize that your attention has wandered away, just bring it back to your breath.

Insight, or Vipassana, Practice

Begin this method by keeping your attention on your breath, as in the preceding exercise.

Then gradually open your awareness to include your other senses, and finally, focus on whatever appears in your awareness.

In learning this practice, it is helpful at first to expand a mindful awareness by directing it to the senses one by one. Later, you can engage in choiceless awareness, being mindful of whatever appears naturally in the openness of awareness.

Start with sounds. Expand your field of awareness to include sounds as they spontaneously call your attention to them and away from your breath.

Allow your attention to turn to hearing the sounds—simply hearing them, without thinking about their source. Be aware of sounds as they appear and disappear in this open field of awareness.

Notice the subtle sounds in the background, paying closer attention to the subtlety. Or simply be with the more obvious sounds in the foreground as they come into your hearing. As sounds appear in awareness, simply let them be known spontaneously.

As you are aware of sounds, also be aware of your reactions to them. Whether they register as pleasant or unpleasant, simply be aware of your reactions without judgment, clinging, or resistance . . . without any preference at all.

As sounds appear and disappear, be aware of the knowing mind, being present to the appearance of sounds as they naturally arise.

When a sound no longer holds your attention, return to the primary object of awareness, your breath.

Mindfulness of Sensations

Let your awareness expand to include physical sensations as they appear naturally. When sensations become predominant and call your attention away from your breathing, focus all of your attention on the sensation, observing any changes in it as you maintain awareness.

Expand your awareness of the sensation of breathing to include any sensation that you notice in your entire body. Focus all your attention on the quality of the sensation—tingling, tension, vibration—and on what happens as you observe it.

See how accurately you can perceive each sensation as it appears in the open field of your awareness. Stay aware of any reactions to the sensations, any clinging or resistance, any reaction that is pleasant or unpleasant.

Stay with the actual sensations that you are feeling, precisely noting the quality of the sensations as they appear, change, and disappear.

What happens as you feel the sensation? Does it intensify? Get weaker? Disappear?

Simply be there, without trying to change the sensation, without evaluating or discriminating, allowing it to appear and disappear, following with your awareness its natural changes.

Keep the knowing mind on the part of the body where the sensation occurs. If you are aware of painful sensations, fine-tune your awareness to feel directly the quality of the pain, whether it's burning, throbbing, or tingling. Whatever it is, be particularly aware of reactions of aversion or resistance as you feel them.

When sensations fade or no longer hold your attention, reconnect with the sensations of breathing.

Thoughts and Mental Images

As strong thoughts pull your attention away from your breathing, be aware of thoughts as they arise in your mind.

Without pursuing thoughts, getting pulled into their story line, or resisting them, simply remain attentive as they arise in your awareness.

Sometimes there are repetitive and familiar patterns to the thoughts. It's important simply to be aware of the appearance of thoughts, without thinking the thought or getting involved in its content.

If we remain unaware of thoughts, they become lenses on our awareness. We interpret our experience through our thoughts— through their concepts, their evaluations, their judgments—rather than being with the experience as it actually is, uncolored by our thoughts.

Watching our thoughts closely lets us see where we get caught by them. When we can watch thoughts in the way a shepherd keeps an eye on a flock of sheep—attentive, but uninvolved—they don't last long, and, with time, fewer thoughts arise.

With mindfulness, we can see their impersonal nature more clearly, not identifying with the thinker, letting thoughts dissolve like waves back into awareness.

Leave your mind as it is, in an open awareness. . . .

Thoughts are like clouds moving through the empty sky, appearing and disappearing in the open expanse of the mind. Let them come and let them go. . . .

When you bring mindful awareness to them, thoughts appear and dissolve like bubbles in water. Thoughts have no solidity, but merely the appearance of solidity because of the power we give them.

If you stay mindful as thoughts appear in your awareness, they reveal their empty nature and eventually dissolve. Let them vanish on their own, without adding to them in any way. If you become too involved with thinking the thoughts, you can reconnect with the sensation of breathing at any point.

Do the same thing with mental images—treat them just as you do thoughts, letting them appear in awareness and then vanish on their own. . . .

Emotions

As emotions arise in your awareness, be attentive to their quality, clearly recognizing and accepting the emotions just as they are, without resistance, judgment, or preference. . . .

When being mindful of emotional states, it's important to remain in a receptive mode. Look openly, with interest.

See if you can note with precision what emotion you are feeling and any underlying emotions, without getting lost in the story line of the thoughts that go with the feelings.

Allow there to be an openness to feel emotions just as they appear, and an acceptance of their presence.

Allow there to be equanimity as you experience the emotion, so it does not become the filter through which you perceive, but rather a full awareness of the feeling. Do this without being pulled into its reality.

Emotions add the qualities of pleasantness or unpleasantness to what the mind perceives. They can condition the mind to cling to pleasant experiences, to resist unpleasant ones, or to become bored with neutral ones. No matter the emotion, simply let it remain in your awareness, without pursuing it.

With more tenacious emotions you can open to a mindful inquiry, reflecting on the nature of the feeling itself, without becoming involved in the story, but keeping an open, investigative awareness.

Is there a place in your body where you experience the emotion most strongly or clearly? Be aware of the effects of the emotion in the mind.

When we can recognize an emotion clearly and openly, our relationship to it changes. We no longer have to resist it or cling to it. We can instead learn to accept it with a clear, nonreactive awareness.

If the emotion is unpleasant, if there is a reaction against it or an aversion to it, be aware of these mind states, relaxing in an open awareness.

Choiceless Awareness

As sounds, sensations, thoughts, images, or emotions appear in the background of your awareness, allow them to remain there, focusing primarily on the sensations of breathing.

As they move into the foreground of your awareness, let whatever predominates become the focus of your attention—a thought, a feeling, whatever appears most strongly in your awareness—opening the field of awareness to include the entire range of experience: breath, sounds, sensations, thoughts, images, emotions. . . .

If you're not sure where your attention should be at any point, you can return to your breathing.

As a thought or sensory experience emerges strongly, let it be in your awareness. Stay with it mindfully, letting it fade and dissolve on its own, bringing your awareness back to your breathing, or to whatever is most predominant in your awareness.

Whatever appears, experience it fully in the expanse of awareness, letting your mind rest without wavering, wherever it goes.

Mental Noting

In some forms of mindfulness, meditators use "mental noting," making a brief mental note or label of what has appeared most predominantly in their awareness. This method of labeling is an aid in connecting awareness with the actual experience in the moment.

For example, if you are meditating on your breath and you become aware of a strong sense of sadness, you would make a brief note in your mind: "sadness." The note can clarify what you experience. At the same time it keeps you from getting pulled into the reality created by the sadness.

Some people find noting a very effective aid to practice, using it as an ongoing method. Others use it only occasionally, as needed. Mental noting can be especially helpful while you're aware of strong emotions and thoughts, particularly for habitual thoughts and feelings, which can pull you into their reality.

Mental noting helps to keep you connected to the experiential level, staying free from the pull of thoughts while experiencing strong emotions or reactive mental states. It can help you stay aware of such states, feeling them while being present and attentive, without identifying with them or getting drawn into the story behind them.

Mental noting can also be a help when you need to focus your wandering, confused, or scattered mind. For example, if you are having trouble keeping your attention on your breath, getting too distracted by other thoughts, you can use the mental note "rising, falling" to track the sensations of breathing as your abdomen rises and falls with each breath. Or you can use the note "in, out" if you are sensing inhalation and exhalation through your nostrils.

If you choose to use noting as an aid, it is important to relate to it as a reminder of what is going on in your experience and as an anchor for attention, not as a way to detach your mind from the experience, but as a method of being with the bare experience without adding other concepts or identifying with the experience.

The noting should be like a whisper in the mind, not like a mantra, or word to focus on. Keep it very soft and light.

As an aid to practice, mental noting can help to clearly acknowledge with precision what is actually happening.

Mindfulness of Eating

So much of what we do in life is conditioned by unconscious habits of relating and reacting. So long as we remain unaware of how those habits are ruling our lives, they continue to control us. The first step in changing such habits is bringing into our awareness what is actually going on.

We need to turn to qualities of effort and clarity to wake up from these strong habits of conditioning, to see them more clearly, unencumbered by habitual ways of perceiving. While this strategy applies to emotional patterns, in this practice we bring a mindful awareness to a neutral activity: eating.

You need some small bits of food for this meditation. A few raisins are a good choice.

> Hold the raisins in the palm of one hand. Before you begin, notice if you have any preconceived notions of what it's like to eat a raisin. Then let go of those assumptions.
>
> Bring your attention to the raisins in your palm, allowing all of your senses to become alive and alert, mindfully noticing the shape and size and texture of each raisin, the play of light and shadow on their surface.
>
> Now, with full awareness, mindfully lift one of the raisins with your other hand as you relax the hand holding the other raisins.
>
> Be fully aware of all the senses. Touching, squeezing, and sensing a raisin with your fingertips, be mindful of the feeling of touch. Then gradually lift the raisin toward your lips, noticing the sensations of the changes in the muscles of your arm as it moves closer to your mouth.
>
> Touch the raisin to your mouth. Notice any anticipatory salivation as you intend to eat the raisin.
>
> Now, with your lips, teeth, and tongue—and noting carefully all the processes involved—lift the raisin into your mouth and begin to chew it.
>
> Be aware of the burst of flavor, the tartness and sweetness, the aroma of the raisin, the texture as it breaks down in your mouth as you chew, the movements of your mouth and tongue as the raisin moves

toward your throat and downward. Then note the absence of the raisin in your mouth.

And notice if you feel a desire to quickly reach for another raisin, for another hit of flavor . . . and so on with the rest of the raisins.

When you've finished, reflect on this way of eating raisins, compared with the way you usually eat them—and whether your experience was different from what you assumed it would be.

We typically eat "on automatic," lost in thought or socializing without paying much attention to the actual experience of eating. If you decide to eat some of your meals mindfully, you might find yourself noticing the taste of the food more and being more conscious of your body's signals of satiety. That often means you will eat less, but enjoy it more.

And as a model of bringing mindfulness to habits that are so automatic, mindful eating is an example of how we can cultivate full attention.

Mindful Walking

While we may find it easier to be mindful while we are sitting still in meditation or doing a focused activity like eating, this awareness can be integrated into the everyday flow of our active lives.

Bringing mindfulness to walking, like mindful eating, gives us practice in surfacing the sequences of unconscious habit in our activities. Mindful walking also adds the practical lesson that we can bring this quality of awareness to any activity—we don't have to be sitting still to be mindful. We can practice mindfulness in the midst of life.

Another benefit of mindful walking is that it raises our energy level. For that reason some people like to do a short session of mindful walking before their daily practice of sitting meditation. Mindful walking can also be a helpful way to calm an agitated state of mind.

The point of mindful walking is not to get somewhere but to become aware of the process of walking itself. For that reason you need only a short path—ten paces or so will be fine—in a room or outdoors where you can walk back and forth. If you do take a longer walk, stay mindful of the experience of walking.

At the beginning, mindful walking is done at a slow pace, to help bring the components of taking a step into awareness. But as you become more familiar with the practice, you can experiment with different speeds.

Standing with your feet about shoulder width apart, become aware of whatever sensations you feel as you mentally scan your body, allowing your mind to become subtle in its perception.

Feel whatever sensations are in your legs and feet: the pressure of your weight distributed on the soles, the sensations in each leg as you make slight adjustments to stay upright. . . .

If your mind wanders or if you become distracted, just bring it back to the sensations in your feet and legs.

Now gradually shift your weight onto one foot. Notice the sensations of the movement, the lightness or heaviness of each leg. . . .

See how accurately you can observe the actual sensations as you shift your weight to the other foot. Just notice whatever you find there, whether it's hardness, pressure, tension, or tingling.

Now slowly lift your foot and place it on the floor in front of you, shifting your weight onto it, experiencing the changing sensations, the contact with the floor, the shifting of muscle as the leg moves. . . .

As you come to the end of your walking path, or need to change directions in walking, first be aware of standing, then of the process of turning as you change directions.

Stay very self-contained, absorbed in the experience of walking and in the sensations in your legs and feet, grounded in your actual experience. When your mind wanders, return with awareness to the sensations of movement.

Walk at a speed that allows you to stay mindful. If your mind is agitated or wanders a lot, try walking faster for a while. As your mind becomes more concentrated, slow down. You can experiment with walking at different speeds to find one at which you can remain aware most easily and walk naturally, with awareness.

4

A Model of the Mind

We were being driven in a battered taxi on an impossibly crowded and chaotic Indian highway. Traffic, none too fast to begin with, slowed to a crawl: a bus had overturned up ahead. ● As we approached the twisted ruins of the bus, I saw a dead man lying peacefully by the side of the road, with what looked like his whole family—wife, children, parents—gathered around him, crying and wailing in grief. What struck me about this tragic scene was how starkly open to the world it was, and, by contrast, how hidden death and grief are in the West, where corpses are immediately taken away, out of sight. In India it seemed perfectly natural to see a family not holding back their grief, with death so matter-of-factly displayed by the side of the road. ● I told that story to one of my clients, Sara, who called me from where she and her three children were visiting with her frail elderly parents. She was feeling fearful of losing her aging mother and father, afraid that they wouldn't be around much longer. Yet she didn't want to feel that fear—after all, she was a busy mother with three children to raise. She had to be a mom first of all. But she felt on the verge of tears, and she didn't want to upset her children. ● She decided to give herself time to be with her feelings. Maybe she'd take a bath so she could be alone and let herself cry. ● So Sara told her children to play by themselves for a while. But the kids sensed something was wrong. The youngest asked, "Mommy, why are you going to take a bath in the middle of the day?" ● Sara decided to be honest with them. She said, "Grandma and Grandpa are very old, and I'm afraid they might die soon. I feel like crying." ● As soon as they understood how she felt, her children gathered around her, holding one another in a big hug. They were all in touch with the poignant sadness of life. They didn't need to be protected from it—they were ready to share it. Sara melted in the arms of her children, feeling soothed by the loving trust that honesty can bring to our close connections.

That episode illustrates for me the power of facing the truth, hard as it may seem. Too often we hide from the dead man in the road, whatever form that hard truth may take in our lives. We feel it's not acceptable to have those feelings. We pretend to be above it, or we try to protect the people in our lives—until we realize the power of genuine honesty, of being natural and matter-of-fact, like the people on that Indian road.

I remember talking with a taxi driver in the Virgin Islands about difficulties people have with one another. His accepting attitude was simple: "Everybody's got *some*thing." But we quickly hide our somethings, in large part because our minds conspire to hide painful truths, not just from other people but from ourselves as well. Yet a path to healing lies in uncovering and exploring those uncomfortable truths, when we can bring into the light of day what lurks beneath the surface.

An Optical Illusion of the Mind ●

The ease with which the mind diverts our attention away from hidden truths stems from its very design. It is something like a trick cabinet that harbors a large compartment where dangerous secrets are kept from prying eyes but which goes undetected because the much shallower exposed compartment fools the eye, seeming to fill the whole cabinet. Once we know about the existence of this secret mental compartment, the key to opening it lies within our grasp.

That key is mindfulness. One reason mindfulness helps so much here has to do with how scary it can be to open such a secret compartment. Mindfulness allows us to feel less overwhelmed by disturbing truths, creating a safe inner refuge, even as it enables us to ferret them out.

But first, some details of that ingenious design. While some of the details in this chapter can be a bit dense, understanding these mental mechanics will help clarify things when we explore the emotional habits that govern our lives.

Here goes.

The mind takes in multiple strands of information that flow through it in parallel streams. As we listen to a friend speak, for example, separate channels of the mind register her tone of voice, facial expressions, gestures, pacing, and meaning—and distill from all that the emotions behind her words. She tells us, "I feel fine," and yet her tremulous voice and teary eyes give us a sense of how upset she really is—a reading that the mind distills from the sum total of these disparate channels of data.

For the most part these channels register what goes on around us in a part of the mind outside of our conscious awareness. We may get a vague sense of how our friend feels, or—if her feelings are obvious—we may consciously realize she's very sad. But more often than not, most of what these channels register stays outside our full awareness—we note her sadness somewhere in our mind without becoming explicitly aware of it.

In fact, less than one percent of all the information the mind takes in actually reaches our awareness. Likewise, most of how we *react* to that information remains outside our awareness; our sympathetic look reveals concern for our friend, even though we are not aware at that moment of our expression. Most of what we register and how we react to it from moment to moment is controlled in those invisible parts of the mind that handle the vast panoply of life's minutiae without bothering us with the trivia.

Yet through what amounts to an optical illusion of the mind, we are under the impression that we *are* aware of all that we take in and all that we do. This illusion persists despite the fact—well known to cognitive scientists—that we are consciously aware of only a tiny portion of our perceptions and actions. To us, that small compartment appears to fill our whole mental cabinet.

A Risky Arrangement ● This is a useful illusion—for the most part. As you hear your friend speak, you don't want to bother to register all the rules of syntax she follows that allow you to make sense of her words. Nor do you want to analyze the subtle changes in her tone of voice and facial muscles that signal her true feelings. Luckily, all of that goes on in your mind automatically and instantaneously, so you don't have to work at it.

If you are driving your car while talking to your friend, for example, your attention is focused mainly on your conversation, and is only occasionally interrupted by a car passing too close or by someone about to cross the street. Dealing with traffic and deciding when to brake, speed up, and use your turn signal can safely be left to that invisible compartment that lies beyond some partition in the mind.

These mental partitions are necessary because our attention, which determines what we notice, is limited. The mind continuously selects some aspects of the world around us to bring within the narrow beam of our attention, while registering a far wider range of data outside that beam. What's registered outside this narrow beam goes behind the partitions in the mind.

While these mental compartments are convenient, they allow us to miss noticing much of importance. For example, a psychologist made a one-minute videotape of three students passing a basketball back and forth. At one point in the video a woman wearing a white Victorian gown and carrying a white parasol strolled through the game; her passage took about four seconds.

The psychologist asked people to watch the video and count how many times the ball was passed back and forth. After it ended, the estimates would come—23, 24. . . . Then he asked the people if they saw anything unusual. The typical response was "What do you mean?" When he then replayed the video, most people were flabbergasted to see, for the first time, the woman walking through the game.

So while the selectivity of attention usually helps us, there is a downside. The limits on attention can mean that we don't notice—and don't notice that we don't notice. Of course, that's usually okay, since we don't want to bother with most of what the mind filters out anyway. But when emotions enter the picture, our mind's selective attention can be less useful: we can avoid noticing something not because it's irrelevant but because it might disturb us.

This was demonstrated by another psychologist, who used a device that tracks the movements of the eye as it focuses on something. He tested volunteers to whom he had first given a psychological test that measured how anxious they were about sexuality. Then he had them look at line drawings of vague scenes. One of the drawings featured the naked torso of a woman in the foreground and a man reading a newspaper in the background.

People who were most anxious about sex had a remarkable response to this drawing: their eyes went nowhere near the woman, but stayed riveted instead on the man in the background! Presumably they sensed the naked woman in their peripheral vision and so guided their eyes away from her body to the neutral part of the scene. When questioned later, they had no memory—and presumably no awareness—of that nude body.

The naked woman had disappeared into the secret compartment in each person's mind in what amounted to a mental vanishing act. This suggests how some of that compartment gets filled, as the mind keeps us from noticing what upsets us.

An amazing number of the things we do and see during a day glide into the mind's secret compartment. This disappearing act involves our automatic reactions as well as many of our thoughts and feelings. When these tricks of the mind become well rehearsed, they act something like a polished magician, lulling us with their smooth illusions.

Noticing What We've Tuned Out ● If we repeat a particular act of inattention over and over again, it becomes automatic, like any other learned habit. While this matters little for the mundane routines of life, the consequences are far greater when those vanishing routines are emotionally loaded.

Consider someone who early in life learned through countless repeated family episodes that disagreements inevitably led to shouting matches or to sulking. Later in life that same sequence might occur when he has disagreements with his wife.

Even though that well-learned habit dictates how he acts, key facts about the sequence itself, including its very existence, will be stored away in that secret mental compartment. Once those facts are locked away, he won't remember having learned the habit in childhood, nor will he be quite aware that even now, years later, it continues to control him. He will be oblivious of the extent to which this habitual reaction determines how he reacts, though he may be aware of its result: that he is the kind of person who responds to disagreements by shouting or by sulking. Just why this is so, however, may mystify him.

Take an example that's not hypothetical. Jake, one of my clients, often lamented that his girlfriend didn't understand his need to be with his three daughters, whom he saw only on weekends, in accordance with the terms of his divorce. "When my daughters are at my house, my girlfriend just sulks," he would tell me.

But when he talked over the problem with his girlfriend, he found that she had another perspective. She told him, "Of course I understand that you and your daughters need time together, and I'm in favor of that. My problem is how you tune me out when you're with them. I'd like to be included, too. And when you make plans with them, I'd like you to consider my wishes instead of going along with whatever they want. But you go into some kind of trance around them, as if I don't exist."

I suggested to Jake that if he wanted to change how he reacted around his daughters and his girlfriend, he had to become conscious of exactly how he *was* reacting. He needed to become aware of what prompted his habitual response and bring more fully into focus a chain of thoughts, feelings, and reactions that ordinarily went on just outside his conscious awareness.

For Jake, that meant becoming aware of a set of fearful thoughts that motivated the trance his girlfriend complained about. Once he began to bring a more precise awareness to those out-of-touch moments, he realized that he had the habitual background thought: "If I don't do everything to please my daughters right now, I'll lose their love." His attentiveness to his daughters and his obliviousness to his girlfriend were both driven by this irrational fear. But once he was able to bring this automatic reaction into his awareness, he could take on a new challenge: staying out of this fear-driven trance.

Unlocking the Secret Compartment ● Here's where mind-

fulness comes in. Just as our habits of attentiveness lead us to tune out many details of our lives, so mindfulness allows us to do the opposite. Mindful attention is fresh and alert rather than operating on automatic. It can notice much of what the mind ordinarily tunes out.

Mindfulness offers an antidote to the numbing effect on consciousness of life on automatic. It embodies the capacity of the mind to know itself by shining a beam of light into that mental realm that ordinarily lies beyond awareness.

With mindfulness, we needn't remain completely unaware of the contents of that secret compartment in the mind. In particular, we may want to examine in a clearer light what's been stuffed in there that offers clues to difficulties in our emotional life. Mindful awareness creates a kind of work space, a place in the mind where we can see and deal with our automatic habits. It's like a private, cozy room where we can read and reflect on the most personal passages in our diary. As one of my clients said, "Mindfulness keeps me in touch with my honesty."

How Repetition Creates Habit ● How does that secret com-

partment get filled with such habits in the first place? "A momentary impulse, an occasional indulgence, a passing whim may by repetition become a habit difficult to uproot, a desire hard to control, and finally an automatic function that is no longer questioned. By repeated gratification of a desire, habit is formed, and thus habitual conditioning can grow into compulsion." This basic formulation of how repetition creates habit was made by Nyanaponika Thera, a Buddhist monk.

It fits well with the modern scientific view of habit as conceived by such neuroscientists as Gerald Edelman, a Nobel Prize winner. Edelman proposes that our habits—our most familiar ways of thinking, feeling, and reacting—take shape at the neural level through the impact of simple repetition on the connections between brain cells. The more often a particular circuit in the brain is used, the stronger its connections become.

As Nyanaponika points out, what was once a mere whim or impulse becomes, through continual repetition, a fixed groove. As we repeat the habit over and over, the neural connections for it strengthen, while those for alternatives to the habit weaken. The brain cells in the chosen circuit develop stronger and stronger links, while the links for alternative responses wither. It's much like a fork in a dirt road: if everyone bears right, over the years that branch will develop deep ruts that will automatically guide the wheels of vehicles to the right.

It's the same with our emotional reactions. When we have a choice between two ways of reacting, the one with the stronger web of connections will win out, like the well-worn branch of a fork in the road. In moments when we can go either way—say, responding to a slight with an angry retort, on the one hand, or sinking into a hurt silence on the other—the one we choose over and over will likely become our automatic response. The alternative will wither through lack of use, as the neural pathways for it thin out.

The Mind's Shortcuts ● The technical term for one of these well-learned habits of mind is "schema." A schema, in the most general sense, is a packet of ways the mind organizes, stores, and acts on a given task. Schemas help us make order out of the chaos that surrounds us. They are at work as the mind takes in the welter of physical signals that enter the eye and ear and make sense of it all. Significantly, they also select for our attention what matters and weed out what they deem irrelevant—in other words, schemas determine what goes into that invisible mental compartment and what comes into the clear light of our awareness.

They also give us a framework to explain what it is we perceive, and a plan for action in response. We have a schema for, say, how to ride a bike or how to go about making an airplane reservation. Schemas are mental models of our experience. When we think about what we have to do to get an airplane ticket, we are calling on a model that includes what we know about airlines and their schedules, credit cards, using the telephone, how to find cut-rate fares, and much more. That mental map tells us what we have to do to make all those elements operate seamlessly so that we end up at the destination we want.

Such models are essential mental devices for navigating a complex world. We use them so often—in effect, rehearsing them over and over—that after the first few times we learn and apply one of them, we don't have to think about it much, or at all.

As we are learning a new mental habit—how to use a new computer program, say—the zones where the brain executes the habit are very active, expending much energy as the circuitry for that habit is strung together and built up. But once we master the habit, those same brain areas expend little energy in executing it—unless, like me, you seem to lack the circuitry for understanding computers! When a mental habit becomes automatic, our mind just rattles off the appropriate schema for what we are doing, without having to put extra energy into the effort. The new schema itself gets stored away in that invisible mental compartment.

The vast majority of schemas are efficient shortcuts in the mind. Much of their efficiency lies in the fact that we don't have to pay attention as we execute them. They simply spring into action, helping us manage our lives like a horde of invisible, ever thoughtful, infinitely resourceful elves who anticipate our every whim and execute whatever is necessary, without having to bother us about it.

But when it comes to one particular category—the schemas that govern our emotional habits—problems can arise. In the realm of emotion, most schemas are helpful, but some can be counterproductive, even self-defeating. In such instances we find ourselves repeating a pattern that we may later realize leads nowhere, but which at the time we seem powerless to change. Somehow we just don't consider the alternatives. Such self-defeating schemas fit what the monk Achan Amaro refers to as "the momentum of habit whereby we are likely to do the same thing again even though the results were painful."

Of all mental habits, perhaps the most emotionally charged are the models of reality for how we think and feel about ourselves and the people in our lives. These personal schemas color and define the most intimate territory in our lives. When these lenses in our minds are clear and accurate, so is our perception of ourselves and others. But when those models of reality are distorted, trouble lurks.

Learning Habits of the Heart ● When you learned to ride a

bike, you may remember, at the beginning you had training wheels. Then later someone steadied you until finally you could do it on your own. But the specifics of going through that sequence are probably a blur in your memory now, with a few specific moments standing out and the rest blending together, and none of it pegged to a particular day and time that you can recall.

The same is true of emotional habits. We were not born with such habits; they have all been learned. We have learned our emotional habits so thoroughly that the repeated episodes where we acquired them are now just a blur in our memory.

Someone brought up in a family where disagreements automatically lead to shouting matches and personal attacks will learn that pattern, or a reaction to it, such as stifling feelings about disagreements in order to avoid such shouting matches, early in life. With that learning will come a set of automatic thoughts and expectations about other people—for example, "The only way to get my feelings and needs noticed is to shout" or "If there's a disagreement, I have to attack before I'm attacked." And while we may not remember exactly how we learned our emotional habits, just as with riding a bike, they have become so familiar to us that they feel natural.

These emotional habits are learned so thoroughly that they operate outside our awareness, and much of their power over our lives comes from the fact that they are largely unconscious. Just as we are unaware that they are being formed as they take shape, and we don't remember most of the specifics about how they became our preferred habits, we remain unaware of how they control us.

Of course many hidden factors control our emotional life, including some that are genetic, like temperament. But here our concern is on the habits we have learned—and that we can change.

Detecting Hidden Patterns ● "I had just gotten back from a vacation and was feeling very relaxed, so I called my mother," a client told me. "She asked about my trip, and I started to tell her. But she cut me off and immediately started talking about herself. That set off something in me. I thought, She couldn't care less about me, and I got sad, then very angry. Within minutes we were arguing again, shouting accusations at each other. I got so furious that I hung up on her. I don't know why this keeps happening to us."

While we are caught up in a maelstrom of anger or panic, everything seems confusing, out of control, overwhelming, and unpredictable. But if we could pull back, see the course of such an episode, and watch it unfold with a symmetry remarkably parallel to many comparable incidents of emotional turmoil, we would start to recognize a hidden pattern—the features of the schema that drives it. We could detect similarities in what triggers the reaction, in its trajectory and mix of thoughts and feelings, in what we find ourselves saying or doing.

After several months of exploring these patterns in her own life, my client can now detect similarities between how she thinks, feels, and reacts to her mother at moments when she feels ignored, and those same reactions as they come up in disagreements with her husband. It's the same pattern, an emotional habit that plays itself out in both these relationships, at times when she feels the other person becoming self-absorbed, and so turning a deaf ear to her own needs or feelings. Her response, she now sees, follows a specific train of thought, emotional reactions, and an angry response that ends in her blowing up.

In our emotional lives much of the chaotic turmoil is imposed by our deepest emotional schemas, ingrained patterns of perception and response that lead us over and over to react to similar triggers with a maladaptive, habitual set of thoughts, feelings, and reactions.

Bringing a mindful attention to our emotional habits as they play out can give us another perspective on what underlies our emotional confusion. As we'll see after reviewing the main emotional schemas, we can bring both empathy and awareness to these patterns.

Schemas dictate their own reality—things as they seem while we are under their spell. But recognizing this hidden pattern helps us see things more as they actually are—not bound by our conditioning, but based on a fuller, more accurate perception. That perspective puts a new frame on our suffering: recognizing the organizing principle at work, we no longer need feel so helpless, victims yet again of the same old reactions. We have a point of leverage, a fulcrum from which we can start to transform our interior landscape.

II

Things as They Seem

5

Emotional Habit

A pithy Zen aphorism goes like this: *To her lover a beautiful woman is a delight; / To a monk she's a distraction; / To a mosquito, a good meal.* ● It makes the point well: how things seem depends on the lens or filter through which we look at them. Some filters are temporary; others can last a lifetime, creating an enduring sense of our reality. ● Long, long before the first modern psychologist—in fact, by the fifth century—the ancient inner scientists who formulated Buddhist psychology had analyzed the often subtle moment-to-moment changes of the mind that shape our reality. It sometimes surprises people to discover that Buddhism contains an entire system of psychology—a mind science—that can be of great value to anyone, Buddhist or not. ● These early inner scientists saw that differing mental states jostle with each other to capture the top position in an ever shifting hierarchy. As one or another rises to the top, it sets the tone for our entire state of mind—whether it be anger, equanimity, or joy. A mental state can last for but a moment, until another state rises to the top of the mind's hierarchy, or it can become a habitual frame of mind. ● If a mental state lasts just a moment or two and then passes, no problem. But when one state becomes a fixed habit of mind, it can define our basic view of the world. The ancient Buddhist psychologists saw that we tend to form mental ruts where a favored mind state dominates our mental hierarchy. When a particular state becomes a persisting habit of mind, it influences a person's entire personality. If the predominant state is negative—agitation or hostility, for instance—what might have been a momentary mood fixates into persisting turbulence. ● One fifth-century Buddhist text points out that people in whom anger predominates much of the time act in typical ways that offer clues to their inner state. They may perform a chore like sweeping the floor in a hurried, impatient way, and they are likely to complain about the food they're served or how uncomfortable their bed is. By contrast, people in whom delusion predominates will sweep the floor carelessly and blithely accept almost anything—bad food, an uncomfortable bed—because they have little of the discriminating awareness that would allow them to judge it.

To the extent that anger or delusion may have become a rut in the mind, it will shape the person's psychological reality. The Dalai Lama refers to such a negative habit of mind as a mental affliction, which he defines as "a mental distortion that disturbs the equilibrium of mind." Our mental afflictions, he observes, "not only create disturbance, anxiety, or unhappiness, but in the long run produce yet further problems."

Maladaptive Mind States ● The ancient Buddhist psychologists

identified some mind states as wholesome, others unwholesome or, in more modern terms, adaptive and maladaptive. Their rule of thumb for classifying a state of mind was simple but profound: it depended on whether the mind state led to inner peace or disturbed the mind. The modern rule of thumb in psychology for classifying a mental habit, or schema, as adaptive or maladaptive is quite similar.

A schema is a powerful set of negative thoughts and feelings. In order to keep from being thrust into the grip of those disturbing mental states, we learn strategies for warding them off. These strategies help us cope with the threat of a full-fledged schema attack, a misery we desperately wish to avoid.

Schema strategies take root because they helped us adapt in some way. We develop them because they were at least partial solutions to an early life problem—working extra hard to please a hypercritical parent, for example, or becoming particularly gregarious to avoid feeling left out by other kids. Though they helped us cope at the time we acquired them, they do not work so well for us now.

Every schema can be seen as an attempt gone awry to fulfill the basic needs of life: safety, connection to others, autonomy, competence, and so on. When these needs are met, a child will thrive. When these basic needs are left unfilled, however, schemas can take root.

Each schema has its own emotional hallmark, a distinctive gut-level, wrenching feeling that takes us over when the schema has us in its grip. These feelings may repeat the emotions we felt during traumatizing events earlier in life that created the schema. During these schema episodes we are once again plunged into abject fear, or we become enraged or depressed.

Nevertheless, these strategies, or emotional habits, can harbor some valuable qualities. For example, people with the schema called unrelenting standards are often highly disciplined and motivated, even driven, in their work. This can make them highly successful at what they do; star performers often have this schema. The pattern becomes maladaptive, though, when they drive themselves so hard that the rest of their life suffers or they exhaust themselves. They need to find a balance—to realize that they don't have to achieve 120 percent. Sometimes it's all right to do just 70 or 80 percent—and to have a life, too.

Or people may have the emotional-deprivation pattern. They feel chronically deprived of love, attention, or caring. They may develop strong empathy and nurturing abilities, which in themselves are admirable gifts. These traits become maladaptive, though, when the person becomes a chronic caretaker in all her relationships, and so feels starved for empathy and nurturance.

Such schema strategies are half-solutions to life's perennial dilemmas, habitual ways we've learned to deal with issues that come up over and over again in life, like the need for close relationships or for love. As partial solutions to pressing problems, such coping strategies ease the pain a bit, though they never really resolve the predicament.

The paradox is that schemas revolve around compelling needs but lead us to think and act in ways that keep those needs from being fulfilled. They perpetuate themselves in a self-defeating cycle. For example, someone with a pattern of emotional deprivation, and the accompanying need for connection and caring, may be drawn over and over again into romantic relationships with lovers who are ungiving and aloof. What drives this self-defeating pattern? The false hope that this time it will be different. This time she will find a partner who *seems* ungiving (which feels comfortably familiar, like home), but who will finally offer her the love and caring she craves from such a man.

Maladaptive schemas lead us to neurotic solutions. On the one hand, these solutions are strategies for filling basic human needs and wishes, like being loved, understood, or accepted. On the other hand, they are self-defeating, because they sabotage the very attempt. Their goals are compelling, but their methods are flawed.

Maladaptive Responses ● While visiting a beach in a nature preserve, I saw a line of seven ducklings without a mother duck emerge from a nearby pond and waddle down the beach at a frantic, confused pace.

They were just a few days old, and they faithfully followed the tallest baby duck, who seemed just as lost and disoriented as all the rest.

They may have sensed the concern of those of us on the beach who saw their plight. They waddled up to several people, any one of whom they might have imprinted as their new mom. For a while they fixated on a woman whose blond hair with dark roots, like the coloring of their own soft down, may have reminded them of their true mother.

As we gently scooped them up into a beach towel to deliver them back to the pond in the woods from where they had come, I had a poignant sense of the panic that must have seized their minds as they searched everywhere for their mother.

I found myself reflecting on the qualities of clients I've had with a strong fear of abandonment. Underneath the desperate attempt to be rescued that many people feel who have this emotional pattern runs a panic so severe that it feels like a fight for life, a fear of being extinguished.

But for those poor ducklings, the panic was appropriate, a fitting response to the danger they were in without a mother to protect them. For those with the fear of abandonment, though, once-appropriate feelings can take over when they no longer fit the actual situation. This remains a crucial distinction: schema responses are overreactions, not appropriate responses to difficult situations.

As we explore emotional habits, we should keep in mind that many or most of our emotional reactions are probably appropriate to some situations. It is only when these reactions no longer work that they become maladaptive.

For instance, I once had a client who was in a relationship with a man who was physically abusive; after she moved out, he even threatened her with a gun. Her fears of him were based in reality. Her reaction—to get a restraining order against him—was completely appropriate. But she also had schemas triggered in that relationship, particularly a fear of abandonment, which had kept her staying with him despite the abuse. It's the maladaptive nature of our responses that set these habits apart from the rest of our emotional repertoire.

Mapping Destructive Habits ● Contrast an adaptive emotional schema with a maladaptive one. A child who is much loved and well cared for, for example, will grow up with the highly adaptive schema that psychoanalyst Erik Erikson called basic trust. Throughout her life this person will tend to first assume that people and the universe pose no threat to her. She'll

see people as trustworthy unless they show themselves to be otherwise. People with basic trust make friends more easily, because they approach people with an attitude of goodwill, assuming the best about others. For the same reasons their relationships tend to be stable.

By contrast, a child who is abused in his early years is likely to grow up with a very maladaptive schema: mistrust. His first assumption about people will be that they cannot be counted on to care about his needs, and he may too readily misinterpret neutral or even positive acts as threats or as proof of his assumption of untrustworthiness. That, of course, was an appropriate self-protective response in childhood. But as adults, those with basic mistrust still approach others with suspicion, and so find it more difficult to make friends and sustain intimate relationships. Because they so readily see hostility or negativity in what people do, their closest relationships become battlegrounds.

This mistrust is the attitude underlying schoolyard bullies: they misinterpret neutral cues as threats and so attack under the false assumption that they are being threatened. A similar dynamic goes on in some husbands who batter their wives: they often have an intense fear of abandonment—that their wife will leave them. This breeds a suspicious radar that perceives symbolic abandonment in something innocuous she does, like walking out of the room during an argument. That simple act—and the misreading of it as abandonment—triggers in them by turn hurt, rage, and inexcusable violence. And so the basic mistrust schema distorts everyday relationships and thrusts people into a hostile and dangerous realm.

This mapping of destructive emotional habits is a modern-day continuation of the task undertaken by the ancient mind scientists of early Buddhism, who spoke of *anusayas,* dormant tendencies in the mind that erupt in episodes of mental and emotional disturbance. Buddhist psychology sees that even though the tendencies may not dominate our lives, their potential for springing into action makes them comparable to a mental minefield. At the least misstep, we are caught up in emotional chaos and mental confusion.

Similarly, modern psychology speaks of schemas as storage systems that preserve specific emotional learning—resentment at feeling treated unfairly, for instance, along with the corresponding range of acts that we have learned to be sensitive to, as well as how we have learned to react when we feel treated that way. These storage systems not only preserve what we have learned but continue to be added to by our experiences throughout life. These patterns lie dormant, waiting for a moment when something happens that brings the schema to mind. Then the old feelings, and the old responses, automatically recur.

Whether because of temperament or serendipitous timing, some children may be more resilient than others, emerging from the cauldron of early life relatively schema-free while a sibling grows up burdened by several such patterns. One reason has to do with the fact that in a psychological sense, every sibling grows up in a different family: an oldest child, for example, may have left home already by the time a parental divorce creates an absent parent for the youngest sibling.

Core Conflicts ● To some extent, our schemas embody ways we have given up part of what is possible for us. Abraham Maslow put it powerfully: "If the only way to maintain the self is to lose others, then the ordinary child will give up the self." Some schemas—and the ways we've learned to respond to them—represent a sense in which we've sacrificed our potential in a bargain to preserve connection.

The task of charting the mental models and propensities that shape our day-to-day reality is a perennial challenge for psychology; Erik Erikson's student David Shapiro offered another intriguing map of this intimate territory. Focusing on people's perceptual habits, Shapiro identified what he called neurotic styles—distinctive, and distorted, ways of perceiving and acting.

Shapiro's styles, a typology of perceptual schemas, read like a modern update of that fifth-century Buddhist list of mental types and their tendencies. People with what Shapiro calls the compulsive style, for example, rigidly fixate on details and dutifully follow the *shoulds* rather than displaying any spontaneity or independence; it's as though they were poring over the rule books of life for guidance. By contrast, those with a hysteric style impulsively react on their first impressions, ignoring the details or even the facts; they read a situation as though they were skimming newspaper headlines, oblivious to the articles that explain them. And people with a paranoid style regard the world with suspicion; such people rivet their attention on a view of life akin to a tabloid conspiracy theory, vigilant for any confirming clue.

Such mental lenses make things seem very different than they actually are, twisting attention, memory, and perception to fit a mental bias. When that lens is built into our core ways of seeing ourselves and others, it shapes not just our way of seeing but our entire life.

Consider a sample maladaptive schema in action:

A man secretly fears that any woman would reject him. He feels like a weak, flawed boy, inadequate for the love of the woman he desires and idealizes.

He hides his fear behind a facade: that of a strong, macho man. With this pretense, he feels self-confident enough to enter a romantic relationship where he charms the woman he idealizes.

As the relationship grows, however, she makes what he sees as overwhelming demands—for his loyalty, time, and attention. But underneath it all, he feels weak and flawed, inadequate to meet her needs. So he reappraises her—maybe she's not so ideal after all. He sees her limitations, starts being rude to her, wants to leave her. She reacts to his rejection by crying, hurt, rage. He feels even more inadequate and finally leaves.

Once he leaves her, he feels lonely. He wants another relationship with a woman. But he secretly fears that no woman would accept him. Once again he feels like a weak, flawed boy, inadequate for the love of the woman he desires. . . .

And so goes the endless round of this man's schema—a specimen captured through the efforts of a team of researchers led by Dr. Mardi Horowitz, a psychiatrist at the University of California. This specimen represents just one of literally hundreds that were brought to light through several years of intensive research into what Horowitz calls maladaptive interpersonal patterns. He sees these life patterns as the outcome of distorted notions that people hold about themselves and the people in their lives—including the hapless man who feels like a weak, flawed boy.

For each of us, a favored schema—too often maladaptive—comes up time and again in our thoughts and words, even our dreams. Some of these fixations are so basic to the outlook and life history of a given person that they are tantamount to scripts that person seems doomed to repeat in relationship after relationship. These core conflicts have themes that play themselves out in a person's most important relationships.

The Anatomy of a Core Conflict ● Every core conflict has three parts, according to Dr. Lester Luborsky, whose team at the University of Pennsylvania has identified thirty or so common fixations. Each one has a wish or need; a typical response that the person anticipates; and the person's typical reaction to that response. Among the common wishes in these core conflicts are these three: I want to be understood, empathized with, and seen accurately; I want to be respected, valued, and treated fairly; and I want to feel good about myself, to be self-confident.

Such wishes, of course, are universal; everyone harbors these desires. The conflict comes from what the person has experienced from other people and so has come to expect in relationships in general. In a maladaptive schema the other person somehow thwarts the wish or need. This results in a rather forlorn list of anticipated responses, including, for example, the certainty that the other person will be insensitive and inconsiderate of my feelings, that the other person will take advantage of me, or that the other person will belittle me.

Understandably, being responded to in these ways will elicit a reaction of rejection and disappointment; anger and resentment; or a feeling of ineffectuality and helplessness.

These recipes for disaster in relationships take shape early and persist in minor variations throughout life. Luborsky borrows an analogy from literature: "the plotline of the fantasy remains the same although the characters and situations vary." So powerful are these plotlines that the same sequence plays out with friends, with lovers and mates, with co-workers. It even dictates the form of the subtle interplay between patient and therapist that psychoanalysts call transference, as the therapist fills the symbolic role of the other person in a replay of the same old familiar melodrama.

The power of such a maladaptive schema in a relationship is clear in an episode recounted by a woman at a workshop. Her core schema made her long for emotional contact, yet fear she would never receive it; as a result she was acutely sensitive to any hint of being ignored. "I came home from work eager to connect with my husband," she said, "just wanting to spend some time with him, feeling close. But when I got home, there he was in the living room glued to a football game on TV, with his papers from work spread all around him. He barely noticed me. I always anticipate that he's going to ignore me, that he just doesn't care about me or our relationship, and there it had come true again."

Her well-rehearsed reaction was to get angry and withdraw: "So I stormed out and went shopping. I stayed away for four hours, knowing it would irritate him. And sure enough, when I got home we had a huge argument. That keeps happening over and over again."

The Common Maladaptive Habits ● When it comes to our maladaptive habits, I'm reminded of those children's puzzle pictures, like the Where's Waldo books, in which the outlines of a camouflaged figure lie hidden within a larger drawing. The challenge comes in spotting the hidden figure. In the same way, our maladaptive emotional habits lie hidden in the rich and confusing texture of the rest of our lives.

To work with them, we must first be able to spot them. For that reason it is immensely useful to have a map that gives us clues to their key features. I do not want to reify these patterns, but it helps to have a conceptual framework to sort them out from what can feel like amorphous confusion. This clarification is essential in the process of eventually letting go of their hold over us.

In graduate school I studied with a psychologist who developed a system of descriptive psychology for classifying these habits. That and other systems I've studied have made clear to me the value of a map, or method, for sorting out our maladaptive habits.

Then, in the mid-1980s, I was one of a circle of colleagues in a case-conference group who contributed ideas to Dr. Jeffrey Young's development of his model of maladaptive schemas. At the time Dr. Young—a protégé of Dr. Aaron Beck, the developer of cognitive therapy—was taking a new direction. He was venturing beyond the traditional boundaries of cognitive therapy into the psychological territory usually covered by long-term psychodynamic therapies: helping people change the deep-seated, destructive emotional habits that carried over into their adult lives from formative childhood experiences.

An Honest Look at Ourselves ● Dr. Young continues to refine and develop his brilliant template on these negative life patterns (if you're interested in learning more about his schema model, read *Reinventing Your Life*). During my work as a psychotherapist, I've found that certain descriptions, based on his model, capture the most common schemas I deal with in my clients—something akin to a generic list of our maladaptive mental habits.

As you read through these descriptions, you may find yourself recognizing patterns from your own life. That recognition is very useful, but it needs to be kept in balance with a broader sense of our general health. Many of us have learned some maladaptive emotional habits. But as Jon Kabat-Zinn reminds us, "There is far more right with us than wrong with us." Mindfulness gives us a way to reconnect with that basic rightness, even at times when "what's wrong" looms large.

Maladaptive schemas can be seen as a kind of mental fog, or emotional cloud. They may obscure our minds for a time, but they still only temporarily cover the clarity and spaciousness of our true nature. Mindfulness helps us hold this larger perspective as we explore these emotional clouds. It gives us a wider view, like seeing the expanse of sky around the clouds. We can learn about our own conditioning without making it too real, being overwhelmed by it, or any longer being completely defined by the limiting beliefs these mental habits foster in us.

If you see yourself in any of these maladaptive schemas, you're not alone: many, if not most, of us have been shaped in these ways, to some degree. These emotional habits can be seen as attempts to manage a painful part of our lives, to avoid disturbing emotions by developing coping strategies. By over-compensating, for example, we engage in maneuvers that push the schema to excess as a way to reassure ourselves that the schema will not overpower us. By avoidance, we tiptoe around the schema to avoid activating it. When such strategies are successful, we temporarily minimize our emotional pain.

These differing strategies can mean the same schema may show up quite differently in the behavior of two different people. In fact, even siblings raised in the same emotional environment can adopt differing coping styles to, say, the trauma of having a parent disappear from their lives after a divorce, an abandonment, or a death.

One child may adopt an overcompensating strategy, becoming very clingy and seeking reassurance in relationships later in life; the other may take an avoidance approach, steering clear of attachment to others lest they, too, leave and make him suffer as he did in childhood. In both cases the strategies develop as ways to keep from reexperiencing the terrifying feeling of being abandoned.

Just why one person chooses one coping style while another takes a different route is not clear. In some cases it may be because of differences in temperament; in others it may have to do with the unconscious choice of which parent or sibling a child models herself after.

I encourage you to bring compassion to this inner exploration. It takes great courage to look honestly into that secret hidden compartment in our minds. Be gentle with yourself.

Remember, too, that every coping strategy is in some way a useful solution to a life problem. They all have, or once had, desirable aspects. But typically these solutions, which worked well enough earlier in life, have become calcified, frozen in place, and are now applied over and over even though they no longer work so well.

Because of the variations in coping strategies, a given schema can manifest itself differently, depending on the approach people have come to rely on. In the descriptions of the schema patterns in this chapter and the next, I'll mention some of the main ways these strategies manifest themselves, so that you'll find it easier to recognize them in your own behavior. But remember that each one of us is unique, and so the descriptions as given may not quite match your own patterns.

Opening up these hidden patterns to the clear light of awareness allows a fresh breeze of change, like remodeling an old attic of the mind. But as with the musty relics from our past that we might find in an attic, some things may be hard to let go of, even if they no longer serve any useful purpose. Sometimes you may prefer just to close the attic door and keep confronting the pattern for another day—or not deal with it at all. But if this is the moment you choose, then this inner exploration can open the way to living life more authentically rather than as the distorting lens of emotional habit makes it seem to be.

Abandonment ● The first schema results from reactions to loss. "I was about three or four years old, and my father, who adored me, had just had a heart attack," one client recalls. "My seven-year-old brother cried, and when I asked him what had happened, he told me our father had died. I felt alone from that moment on. My mother was always too busy keeping things together and traveling for work; I felt abandoned by her, too. From that time on, I always craved reassurance that the people in my life wouldn't leave me. Even now, when they do something that even hints of abandonment—like not calling me back right away or being late to meet me, I immediately feel hurt, then sad. Sometimes I just want to give up on the relationship, even though there's really nothing that wrong."

The ongoing fear that people will leave us all alone lies at the core of abandonment. The pattern can have its roots in an actual childhood experience of being left—by a parent who dies, for instance, or when one parent leaves after a divorce.

But the abandonment need not have been real; a symbolic one, like moving all the time or having an unstable, unreliable, or emotionally distant parent, can have the same kind of emotional impact. A parent who is not reliably there for the child, who is erratic in taking care of the child, or who is unpredictable or alcoholic, sometimes in a good mood and other times a terrifyingly angry one, can also instill the abandonment fear.

For people with this schema, the prospect of being alone stirs up a deep sadness and feeling of isolation. The resulting fear and panic are signature emotions of the abandonment pattern.

The automatic response of a small child to the fear that a key person in her life will abandon her is, of course, to cling harder. That urge is only natural in a child. Holding on for dear life, or constantly seeking reassurance that someone will stay or be dependable, offers an imagined antidote to the feared abandonment. Such a habit is formed early on; typically the clinginess begins as a positive adaptation, a way for that child to calm her fears through seeking a soothing reassurance of consistency.

But such clinginess will be out of place when, as a grown-up, the same fear resurfaces over and over in the person's closest relationships. One coping strategy in abandonment can lead to an anxious attachment, where the person needs constant reassurance that the relationship is steady and secure. But constantly seeking reassurance can sometimes lead to a self-fulfilling prophecy by driving a partner away.

Someone with the abandonment schema can become a worrywart about a relationship, fearing that if she rocks the boat in the smallest way, her lover will abandon her for someone else. An avoidance strategy might lead her to compromise herself by putting up with a bad relationship—again, out of the fear that her partner will leave. Alternatively, she may adapt by running away from a relationship before her partner can leave her—another way to avoid the feared abandonment.

To avoid feelings brought up by being alone, a person with the abandonment schema may be continually scanning for the next person to cling to, always trying to protect herself from the dread of being alone. This desperation leads her to push too hard too early in a romantic relationship, frantically seeking to spend every moment with the man or move in together before he's ready for such a commitment. At the same time, she is hypersensitive to any sign that he is on the verge of abandoning her, and she's always ready to make a jealous accusation that he has another love interest.

This schema makes the person fixate on signs that someone will leave, distorting them to mean the relationship will end. One sign of this kind of skewed thinking is being overly upset by even a short separation from a loved one, such as a spouse taking an overnight business trip. The schema triggers a fear that the loved one will never come back—a primal fear as strong as that of a young child.

The feelings that a temporary separation or the actual loss of a close relationship can trigger in someone with the abandonment schema are far stronger than most other people would feel. The very possibility of such abandonment can trigger a panic as acute as the fear a small child feels when lost from her parents in an amusement park.

If this pattern seems familiar from your own life, it can help to realize that you can be both solitary and content, rather than feeling isolated and despairing. People with abandonment fears need to learn that they will be all right on their own, that they have the inner resources to meet their needs themselves and so will not fall apart if someone leaves them. Along the way to this healing, being especially attentive to the feelings that even a symbolic abandonment stirs up—the hypersensitivity to separation or being left, the desperate clinging to people, the dread of being isolated—will help you track this schema as it starts to take you over. Learning to trust in connections is a landmark along the way.

Deprivation ● One of my clients, the daughter of alcoholic parents, felt basically ignored as a child. "The message I got from childhood," she said, "was that when you ask for what you want, no one hears you or even wants to be near you. That makes it hard to ask for what I want in my marriage. I feel very vulnerable when I bring up my emotional needs."

"My needs won't be met"—that one sentence sums up the core belief of the deprivation schema. This problem often arises from a childhood where one or both parents were so self-absorbed—whether in their work, in their own misery, in a problem like alcoholism, or in a constant preoccupation—that they simply did not notice or seem to care much about their child's emotional needs. In adults, the deprivation schema makes people hypersensitive to—and is often triggered by—signs that they are not being noticed or attended to, particularly in their closest relationships.

The core emotions of the deprivation schema are a deep sadness and hopelessness stemming from the conviction that one will never be understood or cared for. Like a neglected child, as adults people with the deprivation schema often feel angry about their needs being ignored. That anger in turn covers an underlying loneliness and sadness.

The childhood roots of the deprivation pattern can take any of several forms. For some, the deprivation stems from a lack of nurturance, warmth, or affection. Others may have been deprived of empathy because no one truly tuned in to the child's feelings, really listened to the child's concerns and worries, or paid undivided attention. In some cases there was simply a lack of the guidance and direction that every child needs.

The strategies people learn in the deprivation schema can vary. One client, for instance, would get very angry and resentful, attacking anyone who made her feel let down. Yet her demanding attitude made it hard for her family to empathize with her.

Another client with the deprivation pattern was unusually nice, going out of his way for people, doing special favors. But despite his large circle of close friends, he always felt hurt that hardly anyone seemed to care enough to be as thoughtful or caring to him. If he felt in need, he'd become very sad that no one seemed to notice and come through for him—even though he kept his needs to himself. It was almost as though he expected people to read his mind, sensing his needs through his facade that everything was all right.

The first client was too intense in trying to get her needs met, the second too hidden. Same schema, different response—but both had the same result: disappointment.

No matter how much others give to people with underlying deprivation, it never seems to be enough, and so they turn others off with their constant demands. Sometimes they feel other people should just sense their needs without being told. Or they can become self-indulgent, spending far more than they can afford on themselves or overeating in an attempt to give themselves the nurturance they crave. None of this, however, makes up for the real need for emotional nurturance.

By contrast, many children who grow up without nurturing parenting learn, like the second client, to be the caretaker they never had—they become like precocious little adults, sometimes actually acting as a caring "parent" for the inadequate parent. Such children learn early on that if there is to be any parenting here, they will have to provide it for themselves.

While this strategy helps them make their way into adulthood, the learned habit of always being the caring one creates problems for them as adults. For one, people who constantly take care of another person's needs rarely reveal their own. But they can readily feel guilty about not doing enough, no matter how much they are already doing. They desperately want to get the nurturance that they are giving, but, fearing that they will not get it if they let their needs be known, they put on a pretense of constant good humor and capability.

They can seem so together that they need no one to care for them. People see no reason to be concerned about or caring with someone so capable. Sometimes people with the deprivation schema gravitate to careers in the helping professions—social work, nursing, psychotherapy. When such helping is schema-driven, it can backfire, particularly if someone pushes herself to do so much that she burns out.

A variation in the deprivation schema shows up in those who protect themselves from being hurt in a relationship by keeping others at a distance. Such people will be distant within a relationship, never revealing their own feelings or needs, fearing they will not be met anyway. This pattern, learned as a protective strategy in childhood, protects people from once again enduring the hurt of having their needs ignored.

The distorting lens of the deprivation schema fixates on signs of being neglected. This can lead a person to feel disappointed about just one small way in which someone who is otherwise quite caring has let him down, ignoring all the abundant evidence that, in fact, the other person has been there for him. This distortion leads to a trail of chronic disappointments in relationships.

If you recognize the deprivation schema in yourself, you need to become clearer about how your need for nurturance shapes your relationships. Mindfulness, as we'll see, offers a tool for bringing this schema into awareness, so it no longer acts as an invisible pilot in life. You may need to become aware of your tendency to distort how you interpret the other person's actions—for instance, if you think people only want things from you, you need to learn to challenge that thought, to see that people may just enjoy your company without expecting anything more. You can use mindfulness to make behavioral changes, too—for example, by starting to communicate your own needs clearly and appropriately to others, or by seeking out partners who are emotionally available.

Subjugation ● "My mother was extremely domineering," a woman in a workshop told me. "She decided everything for me, even when I was a teenager. I had no voice. She would shop for my shoes, for my clothes, never asking me what I liked. Everything was always her way. Now, in my relationships, I can never speak up for what I want. I just go along with what the other person wants."

The subjugation pattern revolves around the feeling in an intimate relationship that one's own needs never take priority. The other person always rules. The core belief of subjugation is "It's always your way, never mine."

But while people with this pattern give in easily, they build up a hidden resentment that can smolder into anger—the hallmark emotions of this schema. This suppression breeds frustration that can build into rage.

This schema typically originates in a childhood dominated by controlling parents who give the child no say. The parental assertion of power goes far beyond the necessary setting of limits and rules to ignoring completely the child's need for autonomy. The assertion of absolute authority runs a continuum from outright violence and threats to a more subtle control via disapproving looks, frowns, or tone of voice at the least sign of a child asserting her own wishes.

Children who grow up in such an atmosphere learn early that their feelings and needs are invisible or that they don't count, that the other person gets his way. They learn to be powerless, helpless, about their own wishes and preferences. As adults in relationships they may be so used to having the other person dictate to them that they are no longer in touch with what they actually want or need; if asked to decide what restaurant to go to or which movie to see, they can't choose. Someone else has to make the decision.

For children whose parents are too powerful and domineering, passivity—the avoidance strategy—keeps at bay the fear of being yelled at, punished, or disapproved of. By being "good boys" or "good girls"—children who keep their preferences and desires to themselves or who repress them altogether—they can assure a modicum of peace in the home. When this pattern continues into adulthood, they enter relationships overeager to please. Subjugated people can end up in careers chosen by their parents, acquiescing to the demands of a domineering spouse, giving in too readily to their children's whims. But beneath their agreeable veneer, resentment seethes. Frustration and anger over being trapped or having no autonomy are typical in people with the subjugation schema.

Reactions to being subjugated can take several forms. Some people rebel and get into trouble, particularly in childhood and adolescence, typically bringing even greater efforts at subjugation by their overbearing parents. Such rebels can become free spirits, hyperreactive to the least sign of being controlled, quick to express anger at those in authority.

Another strategy with subjugation takes the form of not committing to things, thus avoiding agreements that might make the person feel controlled. People who take this approach may be leery of committing themselves to something as minor as a specific time to meet at a restaurant. Being tied down to an agreement to appear at a given time and place makes them feel trapped. And that kind of symbolic subjugation evokes the old dreaded feelings.

Still another way of adapting is to surrender. Such people end up with an underdeveloped sense of their own preferences, opinions, even their own identity. Their main focus is pleasing other people, while ignoring their own wants and needs. They can go along submissively with partners who are strong and controlling. While they may rankle a bit at feeling trapped, at least they feel secure in such a familiar relationship.

This propensity to please others is out of balance: such people are unable to set limits on what's expected of them, and they end up doing far more than their share of the work or doing too many things for others. They lose sight of what they want, and they fail to ask for their fair share.

You may have the subjugation pattern if, for example, you think of yourself as easygoing and flexible but you rarely stand up for your opinions, preferences, or needs in your close relationships. Despite your easygoing exterior, you feel used or controlled, and you think that people take advantage of you. Understandably, you often feel angry or resentful, but you never express those emotions. You may get back at people indirectly, though, by putting things off, missing deadlines, or being chronically late.

If you see the subjugation schema in yourself you need to get in touch with your resentment and frustration over being controlled. You need to assert your own wishes and needs. Mindfulness can be a useful tool to help you track the automatic reactions, the anger, and the thoughts primed by the fear that you are being controlled again.

Mistrust ● Mary strikes me as a classic example of the mistrust schema in action. Though I've never met her in person, I have read about her in the newspaper: She was featured in an article on women who were abused in childhood. As one of eleven children born to an alcoholic mother, Mary was first sexually molested while still in elementary school, by a relative who groped her repeatedly and threatened to hurt her if she told. She and her sisters, all fearful of further molestation, slept huddled together for protection. When she eventually did tell her mother, the reply was dismissive: "He probably didn't mean nothing like that."

Now, years later, mistrust threatens to poison her relationships. Though Mary can be charming and vivacious, she is quick to switch to mistrust and hostility at the least sign of betrayal. As Mary puts it with candor, "I'm just as paranoid as I-don't-know-what!" She has lost a string of jobs because she got into arguments with co-workers or with her supervisors over perceived slights that she blew up out of proportion. And now her mistrust is seeping into her relationship with her boyfriend: hearing him walk through the house at night, she races to where her young daughter sleeps, to reassure herself that her little girl has not been touched.

Such suspiciousness typifies this schema; its core belief is that people can't be trusted. Along with this belief comes its emotional hallmark: quickness not just to anger but to rage. People with this pattern are constantly vigilant in relationships, fearing that people will somehow take advantage of them or otherwise betray them. Because they are so wary of people's intentions, and so quick to assume the worst, they have a hard time getting close to or opening up to others. Paradoxically, some people with the mistrust schema may gravitate to relationships where their worst fears are confirmed, getting involved with people who do, in fact, treat them badly.

The mistrust pattern often stems from having been abused or otherwise maltreated early in life. The abuse can be physical, emotional, or sexual. When it's physical, a parent's warped perception can make him believe he is simply providing discipline "for the child's good." He sees nothing wrong with severe punishment. If the abuse is emotional, it may take the form of hypercritical, demeaning, and nasty remarks or of "crazy-making" erratic swings between seductive kindness and sudden, extreme rejection.

If the abuse is sexual, all too often the abuser may be a cousin, an uncle, or a family friend—someone whom the victim knows and should be able to trust. The emotional impact is immense: feelings of deep betrayal, fear, shame, and rage. When the abuse is kept secret or denied, the sense of betrayal escalates. Typically, the earlier in life and more persistent the abuse, the stronger the mistrust schema that results.

The mistrust schema differs from most others in that here the parent or perpetrator is being intentionally hurtful and cruel. Given such a terrible reality in a child's life, mistrust can be an adaptive response to a genuine threat: significant people in one's life are *not* trustworthy, and a wary social radar becomes a necessity for survival. The problems arise later in life, when suspicion corrodes otherwise beneficial connections to people who do not deserve to be viewed through the lens of distrust.

This schema can lead to several patterns. In one, the person views everyone with such suspicion that she shies away from any relationship of trust. Or she may at first idealize the other person as a protector or stalwart friend, then blow up at a seeming betrayal and turn against the person. In another variation, she may re-create her original childhood situation: she might be drawn into a string of relationships, each of which becomes abusive.

An abused person can sometimes become an abuser, passing on the abuse to another generation. (Fortunately, relatively few abused children become abusers as adults.)

The mistrust schema can be primed in subtle ways. For example, it can take the form of an ongoing belief that people have ulterior motives—that, for instance, they want to get to know you only because they want something from you. This can lead you to avoid forming new relationships.

If you view life through the distorting lens of the mistrust schema, relationships can seem like dangerous terrain, a place where people secretly harbor an intention to hurt or use you. Whenever someone does something nice, you may automatically suspect an ulterior motive—that they are trying to manipulate you, for instance. Your suspicion may twist things people say or do, making them seem like betrayal. You feel you have to stay vigilant against betrayal, wary that people will turn against you. While these suspicions can emerge in any relationship, they are strongest and most persistent in your closest ones.

If you feel that the mistrust schema applies to you, you need to form relationships where you can genuinely trust the other person. You may want to work with a therapist who specializes in clients who have been abused; once you feel safe with your therapist, the treatment will involve revisiting your memories of the original abuse and expressing your anger at the abuser—an essential emotional step. Mindfulness can help you become aware of your tendency to be mistrustful or to assume a betrayal. You can then challenge those thoughts so as to become more appropriately trusting in your close relationships. A mark of progress will occur when you no longer put up with abuse in your relationships, or when you resist the attraction you feel to an abusive partner.

Unlovability ● The automatic assumption that "I'm not lovable" typifies the unlovability schema. At its core lies a feeling of being somehow flawed, a notion that anyone who gets to know you as you truly are will ultimately find you defective—in fact, this is sometimes called the defectiveness schema.

For Terri, this pattern has recurred in every relationship she's had with a man, leaving her feeling vulnerable and anxious. Terri traces its origins back to her father leaving her mother for another woman: "The message to me was that I was unlovable, since as a female I identified strongly with my rejected mother. My assumption was that women will be found to lack some basic quality by a man, and are easily dispensed with. This has left me in constant fear of being found defective, not good enough, by men."

Shame and humiliation are the most prominent emotions in the defectiveness schema. The sense of being somehow flawed and unworthy of being loved is often instilled by parents who are hypercritical, insulting, or demeaning. A constant message of parental disapproval—"You're just not good enough"—fills the very small world of a child, becoming engraved in his view of himself. That message need not have been articulated in words; children pick up nonverbal expressions of disgust and contempt—the arched eyebrow, the sarcastic tone of voice. And that message has nothing to do with the child's actual qualities or worthiness—it's simply the way he was made to feel about himself.

One way of coping with such demeaning messages can be seen in the child who is so beaten down that he just accepts them. Such a child capitulates, building a definition of himself that has a deeply felt inadequacy at its core. Another child might erect a facade of bravado, an in-your-face boldness that hides an underlying feeling of defectiveness.

Shame takes us over when our weaknesses are exposed to the world or when we fear that they might be exposed. For people with this schema, those defects are deep inside; they believe that as someone gets to know them better their flaws will come to light and they will be rejected.

They may regard themselves as contemptuously as their parents did. In adult relationships, people with this schema are understandably wary that this inner flaw will be unveiled: "If they really get to know me, they won't like me."

Two main patterns are seen in people with the unlovability schema. Some give in to their deep sense of unworthiness. They lack self-confidence and are haunted by the certainty that something about them makes them utterly unacceptable. This leads them to hide themselves, revealing little of their feelings and thoughts, making themselves hard to get to know. Or they go into a relationship dreading the moment of rejection. They may remain deeply afraid of revealing themselves too much, lest they receive criticism or contempt. The cost can be a hollow, false self built up to hide from the world their feelings of unworthiness.

Others hide their sense of defectiveness behind an arrogant bravado that makes them look much better than they feel themselves to be. They compensate for these feelings of inadequacy by making an extra effort to seek adulation. Sometimes they win public recognition, in part to allay their underlying sense of being flawed.

The sense of being unlovable can lead to any number of problems in relationships. Since intimacy and closeness involve the risk of being revealed as flawed, people with this schema can protect themselves through relationships with others who are distant. If you have this schema, it may be hard for you to be genuine and self-revealing in a relationship and to believe that your partner loves you as you are.

If the unlovability schema seems familiar to you, one corrective comes in challenging the thoughts that amplify your faults and self-doubt in your mind; this challenge will give you a more realistic picture of your own actual strengths. The signs of the defectiveness schema are more subtle than most, so mindfulness can be especially helpful in tracking its telltale signs. Typical signs that a sense of defectiveness drives your reactions might include a deep sadness when you are alone, along with thoughts that no would want to be with you; another might be putting yourself down to others or just to yourself. A landmark will come when you learn to feel confident that your loved ones know you and love you as you are.

You may recognize one or another—or several—of these patterns in your own life. It's only natural that reading about our problems stirs them up a bit, along with the feelings that accompany them. It's important to acknowledge your emotional reactions and to empathize with the part of yourself that accepts the schema's existence. I'll go into this in more detail at the end of the next chapter, after we've finished our review of the other major schemas.

If You Want to Become More Aware of Your Schemas

Try to track and explore the times when your schemas are active.

When you are unusually upset, preoccupied by persistent emotions, or behaving impulsively and inappropriately, take these steps.

1. *Acknowledge what's going on.* Try not to gloss over it, put it out of your mind, or move on to the next thing. Instead, bring mindfulness to the moment, at whatever point you can, whether at the peak of your feelings or sometime later when you realize something significant has happened. Realize that you *are* preoccupied, or you're overreacting, or you did or said something inappropriate.

2. *Be open to your feelings.* Use a mindful awareness to explore the feelings connected with the episode that are strongest in you right now. Schemas have distinctive emotional flavors: abandonment triggers anxiety, mistrust elicits rage, deprivation can foster a deep sadness. What are you feeling right now? Have you had similar feelings during past episodes?

3. *Notice your thoughts.* What are you thinking? What are you telling yourself about what happened, what you did or said. How do your thoughts try to justify what you did?

4. *What does this remind you of?* Have you had other episodes similar to this one? Does this remind you of any episodes or feelings from your early years?

5. *Look for a pattern.* Can you see some consistency with other times you've had similar reactions? Does the overall pattern resemble any of the schemas you've just read about? If not, keep the pattern in mind as you continue to read about the schemas in the next chapter.

6

Schemas in the Larger World

The first five maladaptive schemas pertain to our close relationships, showing up over and over again in our love lives, family circles, and friendships. The final five revolve less around these areas and more around other areas, such as school, career, or community life. The first patterns are shaped mainly by our earliest experiences with our parents and family. The rest emerge in part or largely later, as our world expands beyond our immediate family and we meet the challenges of autonomy and competence.

Exclusion ● "I grew up near a small town in Indiana, about two thousand people," a woman told me at a workshop. "The luckiest girls lived in town—they could go to the drugstore together after school and get a soda. I couldn't do that; we lived miles away on a farm, where there was no one to play with after school. I've always felt outside things since then." ● Finding oneself on the outside of things, like being left out of a social clique at school, is a common source of the exclusion schema; "I don't belong" is its motto. The exclusion schema revolves around how we feel about our own status in groups, whether at work, in our own family or circle of friends, or even at a meeting or party. The perceived message boils down to this: "You're not like us, and we don't like you." ● This core belief typically leads the person to stay on the edge of the action, which reinforces the sense of being excluded. The typical emotions are anxiety, particularly in groups or with strangers, and a deep sadness about being alone or lonely. ● While schemas like emotional deprivation and abandonment are primarily formed in life's earliest years, social exclusion typically takes shape later, when acceptance by other kids starts to loom large in a child's emotional life. The needs of children as they grow and develop change over time. Parents and their nurturance reinforced the child's sense of well-being during the grade school years, but as her world expands, peers begin to matter in much the same way. Being included and accepted, even if by just one chum, takes on com-pelling importance. Being the kid others don't want to play with can be crushing.

But rejection by peers is but one source of the exclusion schema. A sense of being excluded can also arise, for instance, from one's family being somehow different from others in the neighborhood. It can even originate from the dynamics within a family—for example, when a divorced parent remarries, forming a blended family in which a child feels left out.

The child who feels excluded may try to adapt by staying on the outside of things or by avoiding the group so as to minimize the hurtfulness of being actively rejected. When this tendency to shy away from groups or keep to the edge carries over into adulthood, it keeps the person from engaging with oth-ers in ways that would result in his acceptance into a group.

This schema operates as a self-fulfilling prophecy: The anxiety a person feels about being scrutinized or rejected makes him socially awkward. In short, the exclusion schema makes him act in a way that ensures that its core belief—"I don't belong"—will come true.

To avoid the feared social rejection, someone who feels inept with strangers might withdraw into a corner at a gathering. Another way to avoid feeling left out is to make an extra effort to fit in: being overly conscientious about becoming the perfect group member.

Another strategy can be an in-your-face exaggeration of the outcast role, glorying in it. That may be going on with some teenagers who adopt the Gothic style: the razorlike Mohawk haircut dyed purple, piercings, black leather clothes. The message these teens project amounts to "I'm different, I don't belong, and I don't care."

If any of this rings true for you, mindfulness can ease your social anxiety and allow you to step back from the thoughts that make you ill at ease, so you can challenge them. You also can learn to counter how you've habitually acted, feeling your fears and challenging them by, for example, making an effort to initiate conversations instead of hanging back. This behavioral shift will depend on an emotional one: learning to master your anxiety so you feel more relaxed in whatever group you find yourself in.

Vulnerability ● "When I was fourteen, my father had a near-fatal heart attack," a woman in a workshop confided. "As he was recuperating, he told me one day, 'You're the only reason I'm trying to live.' I began to fear that his very life depended on me. In college I was a premed; today I'm a cardiologist. I worry about everyone in my life, and I worry far too much. My mother used to do the same. When I went out, she'd ask: 'Do you have your keys? Your money? Your sweater?' I always got the hidden message that something bad might happen. Now I do the same thing. I'll be out on a date and my boyfriend will be locking the car, and I'll ask him in this worried way, 'Do you have your keys? Your credit cards? Your money?' It drives him crazy."

Loss of control lies at the core of the vulnerability pattern. The distinctive emotional signature of vulnerability is an exaggerated fear that some catastrophe is about to strike. Ordinary fears escalate out of control, in what's called catastrophizing: the exaggeration of something small and only slightly worrisome into an imagined, full-fledged disaster.

The roots of vulnerability can usually be traced back to a parent who had the same tendency to catastrophize, or to a time when the person constantly felt as if something bad was about to happen. In either case, the child learns to worry too much, either by following the parent's model or because there *are* real problems to worry about. The message the child gets is that the world is a dangerous place. In adulthood this anxiety can fixate in any of several realms: finances, career, health, or physical safety.

Of course, worrying can be adaptive when it moves us to take safeguards or prepare ourselves for a real risk. Apprehension or anxiety in anticipation of a true crisis or threat serves a useful purpose when it mobilizes us to needed action—like taping up windows when there is a hurricane warning or getting an alarm system installed when there has been a rash of burglaries in the neighborhood.

But the worry habit becomes dysfunctional when it continues well past the point of getting us prepared for a true problem—when it overgeneralizes, leaving us worrying too much about perfectly normal situations and risks, like a loved one taking an airplane trip. Such out-of-proportion anxious thoughts are a hallmark of the vulnerability schema.

This schema can lead people to be overly conscientious in order to ensure a feeling of safety—extra-thrifty to the point of denying themselves any pleasure, for instance, or embracing extreme diet or health fads in the hope of warding off some dreaded disease. It can make someone so risk-averse that they never travel by a means they imagine is too risky or that they never go out at night for fear of being attacked. At its extreme, vulnerability can take the form of a phobia, like fear of flying, of germs, or of driving over bridges. People prone to panic attacks often are victims of this schema.

Another sign of the vulnerability schema can be seen in people who overprepare in order to feel safe or who grossly restrict their activities. Such people may try to assuage their fears by incessantly seeking reassurance.

They may go for unneeded physical checkups or pester investment advisers with fretful queries about the security of their funds. They may even develop private rituals—like checking three times to make sure that the doors are locked—to ease their obsessive worries.

An entirely different, rather paradoxical, picture emerges in people who overcompensate for vulnerability by taking risks. Such people go in for risky pursuits—skydiving, for instance—gambling with fate to show themselves that their fears are misplaced.

If this schema seems to apply to you, one focus for healing is to challenge your fears and, to the extent that they have held you back, gain more freedom in your activities. Mindfulness can help you recognize your fearful thoughts so that you can see that they're simply thoughts, not reality. By mindfully monitoring your thoughts rather than letting them dictate how you behave, you will start to win emotional freedom from your fears. And the calming and relaxing effects of mindfulness meditation will help you as you systematically counter your thoughts by adding a way to quiet the waves of anxiety that course through your body and put you on edge. As you systematically challenge your thoughts with mindfulness, your old fears will no longer dictate what you do.

Failure ● Even as pop singer Janet Jackson signed an $85 million contract—one of the biggest in history—with Virgin Records, she said she felt her success was undeserved. Despite her remarkable achievements, Jackson admitted to suffering from an immense sadness connected with a conviction of not being good enough. That feeling of being deficient despite one's accomplishments typifies the failure schema.

The roots of this pattern in Jackson are typical. Recalling her childhood in an interview, she said, "Kids can be cruel to each other. Or someone has to put someone else down to make themselves feel better, and that happened to me with certain family members. Or at school the teacher would pick on you, make you feel incredibly stupid in front of the entire class. Those are things that really hurt me. And then if you come home and someone else makes you feel the same way, you can begin to see how you feel less-than, not worthy, fraudulent. And that's how I grew up feeling."

Janet Jackson typifies several of the common roots of the failure schema. Sometimes overly critical parents, who make a child feel inept, sow the seeds. Or it can be constant put-down by siblings or schoolmates. Sometimes this schema rises from constantly making negative comparisons between yourself and other children or highly successful parents.

Whatever the cause, the hallmark of this pattern is feeling like a failure underneath it all, no matter how successful you are. A typical thought is that you're just not good enough to succeed at this. The emotions that go along with such thoughts are deep self-doubt and an anxious sadness.

While the unlovability schema stems from feeling flawed as a person and so not worthy of being loved, the failure schema arises in the realm of achievement and career. It centers on feeling that one's successes are undeserved or that one can't succeed at anything, no matter how hard one tries.

The failure schema can lead to pushing oneself very hard to do well, despite the constant fear of failure. This combination can lead to the impostor phenomenon, where people who have done very well nevertheless feel deep in their hearts that they are frauds, that their success was a fluke or a mistake and that they will be found out and exposed. They feel they have fooled people into seeing them as more capable than they truly are. Such people live in dread that they will one day do something that will lead to their unmasking.

The failure schema can be a self-fulfilling prophecy, leading some people to behave in a way that ensures they will not succeed. The conviction that they will fail makes some people take an avoidant path—too leery of trying out new skills or taking on the new challenges that might allow them to succeed. Or they put things off until it's too late, or they manufacture a ready excuse for the failure they anticipate.

If the failure schema seems familiar to you, the arena for change will be in how you regard your achievements—and your ability to achieve. This schema leads to the thought that you can never succeed. But mindfulness can help you identify and challenge the internal put-downs that so easily take over your mind, so you can more accurately assess your actual talents and abilities, or accept that your accomplishments are truly deserved.

Perfectionism ● Shirley went through a litany of complaints: "I work for hours and hours to prepare for the music classes I give. I do much more preparation than any of the other teachers, and I take on more classes than anyone else. I work so hard on it that I feel I have no time left for my own life. And then when a parent makes even a slightly negative comment, I berate myself about it for days."

The roots of this pattern for Shirley are typical: "I can remember when I was a child and brought my report card home, my father would always criticize me no matter how well I did—and I got mostly A's. If I got an A-minus or even an A, he'd ask why it wasn't an A-plus. Nothing I did was ever good enough for him. I still feel that nothing I do is quite good enough."

Shirley's childhood memories reflect the unrelenting standards at play in perfectionism. Parents who are always critical of a child's performance, no matter how good it is, create a deep sense of inadequacy in the child. Such children learn early in life to keep striving and striving, an effort they hope will protect them from losing their parents' love, almost like a magic ritual.

The emotional root of this schema is a sense of failing no matter how hard you try. Beneath that feeling lurks a sadness that you must do ever better to win your parents' love and approval. And with that comes sadness at not being accepted for who you are but only for how well you do.

People with the perfectionism schema see the entire world through a lens of unrealistically high expectations. Their motto is "I have to be perfect." People who harbor this attitude drive themselves to do their best and beyond. They are unrelenting in holding themselves to the highest standards. This can pay off in terms of achievements in career, sports, or other realms.

To blunt the likelihood of criticism, these people drive themselves to work much harder than they have to. But no matter how well one does, of course, it's never good enough, and so people drive themselves until the rest of their life suffers—their health, their relationships, their ability to enjoy life's pleasures. The way they drive themselves heightens the risk of stress-based disorders like colitis or tension headaches. While the perfectionist easily feels impatient and irritated, an emotion hovering in the background is sadness, a melancholy over missing out on life from being too dutiful.

Both the failure schema and perfectionism have to do with our ability to accomplish. The failure schema leads us to expect too little of ourselves; perfectionism, too much. The perfectionism schema drives workaholics. The woman who stays at the office every night pushing herself to get more done, long after everyone else has gone home, may indeed do better in her job as a result. But no matter how well she does, she pressures herself to do more, and her very effort to attain some ever-receding standard means she has no life outside work.

Perfectionism need not be focused on work, however. The same underlying sense that no matter how good you are, you are not good enough, can drive people to push themselves in sports, at school, in physical appearance, for social status, or even to have the best-looking house.

The distorting lens of the perfectionism schema focuses on what's wrong with what you've done. Any flaw in your performance, any slight mistake you made, will be all you will think about. Your self-criticism and self-reproach are relentless.

Some perfectionists try to hold everyone else to the same ultra-high standards they apply to themselves. As a result, they are often critical of other people for what they perceive as failings, even when those people have done a perfectly adequate job or simply see it differently. The critical lens can alight on any situation, always searching out flaws. People with this schema often blur the fine line between a valid discernment and a judgmental opinion; they see their criticism as correct and appropriate.

One sign of the perfectionism schema is the constant feeling that you have to keep pushing and pushing yourself to do more or do better. Another is anxiety about there being too little time to accomplish everything you have set out for yourself. Still another is a grimness about your activities. This can turn an otherwise pleasurable project, like working out at a gym, into yet another tense arena for accomplishment. Perfectionism drives the fun out of life. The perfectionist may fantasize about a day in the future when she can finally enjoy life, but she constantly postpones gratification.

If the perfectionism schema applies to you, mindfulness can help you challenge distorted patterns of thinking and the self-criticism and reproach that drive this pattern, and catch yourself before you once again push yourself too hard. You need to realize that lowering your standards will be a relief to you, making time in your life to get other needs met. Challenging your perfectionistic habits can put your life into a healthier balance, giving yourself downtime in which to enjoy simple pleasures.

Entitlement ● This emotional pattern centers on accepting life's limits. Typical of this pattern is an admission by a client: "I can't stand to drive at the speed limit—I feel I should be able to go as fast as I want. If a slower driver gets in front of me and I'm unable to pass, I get very irritated. The other day I was on a two-lane road and got stuck behind an old man in a large sedan who was driving exactly forty-five miles an hour, the posted limit. I got furious. I honked my horn, flashed my lights at him, kept trying to pull out to pass him, even though it was a curving road with a double line. I was in a rage that he didn't pull over and let me by. When I got to my meeting, all the parking places were gone. So I parked in the handicapped space."

People with the entitlement schema feel special—so special that they are entitled to do whatever they want. Their motto: "Rules don't apply to me." Entitled people view life through a distorting lens that places them above everyone else. Laws, rules, and social conventions are only for others, not for them.

Those with this schema seem oblivious to the unfair burden their entitlement might create for others; they have too little empathy or concern for those they take advantage of. The entitled person will blithely park in a space reserved for the handicapped, help himself to extra servings at a meal when there is barely enough food to go around, or expect his partner to cater to his every need while he attends to none of hers.

This attitude can rise from being spoiled in childhood, treated like a little prince or princess. Children who are brought up in households of great wealth, with servants at their beck and call and all the favors that money can bring, may think they are entitled to special treatment in any and all situations. This can also happen with children, wealthy or not, whose parents set no limits for them, give them whatever they want whenever they want it, rarely punish them, and do not make them take responsibility for anything, even helping with chores. As adults such people can be impulsive, childish, and selfish.

Another source of the entitlement pattern derives from the same root as the unlovability schema: parents whose love seems conditional on the child having a certain quality—beauty, for example, or a gift for sports or academic achievement. Such children may exaggerate their accomplishments, to seem special—and may demand special treatment accordingly. Underneath it all, however, they still feel a sense of inadequacy, even shame, which they cover over with narcissistic pride.

A third source of the pattern can be a reaction to being deprived of attention, affection, or material needs in childhood. Such people feel so aggrieved at having been treated unfairly in childhood that they seem to feel they are entitled to more than their share as compensation for having had so little as children.

This sense of being special should be distinguished from the healthy confidence that genuine competence and ability engender. Well-grounded pride allows people to take risks and stretch themselves toward ever more challenging goals and achievements. The entitlement schema, however, leads people to exaggerate their prowess and abilities, often to prop up an underlying feeling of inadequacy, and so generates a false pride based on a faulty notion of one's abilities. A basic confusion in those with the entitlement pattern is mistaking conceit for a well-grounded confidence.

One sign of the entitlement pattern follows from feeling special: irritation when people say no or set limits on a request. Others are a lack of self-discipline, indulging one's impulses, and gratifying one's desires regardless of the consequences—for example, spending themselves into bankruptcy even while borrowing from friends and family more than they can possibly pay back. The inability to delay gratification in the pursuit of one's goals can lead to chronic underachievement, while giving in to impulses creates a completely chaotic life. One sign might be a home that never gets cleaned, where messes pile up and pile up.

People with this schema typically are blind to its negative impact on other people. They expect the world to treat them as special, and so are surprised and irritated when someone objects to their being allowed to overstep bounds. They feel the pain of the schema only when the consequences of their actions come home: a court date because of unpaid traffic tickets, losing a job because they failed to do what was expected of them, or a spouse threatening divorce because they are so self-centered. In short, when the costs of the schema become too great to ignore.

If the entitlement pattern seems to apply to you, mindfulness can help you learn to spot the impulses building in you—and catch yourself before you yet again overstep appropriate limits. It can also help you connect with the deeper feelings that drive this schema, so you can deal with them more directly. One change that particularly helps break free from the hold of the entitlement schema: start to be aware of the negative impact of your actions on the people around you, and tune in to how you have made them feel. It is also crucial to take more responsibility for your obligations, for your impulsive habits, and for overstepping limits.

Schema Clusters ● While describing the schemas one by one

helps to clarify each of them, in life they often travel in packs and operate in clusters. Natalie's difficulties, for example, revolved around the fact that her husband paid no attention to her needs, always insisting that she do things his way. She found herself giving in, trying to be the perfect wife, scrambling to be sure the kids were good when he was around, doing everything she could to please him. She hated it, but she was motivated by a compelling fear that he would leave her if everything wasn't all just right.

As I worked with Natalie, we uncovered a cluster of schemas that worked together to mold this pattern: deprivation, abandonment, and subjugation. Her deprivation schema led Natalie to care for her husband's needs, never letting him know that *she* felt uncared for in their marriage. And her abandonment schema made her so terrified of his leaving her that it played into her pattern of subjugation: she'd do almost anything he wanted in order to ensure his continued presence. The result: a marriage with no problems—at least on the surface. But beneath that veneer, a deeply unhappy, resentful wife.

Few people, if any, are plagued by just one schema; typically we have several. Some may trigger mostly in one domain of life, like close relationships, while not at all in other parts of life, such as work.

Schemas can interact as they develop. For instance, sometimes a schema acquired quite early in life can make a child more susceptible to certain later-developing schemas. Children who grow up with the unlovability schema, for example, may have a need to prove themselves that can lead to perfectionism. The excellence that perfectionists continually strive for can be a way to buy parental love or attention—bringing home straight A's, winning sports competitions—all in a desperate attempt to earn praise from parents who have made the child feel basically flawed.

Here is another example: entitlement can begin as a way of coping with deprivation or defectiveness. Those schemas set a child up to feel she has to be beautiful or a superb performer or otherwise special in order to be loved. In those who suffered deprivation, entitlement may arise as a feeling that the world owes us special treatment because we suffered through such a hard time. Or, with defectiveness at its root, entitlement can become a way of overcompensating for a deep sense of shame.

Schemas Are Recognizable ● Whatever its origins or way of manifesting itself, each schema has a unique signature, a pattern of typical triggers and reactions. This means every schema can be recognized by the situations that trigger it, the automatic feelings and thoughts the trigger evokes and the habitual reactions that go along with them.

For instance, a woman at a workshop described the trigger for her deprivation pattern: "As my boyfriend is saying good-bye, he'll talk about how busy he's going to be over the next few weeks—but doesn't mention that he'd like to get together again."

Her immediate thoughts: "He's avoiding me. He doesn't care about me. My needs don't matter."

Her feeling: deeply hurt, with a hint of sadness.

Her automatic reaction: to hide her hurt with a cool detachment, as though everything's fine—nothing bothers her. So she responds by acting very cool toward her boyfriend.

The problem with schema reactions, of course, is that they are counterproductive. Her boyfriend picks up on her sudden coolness and asks, "Why do you always get weird when I say good-bye?" She brushes off his feeling ill at ease with a denial: "It's nothing. I'm fine. Have a good week." In doing so she also dismisses what—if she wasn't being controlled by the schema—might have been an opening to talk over her reaction and change the pattern for the better.

"In my family," she recalls, "any expression of strong emotion was frowned upon as a 'dramatic display.' I learned to hide these feelings and express myself with a cool logic. Telling people that I'm angry with them is terrifying to me. I feel I will be completely rejected or, worse, ignored. The background thought I have at those moments is that it's my fate not to be heard, so why bother expressing my needs? They won't be met anyway."

And, of course, the conviction that one's needs won't be met is the credo of the deprivation pattern.

A Reflective Pause ● If you have seen patterns you recognize in yourself while reading these descriptions of maladaptive schemas, you may want to pause to reflect on any feelings they may put you in touch with. These patterns are emotionally loaded, capturing our most compelling needs and fears, hopes and disappointments. Thinking about them inevitably stirs us up.

Right about now we are most likely to say, "Never mind" and turn to some handy distraction. But if you're willing, this is just the moment to keep your attention focused on your emotions without giving in to distractions.

If you resonate with the deprivation schema, for instance, just reading about it can make you feel a bit sad or perhaps angry. The vulnerability schema might bring to mind things you are fearful about, while reading about the exclusion schema might start you thinking about times you've felt like an outsider. One reason for this lies in the way schemas work. Anything that reminds us of our schemas tends to prime these deep emotional habits, if only a touch, bringing out some of the feelings that go with them.

This is a good thing, because we begin to heal when we open ourselves to the feelings that have been holding these patterns in place. It takes courage to face the feelings behind these emotional habits, but that strength of spirit will be your ally in disempowering these tenacious patterns.

Healing schemas starts with an unwavering look at ourselves, hard as that may be. We need to experience the underlying emotional pain or dread, if only to realize that we can survive intact if we let ourselves enter this forbidden territory of the heart. Accessing the underlying feelings that lock in the schema patterns can be deeply reparative, like an immune cell neutralizing the virus that causes a disease. Neutralizing the underlying feelings of a schema deflates what otherwise gives it such compelling power in the mind.

Often when people first hear the descriptions of the schemas, their reaction is, "Oh, my gosh, I've got almost all of them!" We can feel overwhelmed. But no matter how many of these patterns may come up in our lives from time to time, some are more predominant than others. It's advisable to focus on working with just one schema at a time, even though they often overlap and arise together.

While you may eventually get to them all, you want to pace yourself so you are not taking on too much at once, which can be confusing. The interventions for one schema may be very different from those for another. Knowing the schema map can give you a conceptual framework useful for sorting out what's going on. But don't try to do everything at once—a real danger for those with the perfectionism pattern, who bring their need to overachieve even to schema work!

When we open up to our schema patterns, it's important to empathize with the part of us that feels so strongly the emotions that are triggered inside—before we rush to change our reactions. First we need to engage with the part of us that holds the schema's outlook. As we'll see in Chapter 11, we can cultivate a powerful dialogue between the schema's voice and the part of us that is in touch with the innate wisdom of mindfulness.

Our schemas protect us from what might be overwhelming, unbearable feelings. They have been coping strategies, survival mechanisms that let us adapt to adversities. At the point in our lives when we first learned them, they made a certain emotional sense. But we pay a price later as we continue to live our lives guided by the rules of these self-defeating, distorted beliefs, feelings, and reactions.

Our apprehensions about these feelings keep us running from them, preventing us from facing schemas fully and honestly. But once we let those feelings come freely and surrender to their presence, it defuses our fear of them. We see that we *can* survive them intact, that the fear of abandonment or the anger stoked by subjugation do not overwhelm us, after all. The feelings may not be nearly as frightening as we thought they would be. In fact, by letting ourselves feel these repressed emotions, we reclaim a buried part of ourselves, and we feel a more genuine connection with ourselves.

The Can of Worms ● The path to emotional healing, then, involves

a sustained resolve and uncompromising honesty with ourselves. Once we notice the places in our lives where we've kept these emotional patterns alive, we can shake ourselves out of our complacency and reassess who we are, as our old conditioning, our old sense of ourselves, is challenged.

Expect, at some point, to want to run away from all this. It's a little like opening a can of worms, or maybe caterpillars—you may want to shove them all back inside. But as you walk this path, you will also have glimpses of feeling freer, of a more direct connection to your life and the people in it. And once the pull of that greater freedom and authenticity takes hold, it becomes harder to turn back.

It's as though an inner volcano has started to erupt, and despite the danger, we welcome the release. The pain of the truth still feels better than the pain of self-deception. As we settle into the process, at some point we tend to go through a natural grieving as we let go of old identities, familiar habits and ways of being. Eventually those caterpillars disperse, weaving themselves into protective cocoons while shedding their former identity. Unraveling the membranes of our schema patterns, we too begin to emerge from our cocoons, feeling lighter and more alive—as if, metaphorically, we were growing wings.

As they go through this mindful investigation, people often find a growing confidence in their own wisdom. Some describe it as though they were getting more familiar with a wise inner being to whom they can turn for guidance. They learn to trust that intuitive, wise voice more and more.

As a client of mine said, "In intensely difficult emotions, if I can step out of the way, it's as though my organism knows exactly what to do: how to cry, how to release painful feelings. It all happens so naturally, as if it had a life of its own. I can let go of having to control everything and let a healing process occur by itself."

The original meaning of the word "emotion" derives from *emotere*, the Latin word for "to move out." Emotion implies motion. I experienced this movement of emotion during a spellbinding live performance by the legendary blues musician Buddy Guy.

The blues can make you feel at home with your feelings—deeply passionate, deeply painful, whatever. Any feeling is welcomed into this soulful embrace, with the carefree attitude, "Let it in—we can handle it." Feelings are held, but not held on to. The spirit of the blues allows the feelings to move through you in a way that opens you to the sensual realm of emotion.

Mindfulness can be like this soulful embrace, intimately connecting us with our raw senses and tender feelings. Not evaluating them, not rejecting or holding on to them, just feeling them naturally and letting them move through us, embraced by an empathic awareness.

If You Want to Know More about Your Own Schemas

Learn to recognize the schemas' signature patterns. Acknowledge and get to know them.

Since every schema has distinct identifying elements, parts of the pattern that come up time and again, becoming familiar with these parts of our schemas gives us a powerful tool in recognizing when we are caught in a schema attack. We can use that familiarity as a cue to ourselves that the schema has been activated again.

Recognizing, for instance, "Oh, I'm having *those* feelings again," or "Here come my schema thoughts," gives us the freedom to wake from the schema trance. But that recognition can be enhanced with mindfulness, the ability to observe our experience without being swept away in it.

You can begin acknowledging the schemas by simply becoming familiar with the signs that come up most often in your life. You can do this by keeping a schema journal for a week or two, or more, jotting down clues to the schemas that may be operating at times when you feel upset in some way—particularly at times when, looking back, you suspect that you were overreacting. The realization that the reaction didn't fit may come later on, as you reflect back on what happened: He couldn't help being late—why did I feel so hurt and angry? Sometimes it helps to refresh yourself—to warm up the feelings—by talking about your overreaction with a good listener, to reflect on it by writing in your journal, or simply to mull it over in your mind.

Any element of a schema can be a clue. Track any parts of the pattern you can readily identify:

1. First, ask yourself if there was anything *maladaptive* about how you reacted? Did the resulting interaction work out well, or did your distorted thoughts, intense feelings, or overreactions leave you feeling upset? This is an important distinction, a general signal to you that a schema, rather than a useful response, is at play.
2. What was the *trigger*? Did you feel left out of a group at work or at a party? These are signs of the social exclusion schema. Each schema has unique triggers, so the situation that sets you off is another clue to which schema might be involved.

3. What were your *feelings?* Each schema has its own distinctive emotional flavor. For example, failure can trigger a sense of shame; vulnerability unleashes a flood of worrisome fears; subjugation results in resentment or rage. You can identify whatever schema may be at play by identifying your visceral reactions.

4. What were your *thoughts?* For example, did you worry that you had a severe illness like pneumonia when it really was just a minor cold? That signifies the vulnerability-to-harm pattern.

5. What did you *do?* Like your thoughts and feelings, the actions you take when a schema is activated can be just as automatic and habitual. Avoiding contact at a party could well be a sign of the social exclusion schema.

6. What might be the *origins?* Does this resonate with experiences in your early life? For example, your intense anger when your partner is late to meet you and fails to call may remind you of times in your childhood when a parent was unreliable or did not show up—typical of the deprivation schema.

Start to map the schemas that come up most often for you over the course of a week. Keep a journal or notebook handy to jot down each of these elements, so you can learn to recognize their telltale signs as they are occurring.

7

How Schemas Work

An old story tells of a young man who keeps hearing about a wonderful tailor, Zumbach, whose suits can make anyone look handsome and stylish. One day the man goes to Zumbach and asks him to make a suit. So Zumbach takes his measurements and tells him to come back in a week. ● A week later the young customer eagerly goes back for his suit. Zumbach, with great ceremony, brings out the suit and has the man try it on. It looks wonderful—except that one sleeve is longer than the other, the buttons don't match up, and the trousers are too short. ● So the customer complains. Zumbach, deeply affronted, says with great indignation, "It's not the suit. The trouble is the way you're wearing it. If you crook your left elbow just a bit, the sleeves will be perfect. And if you hunch forward and raise your right shoulder, the buttons match up splendidly. Then if you'll just bend your knees a bit, you'll see the slacks are just right." ● The customer tries it and, lo and behold, the suit fits like a glove—and it's gorgeous! ● Like Zumbach's suit, schemas twist our perceptions and bend our responses to suit their warped version of reality. They convince us that their twisted version of reality is how things actually are. They define our own view of who we have to be, and what is acceptable. In short, they keep us from displaying our natural flexibility, creativity, joy, and compassion by confining our lives along the arbitrary lines of thought, feeling, and reaction they lay out for us. ● Schemas give us a single way of seeing, thinking, and feeling about things and one habitual way to react to them. And that reaction not only confirms how the schema tells us things are, but drastically limits our options. ● It's like that exercise where people are asked to connect nine dots laid out in three parallel lines by using just four straight lines without ever lifting the pencil from the paper. As long as we labor under the assumption that we can't stray beyond the area of the dots, we can never see the solution, which demands the lines go outside the square of dots.

It's the same with schemas: they keep us from broadening our perspective and making flexible responses. They confine us to a narrow way of thinking about the problems we face—like a Zumbach suit for the psyche.

Emotional alchemy entails an education about schemas. The workshops I give are designed to increase people's insight into and conceptual understanding of how schemas operate and how to begin to work with them— how, in other words, to know yourself. Understanding schemas in depth is a first step to freeing ourselves from these mental prisons.

Tunnel Vision ● You may have witnessed a classic example of the reality created by the perfectionism schema if you've ever seen a figure-skating competition. Watching a world-class skater perform is an edge-of-your-seat experience. You know she's pushed herself past her limits, practicing endless hours to perfect the moves. You're awed by her confidence and the graceful precision of her skating, amazed at what the human body is capable of accomplishing.

Then, when she goes into a spellbinding triple lutz, you're stunned to see her lose her balance and tumble to the ice. She quickly recovers and skates on, giving the rest of her performance her all. But at the end the applause is halfhearted, and she seems deflated.

You listen to the announcer analyzing her mistakes with a tone that mixes regret with judgment. Her fall is replayed in slow motion while the announcer emphasizes point-by-point precisely how she failed to accomplish the perfection everyone expected of her—how, in a sense, she let us down. You watch the skater hold back tears as she skates to the side, her disappointment in herself palpable. No one—least of all the skater herself—gives credit to the 98 percent of her performance that was sterling; the focus is entirely on that moment of failure.

She slouches beside her coach as the judges' scores are posted. You wish someone would come along and praise the rest of her performance, let her know that, for the most part, she did superbly; reassure her that she's not a horrible failure in life because of this one mistake. But there is no forgiveness for her, no larger perspective. She wants to run, to hide. You sense that this moment will haunt her for a very long time.

That dismal scenario captures the claustrophobic universe created whenever a schema captures the mind. The result is akin to a possession state, dictating our experience at that moment. Because schemas influence our perception of events, becoming part of the lens through which we see reality, they have the power to select what we attend to and what we ignore, without our being conscious of their role. The way they present reality to us seems to be as it really is. The single mistake looms large in the mind of the perfectionist, who remains oblivious to the excellence of her performance.

While we are victims of a schema, we can easily be blind to the role of that pattern in our life's repeated disasters. The schema's reality defines what we perceive and remember, but leaves us impervious to the fact that the schema itself is at work in our minds. So we see the problem as "out there" rather than in our minds.

A person who is under the spell of a schema can seem like the man in the apocryphal tale who complains to his therapist, "I've just gotten fired for the fourth time in the last few years. My marriage is on the verge of collapse, and I've already been divorced five times. Please help me understand why there are so many messed-up people out there."

Absurd Mental Habits ● "As for the mystery and enigma in my painting," the Surrealist painter René Magritte once commented, "I would say it is the best proof of my break with the absurd mental habits that generally take the place of an authentic feeling of existence."

Maladaptive schemas certainly fit what Magritte called "absurd mental habits." They keep us from experiencing the moment in an immediate and direct way. The distortions they impose on our perception render life as it seems to the schema, hindering us from registering and responding to things as they actually are. And that in turn robs us of our spontaneity and flexibility. Instead, we are caught in the rut of habit, reacting to some packaged pattern of seeing and reacting. These imposed habits keep us from a direct experience of what is actually going on in the moment—a genuine presence that Magritte called "an authentic feeling of existence."

Several mental and perceptual distortions are typical of schemas at work in the mind:

SELECTIVE PERCEPTION. Seeing things only one way, while discounting all evidence to the contrary. A student with the perfectionism pattern, for example, might do well on a term paper but get a single negative comment. He will then ruminate on that comment in a tape loop of self-criticism, ignoring the overall good grade.

OVERGENERALIZATION. A single event signifies a perpetual pattern. Clues to this distortion are in the use of words like "always" or "never." Someone with the failure schema who gets passed over for a promotion because someone else has more appropriate qualifications will tell himself, "I never succeed at anything."

MIND READING. A mind reader attributes the worst motives or thoughts to others to explain what they have done; she seizes on these arbitrary explanations as though they had been proven true. Take someone with the abandonment schema who ends up waiting and waiting at a restaurant for a friend who is late. While sitting there, she starts assuming this delay means her friend will stand her up. She will then review things she has said or done that might have caused her friend to want to end their relationship.

JUMPING TO CONCLUSIONS. A schema concludes that its worst beliefs are valid despite the absence of real evidence. The moment someone with the social exclusion pattern enters a party, for example, the automatic thought will come: "No one here wants to talk to me. I don't belong here."

EXAGGERATION. A trivial fact is mistaken for a catastrophe. For instance, someone with the vulnerability pattern will notice the first symptoms of a sore throat, and will suddenly be convinced that he is coming down with life-threatening pneumonia.

A Poet's Logic ● Our schemas flavor the raw experiences of our lives with their particular passion. They determine what emotional implications we read into the facts, and so how that information makes us feel.

The "truth," for a schema, lies in the emotional implications it reads into a simple statement or thought, and in the dire predictions, expectations, attributions, and assumptions we find hidden there.

Schemas are triggered by *symbolic* realities. In this sense, a schema operates more like a poem than like a declarative sentence. The meaning of a sentence is relatively straightforward, conveying some specific information. But a poem can't be understood in terms of the literal meanings of the words. Its meaning lies in the symbolic significance of its words, their emotional implications, and the free-wheeling associations to them.

Like poems, schemas follow a certain irrational logic, something akin to the childlike mode of thinking that Freud called primary process, in which facts are bendable and reality can be distorted to fit different ways of seeing things—as in a dream.

Exactly what implications we read into the bare facts of a moment depend on the specific maps of experience our personal history has shaped. Take this sentence: "I failed the test." As a statement its meaning is simple. But the emotional implications, especially for a person prone to the failure schema, can be vast, something like those of a semi-poem that might begin this way:

> *I failed the test.*
> *I fail.*
> *I fail at everything.*

That short quasi-poem could well summarize the core thought in a failure schema. It could go on: "I always fail. I never succeed. I just don't have what it takes. . . ." This mental map might well conclude that one is not just incompetent but worthless. Thus the fact—failing the test—takes on the dire and gloomy meanings of the "poem" above.

The failure schema, as we've seen, typically builds upon repeated early experiences of failure or hurtful put-downs. By contrast, for someone with a personal history of overcoming setbacks and a stronger sense of competence, the corresponding mental map would be more optimistic. The implications read into the same fact—failing the test—might be "I'll study harder next time and do better," with the underlying assumption, "I can succeed." And instead of a devastating sense of worthlessness and depression, the person would feel hopeful. In this way schemas determine the impact of events in our lives.

The Anatomy of a Schema Attack ● "I once had a boyfriend I had met when we both worked for the same company," Teresa recounted in a workshop. "After several months we broke up. Two weeks after our breakup, I saw him pull into the parking lot one morning—and there was a woman in the car with him.

"I was hurt and furious. I thought, 'They've slept together. He's done this to me already!' I felt completely betrayed, even though since we had broken up I had started dating another man.

"So I stormed right in front of his car, seething with fury, making sure he could see me, then stalked into the building and slammed the door. . . . Days later I found out that he and the woman weren't together at all. He had just given her a lift because her car had broken down on the way to work."

Perhaps anyone would have been at least a little upset at seeing an ex-lover with someone new. But Teresa's reaction went way beyond ordinary jealousy: she was seething with fury. The added rage, Teresa saw in analyzing her own schemas, traced to a strong fear of abandonment that stemmed in large part from her childhood, when her father had actually abandoned her mother and her and moved in with another woman. The resulting hurt and anger that Teresa carried was triggered by her ex-boyfriend's symbolic repetition of that childhood trauma.

When, like Teresa, we find ourselves swept away by overwhelming feelings—whether rage, hurt, fear, or sadness—the brain's emotional centers have seized power from the more rational, thinking brain. This rational part of the brain might have cautioned Teresa to consider other possibilities before exploding in rage.

Such overreactions are schema attacks, emotional explosions triggered by our schemas. The telltale signs of a schema attack are an overreaction that is very quick, very strong, very inappropriate—and that, on a closer look, reveals a symbolic meaning that triggers the schema. For example, we may isolate ourselves on the edge of a party in reaction to someone's frosty tone of voice, which triggered our social exclusion schema—the cold tone symbolizing the social rejection we fear, flooding our mind with the thought that no one would want to talk to us, and the familiar anxious feelings that go along with that notion.

A schema attack like Teresa's tantrum originates in the emotional centers, an ancient part of the brain that has enormous power. Emotions serve a crucial purpose in survival: they are a way the brain can ensure that we make an instantaneous response that could rescue us from some threat. The brain's design still gives our emotions the power to take us over in an instant if the emotional centers perceive an emergency, whether that emergency is a real physical danger or just a symbolic one.

The Schema Warehouse ● The anatomical trigger for such a schema attack is the structure in the emotional brain called the amygdala, mentioned earlier. It holds the key to understanding how someone like Teresa can, in an instant, do something that in hindsight she regrets. The amygdala acts as the brain's storage center for our negative emotional memories, something like a vast archive of electrifying, terrifying, and infuriating

moments from our lives. Whenever we have been flooded with anger or anxiety, overwhelmed by sadness, or torn by hurt, that emotion has left an imprint in the amygdala.

So, presumably, have those emotionally charged moments over the years when our emotional habits were being shaped. Along with each emotional imprint, the amygdala dutifully stores whatever reaction we learned at those moments, whether it was freezing in fear, lashing out in rage, or tuning out and going numb. In short, the amygdala acts as a schema warehouse, the repository for our repertoire of negative emotional habits.

Our memories of past upsets—and what we learned to do at such moments—act as emotional radar, scanning everything we experience. When there is a seeming match between something happening now and something from our past that was emotionally distressing—"He's rejecting and abandoning me, just as my father did when he deserted the family and ran off with another woman!"—the match triggers whatever reaction we learned to make to that earlier event. The result: a schema attack.

In these moments, the amygdala falls back on whatever response is most familiar, something like a default option in a computer. The amygdala searches for a quick response and takes whatever comes immediately to hand. The amygdala favors one way to respond—whatever habit it has overlearned through countless repetitions—so it readily follows the well-practiced script of a schema.

Say someone's romantic partner doesn't call her when he said he would, and her mistrust schema sends her into a fury over what she perceives as his betrayal. The rut in her brain has become so well-worn that there is little choice once the schema attack begins: we play out the same response over and over, even though we may realize rationally that it makes no sense.

The Design Flaw ● There is a neural back alley, a one-neuron-long link between the thalamus, where all we see and hear first enters the brain, and the amygdala, where our emotional memories scan all we experience. But there's a problem with this arrangement: The circuit to the amygdala gets only a small portion of the information coming into the brain—what amounts to the fuzzy picture of an out-of-focus movie. Only about 5 percent or less of the signal coming in from the senses goes through this shortcut from the thalamus to the amygdala; all the rest goes up to the neocortex, the thinking brain, where a more systematic analysis goes on.

The amygdala makes its snap judgments on the basis of a dim and foggy picture of things, while a much clearer image goes up to the centers in the neocortex. Because the neocortex is more thorough in coming to its conclusions, it yields a more measured and accurate response.

The amygdala comes to its conclusions much, much faster in brain time than do the more rational circuits in the thinking brain. In fact, this emotional snap judgment can be made before the thinking brain has time to figure out what's going on.

That's where the problem begins. The amygdala bases its reactions on a fuzzier picture than the thinking brain gets, and does so with lightning speed. This must have worked well enough during most of evolution, when there were so many real, physical threats. But in modern life we still respond to symbolic threats—like the sight that triggered Teresa's hurt about abandonment—with the same intensity as though they were actual physical dangers.

This design flaw in our neural architecture means a snap decision based on a blurry picture can readily lead to a schema attack. A brain response that worked so well in ancient times can today lead to disaster: Teresa overreacts with all the speed and force that we need to dodge a speeding car when she sees her ex-boyfriend driving up to work with another woman.

Schema Priming ● When the amygdala gets triggered, it floods the body with the stress hormones that prepare it for an emergency. These hormones are of two kinds: one variety provides the body with a quick, intense shot of energy—enough, say, for one vigorous round of fighting or running, the ancient survival responses that, in evolution, paid off. Another kind is secreted more gradually into the body, heightening its overall sensitivity to events, making us hyperalert to any coming danger.

These biological responses mean that the small crises of a stressful day build up progressively higher levels of stress hormones. More to the point, when something comes up that resonates with a schema—say, seeing a TV show about a domineering mother who bears a strong resemblance to your own mother—it can prime your own subjugation schema. You become hypersensitive to events in your day that feel like subjugation.

Schemas can stay primed for hours, while those stress hormones surge inside us. And because a primed schema can make us more susceptible to more schema reactivity, the process can be self-sustaining, going on over days or weeks as one event after another continues to play on our sensitivity. In fact priming may be the way we experience schemas most of the time—not in a full-fledged schema attack but as a subtle, ongoing undertone to our day.

Schema priming, in turn, leads us to engage in whichever coping strategy we favor for that schema. If we have learned to overcompensate for subjugation, we may become bossy and domineering ourselves; if we have learned an avoidance approach, we become more submissive.

The hormones that prime our brain to be ever more vigilant make us biologically more sensitive and reactive. We become more vulnerable to seeing difficult moments through a schema lens and so as upsetting rather than just as something else to deal with in our day. Our schemas are set on a hair trigger, ready to unleash their load at any handy target.

When the brain becomes hypervigilant, the lenses through which it scans our world put our schemas toward the top of the hierarchy. The set point for a schema attack becomes much lower: we are ready to pounce on someone for something that, were we in a more content frame of mind, would pass peacefully. And while the schema stays primed, we are more likely to enact yet again our familiar ways of coping with the schema.

Brain studies show that a highly activated—or hot—amygdala impairs our ability to turn off our negative thoughts and emotions. So if we have already been upset by something else, and then a bit later a schema attack gets launched, we find it even more difficult to stop.

Tellingly, a hot amygdala floods the body with high levels of cortisol, the hormone released by the brain to marshal the body's emergency responses. Cortisol makes the whole situation worse. The brain structure that matches our actions to the situation and makes sure they are appropriate is called the hippocampus. It turns out that the hippocampus is thrown off-kilter by the flood of cortisol unleashed during a surge of negative emotion like that of a schema attack.

Inappropriateness, remember, is one hallmark of a schema attack. Social exclusion, for example, makes people overly timid in groups; the abandonment schema leads to anger at signs of being left that are merely symbolic. From what we know about the brain, it seems that the more upset we are even before a schema is triggered, the more likely the ensuing schema attack will be inappropriate—the wrong reaction to the wrong person at the wrong time.

Multiple Selves ● The power of schemas to dictate our reality parallels a notion in classical Buddhist psychology which posits that whatever mental state dominates our mind at a given moment will shape how we perceive and react to whatever is going on. As these mental states shift, so do our perceptions and reactions.

In a sense, these shifts make us a different person depending on which emotional states dominate our mind in a given moment. This view of the multitudinous selves that populate our mind fits recent thinking in modern personality theory and cognitive science. Instead of seeing personality as a fixed set of tendencies, modern psychology is coming around to a view that who we are shifts, sometimes radically, from moment to moment and from context to context—though the coexistence of these differing realities does not release us from responsibility for what we do.

Each emotion, in a sense, is its own context. A strong emotion like anger or fear will control our priorities in attention and in memory. We recall to mind or fix our attention more easily on whatever fits the emotion of the moment. A schema can be seen as a mini-self, a constellation of feelings, thoughts, memories, and propensities to act that define our reality at that moment.

Sometimes schemas remind me of that famous scene in the movie *Alien* where a piranha-mouthed monster bursts from the stomach of a spaceship crew member. Schemas are almost like living beings inside our mind. Like an alien parasite, they struggle to survive—for the most part, quite successfully. These emotional habits have a life of their own. Even if we try not to let them affect us, they come into play despite our best intentions.

In a sense, the twists and turns that schemas impose on reality and on our emotional lives may help to ensure their survival. This schema survival tactic can be seen in how the very reactions a schema dictates for us result in outcomes that justify the schema's own distorted beliefs. They act as a kind of self-fulfilling prophecy, a working theory or assumption about ourselves, other people, and what we believe to be the inevitable nature of our relationships with them.

Someone with the mistrust schema, for instance, will approach people with the belief that no one can be trusted, and so will act wary, with a too-ready suspicion, pouncing on any sign that someone has betrayed him. The guardedness of someone who believes people can't be trusted makes others uncomfortable and so less likely to be warm and open. If he is guarded in return—as this attitude might well promote—the relationship will not grow into a close, trusting bond.

Schemas also have survival power because, in some primitive way, they seem to work for us. Remember that we learned our schemas as ways of responding to upsetting situations. They are tactics for making ourselves feel better, for protecting ourselves from feeling terrible, or for responding to an unsettling situation.

Our schemas have been much used precisely because they serve a useful emotional function, at least in part. For instance, the vulnerability schema has an almost desperate goal: to ensure that some feared calamity will not occur. Worrying, of course, can be adaptive, particularly when it moves us to prepare for a potential danger. But a kind of magical thinking drives this schema, as though by worrying and obsessing about the feared catastrophe, we are doing something that will prevent it from happening. This almost superstitious belief leads people to go through the same ritual of over-worrying time and again, even though it erodes their own peace of mind and that of the people close to them.

One client said of this pattern that she knows her constant apprehension bothers everyone, but she adds, "I can't seem to stop myself. If someone in my family or a boyfriend is going on a trip, I'll make myself sick with worry that something bad is going to happen to them. I'll get these fearful fantasies of someone breaking into their hotel room, or something worse. And I'll have to call them up—even when I know it's too late to call—just to be sure they're okay."

Paradoxically, because the vulnerability schema impels her to over-worry about situations that in reality are benign, it *seems* to pay off. The magical thinking goes like this: "Because I went through my ritual of worrying, nothing bad happened. Everyone is safe, and I feel relieved once again." It's as though her extra worrying had some protective power.

Despite its illogic, the constantly repeated sequence in her mind, in which over-worry seems to lead to emotional relief, powerfully reinforces her habit. Such continual reinforcement and repetition make schemas like vulnerability particularly tenacious habits of mind, difficult to change. But we *can* change them, nonetheless—with the right awareness tools.

So Now What Do I Do? ● Someone I know had a frustrating pattern: She was attracted to emotionally withdrawn, ungiving men who made her feel neglected and forlorn. Over and over she would be drawn to someone, get into a relationship, and find—once again—the same disappointment.

One day I asked if she thought there might be a connection between her tendency to be drawn to such rejecting men and her lifelong travails with her cold and distant father.

Her first response was "Can we change the subject?"

But after we talked for a bit longer, she finally confided, "I know there's a connection—I just don't know what to do about it."

Many of us have this frustration from time to time. We are aware that something isn't right in our lives, and we are even able to make the connection between what isn't working in our lives now and the continued pattern from our early life conditioning. It takes a good deal of insight and awareness even to get to this point. But that leaves us with the question, "Now what?"

People sometimes wish they had never opened up the emotional can of worms in the first place. As a friend said recently, partly in jest, "I know I have unresolved emotional issues—I just prefer to shove them inside and pretend they're not there!"

Her sentiment, poignant as it is, is all too common.

I've felt that way myself when facing a schema trigger. Even after years of working on my own emotional habits, an inner voice would remind me of a line from the old Laurel and Hardy comedy classics, where a flustered Stan says to his sidekick, "Fine mess you got me in, Ollie."

But on the other hand, there are moments of emotional freedom that give us hope: that we no longer have to put up with being treated unfairly by people, with not getting our need for caring met, with living in fear of catastrophe, or with feeling left out—moments that show the way out of the conditioning that has encrusted into our core models of ourselves and of the people in our lives.

At these moments we can feel the exhilaration and relief of a break from the relentless grip of conditioning, the driving force behind so much of what we believe and act upon. Such moments make us realize that we are not trapped by the patterns that make us feel so frozen.

But before we can be free, we need to acknowledge the ways we are caught. It's crucial, of course, not to stop there, at a place of hopelessness, but rather to see this suffering in our lives as the result of learned habits. And then to see that we have a choice not to let the tyranny of these habits continue.

By understanding the mechanics and the map of schema patterns and by realizing how they erupt in our lives and relationships, we allow for the possibility of becoming more aware of them and of making real, lasting changes for the better. This takes time and effort; there is no quick fix. But our emotional habits are like any other habits: they can be brought into awareness and changed.

Four Noble Truths and Schemas ● When someone is in the grip of a schema, we can't simply say, "Oh, that's just your deprivation

schema acting up again." Understandably, people experience such easy categorization as a dismissal of the validity of their feelings at the moment. Empathy is needed first, before any attempts to change.

As a therapist, as well as in my own inner work, I've learned that it's important first to understand how the person experiences and interprets a situation, and to empathize with his symbolic reality. Once the part of him that identifies with the schema reality feels empathized with, he can begin to be open to other perspectives. That includes starting to see how the lens of the schema distorts his perceptions and reactions.

We can start this work, then, by getting in touch with and expressing the underlying feelings that have been locked inside the holding patterns of our schemas. The means for this is a mindful empathy—just *being* with feelings without trying to change them. As we experience these deep feelings, we often spontaneously start to make connections between memories of the origins of a schema and our present feelings and responses. Insights can come to us, new ways of seeing old habits or different perspectives that challenge our old assumptions.

This process of working through our emotions has an organic feel, unraveling memories, feelings, patterns of physically held tension, energy blocks. Insights have their own natural timing, which vary from person to person.

Once we are willing to empathize with our schema feelings, we are less motivated to be overly rational or to engage in emotional distancing. It's not that we need to stay only at the feeling level, but it's important that we not resist and avoid it.

Part of us at some level may know the schema doesn't work or does not make sense, but we may not be fully ready to act on that insight yet. With empathy it's more likely we'll see the distortions more boldly. Mindfulness allows us to be more present with old feelings and patterns, not so influenced or defined by them.

Then we can more freely explore all the dimensions of relating to our emotional life—cognitively, emotionally, behaviorally, and spiritually. Reframing, investigating, and challenging our thinking patterns and gaining insight into emotional reactions is sometimes most useful. At other times, intentionally behaving in a new and different way is reparative. For some of us a physical expression, or accessing and freeing emotions in physical blocks, offers an effective vehicle. And some of us may be more drawn to reparative emotional experiences, both internally and through our relationships. Finally, some dedicated spiritual practitioners prefer to dissolve emotions through awareness alone.

Whatever we are naturally drawn to, whatever works best for us, it's important that we make this inner work our own, staying connected, each in our own way, with the motive to be free from these relentless patterns.

Buddhism distinguishes among several varieties of suffering. Schemas fall into the category of suffering due to our conditioning, our learned habits. At the heart of Buddhist teachings are the Four Noble Truths, which describe how we experience our suffering and how it can end. At the relative level, they apply to steps in emotional alchemy.

The first of these truths is simply to recognize our suffering, which is what we do when we acknowledge our schemas. The last few chapters have emphasized this through acknowledgment of the truth of our schema suffering.

Once schemas are recognized and empathized with, we can begin the work of changing them. Seeing what keeps our habitual patterns in place is akin to the second truth, the cause of our suffering.

The third truth is that we can free ourselves from suffering, which we do as we begin to become aware of our schemas and start to challenge them. And the fourth truth, the details of the path to being more free from the suffering caused by our emotional patterns, is what the rest of this book is about.

III

A Mindful Therapy

8

The Many Uses of Mindfulness

Wisdom, free from the clouds of the two obscuring veils
Altogether pure and shining brightly like the sun
Waking us up from the sleep of our disturbed emotions
*   and the chains of mental habit*
Scattering the darkness of not knowing.

These lines from an ancient Tibetan prayer have been a continuing inspiration. This description of the power of wisdom to bring a transcendent clarity to the mind so perfectly portrays how mindfulness can help us remove the obscuration created by our schemas. ● The word "obscuration" occurs frequently in Buddhist texts to denote whatever distorts, blocks, or biases our perception. From the Buddhist perspective, obscuration takes the form of thoughts or emotions. Mindfulness helps us cultivate a refined awareness, detecting the subtlety of our emotional and cognitive patterns, which we otherwise so easily overlook amid the distractions of everyday life. It allows us to distinguish between distortion and reality—that is, between how things seem and how they actually are. ● In the chapters to come we will see how the integration of mindfulness with the conceptual framework and interventions of schema therapy works to clear the obscurations created by our maladaptive emotional habits. The mind has immense power either to obscure itself with habitual emotional reactions or to burn through these obscurations to its natural, open clarity. ● This integration came together very naturally years ago, when I was training in schema therapy. In those same years I was also participating in intensive mindfulness retreats. As I started to integrate the two approaches in my therapy practice, and in my own inner work, I was struck by the ways the two approaches to our obscurations overlapped and worked well together, complementing and enhancing each other.

Schema therapy focuses on four domains: our thoughts, our emotions, our actions, and our relationships. Emotional alchemy applies mindfulness to clearing obscurations in the cognitive and emotional realms within the mind, as well as in the outer realms of our behavior and personal relationships. Mindfulness has specific applications in these four realms, as we will see.

To be sure, every person is different. In my therapy practice I tune in to how I feel a person needs to work, and I respond accordingly instead of imposing a uniform structure or path that everyone must fit into or follow. Some people are more naturally sensitive to the tides of their emotions and so find working directly in that realm most powerful; others find a special power in challenging their thoughts. Still others feel that changing a key maladaptive habit, or working in the arena of relationships, offers the best focus for their efforts.

But whichever seems most relevant at first, this work incorporates all these areas, since they operate in a chain of connection. For instance, focusing on the distorted thoughts that typify a schema, without attending also to the raw emotions that fuel the pattern only does part of the task. Failing to empathize with the feelings of the schema and so trying to fix things too soon may result in an artificial change.

Our actions are our thoughts and feelings laid bare. When it comes to changing the habitual patterns that schemas drive us to repeat over and over in our lives, schema therapy seeks to loosen the hold of habit and so give us more flexibility and free range in how we respond. The more we repeat a habitual response, the stronger it becomes—and the more likely we will automatically go down that route again.

Emotional alchemy is mindfully enhanced schema therapy. When it comes to breaking the chain of habit, mindfulness presents a tool of choice. If you can see an emotional habit with mindfulness, with a neutral, clear awareness, you will be able to challenge it even while it has started to hold you in its sway. Challenging emotional habits with mindfulness, in the very moment you are starting to lose it, offers the most effective way to work with these powerful emotional habits.

For one of my early clients, mindfulness became a way to short-circuit her panic attacks. When she first came to me she had classic panic symptoms. She would suddenly have overwhelming fears that something catastrophic was about to happen. Her anxiety would make her hyperventilate, and that led to a vivid fear that her heart would stop or that she would not be able to breathe and so would suffocate. Her habitual tendency to anticipate catastrophe meant that her fears would quickly spiral into a panic.

But once she had practiced mindfulness for a while, she learned to apply a mindful awareness the moment she noticed the onset of her symptoms. Then she could see her mind start to exaggerate the danger into a catastrophe. But instead of giving in to the tidal pull of panic, she would use these very thoughts and feelings as a cue to tune in to simply concentrating on her breathing. At first this made her feel a bit more anxious. But after more practice she found that it actually helped calm her and let her think more clearly, even challenging her panicky thoughts instead of letting them take over her mind. She would remind herself that in reality she was safe despite her fears, or that her hyperventilating was only a sign of temporary anxiety, not a sign that she would suffocate.

Being in the present rather than getting lost in anxious thoughts offers a mindful antidote to panic. My client's mindful awareness short-circuited the spiral into panic: instead of a torrent of frightened thoughts and fears building on one another, she would become calm and so avoid the onset of full panic. Eventually she was even able to stop taking the medications she had been given to alleviate the symptoms, and her panic attacks finally ceased altogether.

Observing our emotional habits with mindfulness eventually allows us to be less limited by them and more able to disengage from their distorted view of life. Gradually, as these patterns lose their power, we begin to see things in a more balanced way, allowing for a more flexible response instead of a single, invariable automatic reaction.

Moments of Mindfulness ● Mindfulness changes our relationship to the moments when we are most upset and distressed. Instead of seeing those moments in a purely negative light, if we bring mindfulness to them we can see the possibilities for change they offer. As the late Tibetan teacher Chogyam Trungpa, an expert on Buddhist psychology, put it, "When problems arise, instead of being seen as purely threats, they become learning situations, opportunities to find out more about one's own mind and to continue on one's journey."

When we practice mindfulness, the effects can show up in many different ways in life. Sometimes it may be in responding differently to an irritation, without being provoked; sometimes it means getting in touch with a feeling you would have ignored before, and listening more closely to the messages that feeling offers. Sometimes mindfulness gives you more empathy for someone—or for yourself. Other times it may allow you to get an insight into why you're having an emotional reaction, or you may realize that your reactions now make you feel less overwhelmed.

The specific effects of mindfulness for a given person at a given time are unique. One client told me, "Since I've started practicing mindfulness, I notice things more. I take the time to listen to someone, where before I might have felt too busy, impatient, or overwhelmed to take the time." She found that this more mindful stance made a palpable difference in three very different relationships: with her partner at work, with her husband, and with her teenage daughter. In her business she noted a marked decrease in the number of times she and her partner fell into bickering. She also noticed that her husband seemed to be more interested in *her* concerns because she was engaging more with his. And she knew things had changed when one day her daughter said, "You know, Mom, it's so much easier now to talk to you about stuff."

Another client was tormented by performance anxiety, a constant battle for her, since live stage performances were essential to her career. When she was about to go onstage, and even when she was in the middle of a performance, she would find herself obsessed by the thought that people in the audience were criticizing her, finding her performance awful.

After some time in therapy, she was able to use mindfulness to become more aware of these thoughts as they were happening, to see how these knee-jerk fears were controlling her. So before going onstage, she would become mindful, catching those self-critical thoughts as they were starting on their usual rampage, and challenging them. She would remind herself, for instance, "I'm not defined by what the people in this audience think." She used a mindful pause to talk herself through her fears, so she could put her energy into creative expression in music instead of being preoccupied with what people in the audience might be thinking about her.

Another told me, "Feelings aren't so scary when you stop avoiding them." She had realized that using mindfulness practice allowed her to face and stay with the hurt and sadness she felt in key relationships—with her mother, with certain friends. She found that as she investigated those feelings and started to detect the patterns within her that triggered them, she was becoming less reactive in these relationships.

These changes were all the result of people taking moments of mindfulness. Any time you wake up to what you are doing on automatic, bringing it into awareness more clearly, you are being mindful. Mindfulness helps us have wake-up moments when we need them most: in the midst of life, when our emotional reactions are in full swing.

"Sometimes I'm working with a situation that would ordinarily have triggered an angry explosion in me," a client told me, "and instead I see what's going on, what would usually build up inside me. I'm aware of an internal flicker, but this time it chooses not to ignite. I'm starting to see that I don't have to let it continue to control me."

A Mindful Radar ● Mindfulness enables us to catch schemas as they begin to take us over. Our normal haste means that our emotional habits fly into action without our noticing what's happening—our minds are off somewhere else. Mindful awareness of such moments slows the mind's velocity, allowing us to see more clearly what's happening and so have more choices instead of just racing into our automatic response. As one client said, "Mindfulness is like a parachute—it slows things down so you can notice more."

When we see more clearly into a state of mind, our relationship to it changes. If we are mindful of a reactive state—being angry, say—our perspective on it is fresh: we can experience angry feelings fully in our bodies and in our minds, rather than simply being swept along by those waves of anger. We can be aware of the feelings and let them pass. If we do not resist unpleasant feelings or try to prolong pleasant ones, we can be with our emotions and mental states as they are. Instead of being swept away by an emotion, and so just automatically reacting as we have hundreds of times before when we felt that way, we have a choice: we can be creative in our response.

There are many ways to apply mindfulness to our disturbing emotions; any of three different intensity levels of mindfulness can be brought to bear, depending on the tenacity and strength of the feelings. Nyanaponika Thera, in *The Power of Mindfulness,* offers a rule of thumb for being mindful of varying intensities of our inner turbulence: put the least effort into dealing with a disturbing feeling that will do the job.

A light touch, without much emphasis on or attention to details, may be all we need to keep at bay a mild emotional disturbance so we can get on with other things. A brief act of noticing the disturbing thoughts and feelings, just an acknowledgment, like an inner nod—rather than a mental conversation with them—can sometimes suffice.

Such a light touch of mindfulness can sometimes clear the mind. If the disturbance is not very turbulent, if the schema is only slightly activated or is losing its hold over us, or if our powers of attention are strong, simply noting the disturbance may be enough to dislodge it from the mind.

Mindfulness heightens our ability to hear whispers of the subterranean feelings and thoughts that roil beneath the depths. Mindfulness helps us detect and capture the automatic thoughts that, if allowed to continue down the track, could foment a schema attack. For instance, the social exclusion schema's trigger goes something like this: "I'll never belong in a group; I'll always be an outsider." The subjugation schema: "I feel controlled." These thoughts act invisibly, outside our awareness, to trigger a full-fledged schema attack. But if we can use our mindful radar to bring these stealthy habitual thoughts onto the screen of our awareness before the attack begins, then we can challenge them and abort the attack. This lets us remind ourselves of our schema vulnerability, rather than letting the schema fears and thoughts control us.

These automatic thoughts prove remarkably flimsy once we bring them into the clear light of awareness and counter them with evidence to the contrary. For instance, just bringing to mind reassuring memories of times when someone's lateness had nothing to do with signaling a troubled relationship, or of times when we've met strangers at a party with whom we felt completely comfortable, can sometimes be enough to vanquish schema-triggering thoughts of abandonment or exclusion. Of course, becoming mindful doesn't necessarily mean we will instantly have clarity on what is happening. The point is to be with our experience in an open, accepting way, so that whatever is happening, and however it changes, we will stay present with a sustained gaze.

If our mindfulness has enough power to stay steady as we bring these hidden feelings and thoughts to the surface, says Nyanaponika, they sometimes can "reveal how poor and weak they actually are"—like the grand illusions of the Wizard of Oz. Once we look behind the curtain that hid them from our gaze we can begin to question the shaky assumptions and knee-jerk emotional habits that have given such a grandiose power to our schemas. Our fears can shrink back to manageable proportions—or maybe vanish.

Sustained Mindfulness ● But if a schema is more strongly aroused, and if disturbing feelings persist, then we need to marshal a corresponding persistence in mindfulness. And more often than not in this process—particularly at the beginning—such feelings *do* persist. So mindfulness needs to be sustained, with each surge of disturbance being countered by a corresponding application of calm and steady attention. If we can persist, this firm, determined, and steady mindfulness can often make the intensity of the emotion dissipate, like a fire starved for air.

At this level of mindfulness, it may help to use the method of naming—

bringing to mind a single word that identifies the nature of the disturbance. If, for instance, you are being assailed by feelings of hurt because your abandonment schema has been triggered, you can lightly repeat in your mind a word—"fear" or "loss" or "abandonment"—to help you notice what's going on without being drawn deeper into it. Each time you sense the disturbing feelings as they ebb, you can repeat that word in your mind, not as mantra that you focus on but with equanimity, as a nod of acknowledgment.

Miriam, one of my clients who is also an enthusiastic mindfulness meditator, was at a three-month meditation retreat with the teacher Joseph Goldstein. In one of his talks, he had likened acting out of habitual reactions to the arms in an old jukebox that automatically swing out, pick up a record, and place it on the turntable. He playfully suggested that whenever the meditators saw their mind swing into such a habitual act, they simply give a label to each such habit—something like "B3," like a selection code on a jukebox.

"One morning," Miriam told me later, "I tried this with my habitual morning thoughts. These are the schema thoughts that kick in after I wake up: 'I can't do this,' 'I feel overwhelmed,' and 'I hate myself.' So I labeled them 'M1,' 'M2,' and 'M3,' for 'morning tape thoughts.' This way I can more easily watch the habitual play of thoughts running through my mind, without taking them too seriously or getting hooked in."

As we become more familiar with tracking these habitual emotional patterns we can trace a chain of associative thoughts, using mindfulness to track and identify the moment the thought arose in our awareness, then took us over so that we believed the thought. But with mindfulness, these thoughts can be seen as akin to sensations of the mind.

Tranquillity and concentration practices are also effective for calming activated schemas and their turbulent emotions. When a schema trigger disturbs your equilibrium, stirring strong feelings and reactions, it can be quite helpful first to calm your mind down and neutralize your feelings by, for instance, meditating on your breathing for a bit.

Concentration can induce calm, help us feel more centered, and free our attention from the gravitational pull of the schema reaction. After you have more equanimity and focus, you can shift to a mindful investigation of the feelings and mind state, gaining a more subtle understanding of the workings of the schema when it is activated.

But if these applications of mindfulness aren't enough, and if the disturbing feelings continue or grow stronger, you need to take a more active stance, turning your full, deliberate attention to the thoughts and feelings that empower the schema. Mindfulness, joined with methods of schema therapy

I'll review in the coming chapters, marshals an assertive challenge to the thoughts that trigger the disturbed feelings.

A mindful attention helps us distinguish between distortion and reality, so we can see clearly the distorted thoughts, personal myths, and emotional patterns that entrap us. We can then work to free ourselves from their hold. At this third level, the use of mindfulness diverges from traditional meditation practice, in which attention is not directed but remains as a steady monitor of whatever arises naturally. Here we use a conceptual investigation of the pattern.

This can take the form, for example, of holding a question in mind: What can I learn from this? What thoughts are behind these feelings? What schema is at work now? What distorting lens am I looking through?

Investigating Schemas ● There are two dimensions to mindfulness. The calming aspect can help us quiet down the disturbing emotions of a schema attack, while the investigative nature fosters insights. The two dimensions can be used in tandem.

Carolyn, a professor, was looking through the college catalog at descriptions of course offerings, including her own, when her perfectionism schema triggered a spiral of negative self-judgment: "The other teachers' courses all sound so together. They're more organized and more professional than I am. Their courses sound so much more interesting. No one's going to want to sign up for mine."

When she told me about it later, I said, "You can take either of two approaches. The calming approach would be to say to yourself the moment you have your first self-critical thought: 'I know I'm vulnerable to judging myself and comparing myself adversely to others when I read through catalogs like this.' Then put the catalog away and stay focused on something else, or just on your breathing, until you drop the thoughts and calm down.

"Or you can take the investigative approach, working mindfully with the emotional reaction of judging and comparing yourself while you're having it. With an observing awareness, notice how you are being affected—while not getting pulled deeper into the reaction or its story line—and see it as a learning opportunity."

Investigating schemas in this way can lead to a more precise understanding of them. Among the psychological insights to be gained from this sustained attention are a sense of what triggers your schema, a recognition of the emotional patterns that go with it or hold it in place, and memories of early events in your life that shaped or gave rise to the schema.

In this form of schema inquiry, you get more involved in the story behind an emotional state than you would while practicing meditation. But this extension of mindful investigation into your life can help sustain a clearer awareness in situations that might otherwise be disturbing.

As a therapist I very often find myself during a session trying to keep people focused and attentive to emotions and patterns that need to be investigated in order for healing to occur. But I also urge my clients to sustain their awareness on their own until the strong emotional state comes to its natural end.

If you are in psychotherapy of any kind, this sustained awareness will complement the work you are doing with your therapist. There are several reasons for this. One is that becoming a diligent observer of what you experience between therapy sessions lets you take fuller advantage of the session itself by bringing to it the best specimens of what you are dealing with from day to day. Another reason is that mindfulness extends the reach of the therapy session, letting you spontaneously notice moments to apply the insights from therapy into your life.

Wise Reflection ●
Wise reflection is another extremely useful process of mindful investigation. Achan Amaro, who trained for many years in Thai forest monasteries, describes wise reflection this way: "You start doing some concentration practice for a while—to focus your attention—so it doesn't just wander off. Then you shift to an investigative mode where you take something you want to investigate and drop it into the mind, into awareness. You let the mind investigate in a reflective way, without thinking about it. The moment you find yourself wandering off, you come back to the breath for a while to gather concentration."

He continues, "Then you drop it into awareness again, getting a sense, in a more intuitive way, of any insights that arise about what you are reflecting on. This is very helpful in working with habitual patterns—to bring them to mind for wise reflection when you're not in the middle of your life where they are usually playing out. You want to reflect on them wisely, when you have a more mindful, investigative quality of awareness. Otherwise the habitual patterns keep playing out over and over, until you bring more awareness to them and break the chain of habitual pattern."

Wise reflection can occur at different levels. Sometimes it is more conceptual, thinking things over, at other times more grounded in deep practice, where a strong intuitive sense can emerge. One of my clients told me about using this approach.

"As I started to meditate this morning, I immediately noticed the agitated quality of my mind," she said. "There were many unsettling issues jostling for my attention, issues I'd been grappling with for some days. I'd had another run-in with my mother, who is constantly critical. I'd blown up at her and hung up the phone. My awareness was continually distracted by wanting to make sense out of what was happening, even if things couldn't be changed.

"After some time, settling into practice, the mental agitation settled down, as a clarity began to emerge and my mind quieted," she continued. "It was almost like diving into a reservoir of clear awareness. After a while I reflected on some of the same issues that had preoccupied me: Why am I so vulnerable to my mother's criticism? What can I do to change this pattern?

"Now I felt an expanded perspective that made everything seem more workable, more acceptable. I connected what had happened to my thoughts about my perfectionism and unlovability schemas. I could see that I had reacted to her just the way I've done all these years when she puts me down. I could feel myself tense up again as I thought about her, starting to get upset all over again. So I just went back to the meditation for a while.

"Then, after I felt more centered, I reflected on it again," my client told me. "Now I felt—maybe for the first time—that I didn't have to react that same old way with her. That there was something in me now that allowed me to catch myself, to say something to her that would de-escalate instead of being a counterattack."

When meditating, if we cultivate a mindful awareness, we may find within us a source of insight that has a way of transforming emotional states. The mind may be grappling with some problem, or just lost in confusion. Then a process of transformation may occur, where what is not realized or understood can settle into an intuitive knowing. The wiser qualities of a mindful awareness become available to us. There is clarity, focus, and calm. Intuition and trust connect us to a part of ourselves that can make sense out of the confusion.

By contrast, the agitation and fear caused by our schemas—and the habitual impulse to resist suffering—stem from our losing touch with this reservoir of mindful wisdom. We let the schema define our experience. But if we apply a wise reflection, we have a means of understanding that experience in a new way.

The Power of Practice ● In order for mindfulness to work for us, we need to make an effort to strengthen our ability to be mindful. That

means, essentially, developing a regular meditation practice and, if possible, going to a retreat. Meditation, remember, requires us to retrain our most basic habits of attention.

Ordinarily we are easily distracted, but mindfulness strengthens the muscle of concentration so we can maintain our focus. Where our attention tends to go from one thing to another, staying on the surface of things, mindfulness cultivates the ability to sustain an investigative awareness, one that goes deeper into our experience.

If we are going to be able to bring these qualities to bear on our schemas, we need to make practicing mindfulness meditation an ongoing part of our life. Like any new skill, it takes doing it over and over to attain a meaningful level of mastery. With meditation, regular practice can become easier and easier, because it is in itself pleasant, an oasis of peaceful time with ourselves amid the frenzy of our lives.

I remember a man coming to see me after a workshop. "You may not remember me," he said, "but a friend brought me to a workshop you taught years ago for beginners in meditation. I was addicted to drugs then, but not anymore—now I'm addicted to meditation." Meditation, of course, amounts to a positive addiction, like regular exercise: something that has benefits and that you do regularly because you love doing it.

Mindfulness during Schema Attacks ● While mindfulness comes more easily in quiet moments while we are in a contemplative mood, it is most useful in the heat of a schema attack. This is one reason mindfulness needs to be a daily practice: so we can rely on it when we need it most, in those moments when we are acting mindlessly. One client described taking a mindful pause and a few breaths as a way to become more present, clear, and emotionally available when her child was in a frustrated meltdown.

The challenge is to maintain our equanimity *while* we are upset or as soon as possible after the peak of the disturbance. Holding your attention evenly on an intense emotion may allow the feeling to intensify for a while before it fades or changes. But even if it doesn't go away, mindfulness can let us see its transparency more clearly.

If what comes up is, say, anger, a mindful stance toward it is simply to observe it without getting caught up in it—not identifying completely with the rage and with thoughts like "I hate you!" but having a simultaneous awareness that "This is anger I'm feeling." The idea is neither to suppress such feelings nor to act on them, but simply to be aware of them.

A mindful person focuses on the *process* of awareness without getting caught up in the *content* of awareness. She notices the feeling of anger, for example, but does not get drawn into the specific details or content of the anger. If she starts to get lost in the reason she is angry—thoughts like "I can't stand it when he does that to me!"—then she is no longer being mindful; she has identified with the anger rather than simply noticing it.

Mindfulness is not repression, however. You want to allow yourself to fully experience a feeling like anger. Notice the thoughts that come up in your mind, the feelings in your body, the impulse to act, or the actions you find yourself taking. You may notice, for example, a tightness in your gut, or your arm muscles may become tense, as though you want to strike someone or make a fist, and your mind may spin with indignant thoughts.

In short, you experience the anger as meticulously as you can. If you act in response to whatever is causing the anger, you would do so mindfully, which should make your response more skillful. Being mindful of the anger tends to change your relationship to the feeling of anger, making you more fully aware of what is going on. You can express your feelings about the cause of the anger and be aware with mindfulness at the same time, but that reaction is different from the usual kind, which is mindlessly acting out of anger.

If you're very mindful, you're more able to do what Aristotle observed was so difficult: "to be angry with the right person, in the right way, at the right time, and for the right purpose."

Catching the Buildup ● All too often in life we become aware that we've had a schema attack only after the whole sequence has played itself out, if we notice at all. We look back and realize, Oh, I've done *that* again. But mindfulness gives us a way to spot schema attacks as they are building up inside us—hopefully before we repeat our habitual response yet again. Mindfulness is key: the more powerful our awareness, the more able we will be to notice the attack as it is coming rather than long after it has gone.

A client told me about going back to work after having been away on a mindfulness retreat: "I needed to go back to work the other day, and I was very aware of how reactive my mind was. I tried to stay aware of the feeling tone of those reactions.

"One woman I work with is particularly annoying. She barges into conversations, then talks endlessly about her complaints and opinions. Usually that would lead me to get angry and be sharp with her. Then I'd be in a bad mood for hours. But this time I stayed mindful. When she said things I didn't agree with, I saw my mind start to close around a critical thought, as usual. So I reminded myself just to be aware of the unpleasant feelings that went with those thoughts. As I stayed mindful of these unpleasant feelings, I watched them dissolve into nothing, followed by the pleasant sense of not being so easily upset by unpleasant experiences. It's a relief to live life with more equanimity."

In that mindful pause my client was able to step far enough out of her own habitual response to bring clarity and equanimity to what might otherwise have been a mental tirade of criticism. Such moments of mindfulness bring self-awareness to the raw feelings and impulses of the emotional center. Ordinarily, when we are swept away by an emotion, our feelings lead us to act without thought about what we are about to do—we just react.

But mindfulness allows us to bring to the emotional process a precise awareness that makes distinctions among the thoughts, the feelings, and the impulse to act. An enhanced ability to notice the moment of intention—the mental movement that comes before we act—gives us more choice.

Mindfulness gives us freedom at that critical choice point. If we can attend to that moment mindfully, for instance, we can stay with the sensations aroused by angry feelings and thoughts, following them until they fade or lose their grip on us rather than letting them dictate what we do. Or we can choose an alternative response, perhaps clearly articulating and asserting our needs rather than just reacting with an angry outburst.

Refining our self-awareness means noticing the impulse even *before* we act on it so we can more readily decide not to follow the impulse to the action. The main principle: The earlier in the course of a schema attack that we can catch what's going on, the more able we are to short-circuit the sequence.

If we can notice the familiar feeling in our body or the familiar thoughts which signal that the schema has been activated, we can have more choice over what we do next. The more subtle the level at which we notice the onset of a schema attack, the better. Mindfulness offers us that sensitive inner radar.

Subtle Understanding ● Schema activity does not always announce itself blatantly. Very often long before an attack takes us over, there is a quiet period of buildup, during which the schema has been primed and lurks in the background of our awareness. Or the schema may stay primed for days or weeks, only occasionally erupting into a full attack.

Signs that a schema has been primed can include more frequently having the thoughts that typically go with the pattern, the associated feelings it activates, or the typical impulses to react in accord with that schema.

A prolonged episode of schema priming can begin with a close brush with a schema attack that simmers within you. Because the primed schema sensitizes you to the least hint of events that set you off, moments that otherwise would have gone by unnoticed now become mini-triggers, keeping the schema primed.

For example, if you have an encounter with someone who often triggers a schema—say deprivation—even an innocent interaction might start the priming. You might find yourself, for example, wary of people's motives as the fear they will take but not give back moves to the forefront of your mind. You might start interpreting someone failing to thank you for a kindness as a sign that they only want things from you, without reciprocating—a typical thought for the deprivation schema.

When a schema is primed like this, it can become an underlying, self-sustaining mood that taints your perception of people so subtly that you barely notice it. But one sign will be how easily thoughts related to that schema come to mind.

Learning the mechanics of our schemas can be extremely clarifying, offering helpful clues to what is actually going on. For example, if you resonate with the deprivation schema, you may find that even a slight instance of thoughtlessness—say, a friend at work forgot to bring you back the coffee you asked her to pick up when she went out—primes the pattern. You might find your thoughts wandering to other times when friends or relatives have let you down or ignored your needs or feelings. You might feel a tinge of hurt, sadness, or annoyance at your friend's thoughtlessness, or you might want to go out and do something extra nice for yourself, like indulging in a rich, tasty muffin with your coffee, to make yourself feel better.

These are typical schema reactions, of a quiet kind that can easily go unrecognized as such. Sometimes our schema reactions are so subtle that all we know is we feel funny about something but do not quite know why. Becoming mindful of these subtle signals opens the possibility of detecting the activity of a schema that might otherwise escape our radar and so control our reactions yet again.

Mindfulness of a Primed Schema ● These subtle feelings and reactions often develop into a sustained mood—a longer-lasting reaction that can create a lingering skewed filter on our awareness, clouding our perception. Bringing a more precise mindful awareness to these schema-

induced moods can let us see what actually drives the feelings and their accompanying thoughts.

Take my client Kimberly, whose deprivation schema had been primed. At first all she noticed was what she thought of as a bad mood. When she paid closer attention, she became aware of a sensation of heaviness in her chest and abdomen. Continuing to observe her reaction with mindfulness, she noticed a predominance in her mind of the familiar patterns of thoughts associated with deprivation. For instance, after getting a message that a friend had called to ask for a favor, she automatically thought, "Why does she only call me when she needs a favor?" Along with that thought came resentment. Paying still closer attention, Kimberly noticed a sadness along with the resentment.

So she asked herself with a tender empathy, "You're feeling sad about something, aren't you?" She found tears rolling down her cheeks. Memories came to her of a recent disappointment by another old friend whom she hadn't heard from for years, but who called up out of the blue to ask for a loan. That, she realized, was the incident that had primed her schema, setting off this bad mood.

By getting in touch with all the subtle ways we are affected when a schema is primed, we can begin the process of releasing ourselves from the dense fog of moodiness. Realizing what was going on led Kimberly to try what for her was a proven antidote. She no longer felt helpless, trapped by the mood; she could now take steps to end it.

In her case, two approaches helped. One was simply being mindful of the mood and its underlying causes. That mindfulness alone offered her some relief. Kimberly also talked over her feelings with a caring and understanding friend. The combination of inner and outer nurturance broke the schema spell.

Mindful Schema Work ● As we will see in the following chapters, mindfulness has a particular quality to offer each of the four areas of schema work: our thoughts, our emotions, our habitual behavior, and our relationships. While of necessity I will describe these areas one by one, when it comes to the actual work of emotional alchemy, they operate simultaneously along parallel tracks. And to some extent the boundaries between them are artificial. Emotional work, for instance, also involves dealing with the thoughts that drive a schema.

Emotional Alchemy

Take, for example, how Kimberly, another time, worked in a different way with her emotional deprivation schema. On the cognitive level, she often assumed that other people were intentionally depriving her, or she felt that they should read her mind, knowing what she needed without her having to say anything. In bringing mindfulness to bear on these thoughts, she used it as inner radar. When she caught herself having a schema thought, like "Nobody really cares about my needs," she would pause long enough to challenge that thought rather than letting it control her or distort her reality.

Deprivation carries a high emotional charge, and so Kimberly often found herself feeling intensely sad or angry without really knowing why. Here mindfulness played several roles. When it came to sorting out this welter of confusing feelings, she practiced sustaining a mindful awareness in their midst. That helped her detect the telltale signs of her deprivation schema. When these feelings started to come up, she was able to use mindfulness to connect with them despite the impulse to avoid them by focusing on something else.

The sadness and indignation that fuel deprivation are at the core of this schema. For Kimberly, connecting with these feelings with mindfulness was a helpful step toward letting them go. Here she used a journal to reflect on the feelings and their origins in her childhood. Sometimes she would have an inner dialogue with the deprived little girl who was frozen in the schema patterns. She empathized with the child's feelings, acknowledging the sense in which they once seemed appropriate. Mindful awareness can be like a soothing, nurturing presence, and Kimberly was able to maintain an attentive mindfulness to her painful feelings, which acted as a kind of symbolic replacement for the attentive presence she had yearned for as a child.

Kimberly sometimes found herself resenting and withdrawing from other people—particularly her husband, her mother, and her closest friends—but, again, not knowing exactly why. Mindfulness can intervene in such habitual schema-driven behavior by helping us track the sequence in which the schema thoughts and emotions drive us to do something maladaptive or just inappropriate. As Kimberly became mindful of the thoughts and feelings that were making her withdraw and sulk yet again, she found she now had a chance to respond differently—to change what she did for the better. Rather than angrily assuming her needs would once again be ignored, and so withdrawing, she started to express to those closest to her what she needed from them.

Here she had an opportunity to work on making her closest relationships more satisfying. She had always been the caretaker in these relationships, ever ready to attend to others' needs but never expressing her own. She now took active steps to change those habitual patterns of interaction, again using mindfulness to catch herself when she was about to slip into her schema habits. With her husband, who also became intrigued by schema work, she started to use their conflicts as an opportunity—after things calmed down—to go back and look at which schemas had triggered the fight. There were, however, two friends who simply could not seem to change—who somehow felt entitled always to be the ones whose needs were met, but who were unwilling to reciprocate. No longer feeling drawn to friends who were so self-absorbed and depriving, Kimberly had less contact with them and put more energy into those friends who were able to be as giving and nurturing as she was.

So emotional alchemy progresses along many lines as we take on a given schema. In many or most of these steps, mindfulness operates as an ally, complementing schema therapy, as we shall see in the chapters ahead.

If You Want to Free Yourself
from a Schema Reaction

Try bringing mindfulness to strong emotions.

1. *Notice when you are having an inappropriate emotional reaction.* Common signs that a reaction is inappropriate include an extreme overreaction, like intense anger at an unintended slight, or deep sadness when someone leaves. Or it may be an emotion that does not fit the situation, like hurt instead of anger, or even the absence of an emotion, like going blank, when most people would feel anxious or angry.

2. *Become mindful.* You may notice yourself reacting inappropriately while in the heat of the reaction or not until minutes, hours, or even days after the feelings have peaked. It's best, of course, to become aware at some point *during* the reaction, and to use the realization of an overreaction as a cue to become mindful. As your mindfulness strengthens, you'll be able to awaken at an earlier and earlier point in the arc of reaction.

3. *Notice what you are feeling.* There typically is a mix of emotions, some stronger than others. You may, for example, experience anger as the most obvious emotion but detect a mixture of hurt and sadness behind the anger.

4. *Notice what you are thinking.* There are different levels of thought during an overreaction. At the obvious level are those thoughts that are specific to the moment and that feed your emotional reaction. More subtle are the background thoughts that trigger these obvious ones: "He can't treat me like that!" expresses a righteous indignation about being treated unfairly, which in turns fuels an angry retort. Extremely strong emotional reactions of any kind are often a clue that what happened carried some deeper symbolic meaning for you and that the intensity of your reaction stems from the symbolic reality rather than what was actually happening. Your automatic thoughts typically revolve around the symbolic reality, interpreting what is happening from that perspective.

5. *Be mindful of your actions or impulses.* Again there are differing levels. There are the obvious ways you behave—what you did and said,

the tone in which you said things. And then there is a more subtle level—for instance, the impulses you had that you did not act on.

6. *Notice how your reaction changes.* This sixth step takes note of how becoming mindful of your overreaction allows your habitual lock-step pattern of reaction to loosen and shift to responses that are more adaptive or positive. Notice what habitual reactions start to come up. Talk yourself through it while staying open to whatever the experience is. And watch for any ways in which your reaction is transformed as you let the old familiar impulses, thoughts, and emotions simply be, without letting them control you yet again.

The Mindful Alchemy of Anger

As an example, consider how this approach can begin to transform your anger.

First ask yourself if this anger is inappropriate. There are situations—like being treated unfairly or seeing someone being victimized—where anger is natural and appropriate. But more often than not, our anger arises because of the symbolic meaning of an interaction—how a schema leads us to interpret what is happening. In these cases the anger is inevitably an overreaction.

We can learn to use such an angry moment as part of emotional alchemy. When we're angry, we can ask ourselves these questions: What fuels this anger? What was the trigger for it—was it someone's words or tone of voice? What thoughts are racing through my mind? What am I telling myself to justify my anger? Anger tends to gain momentum by feeding on these self-justifying thoughts, leading us to believe there is nowhere to go but to erupt like a volcano.

Some time when you're simmering with anger, try this experiment:

Sit still and mindfully experience your anger. Don't let yourself get swept away or caught up in what you're angry about. Pull back a bit from your thoughts so you can observe them *as* thoughts.

Just be present with your experience, without thinking about it. Stay aware of what is happening in your mind and body without getting caught up in more thoughts about your experience.

You can simply be aware of your experience, with choiceless awareness. Or, if you find it hard to maintain a mindful stance, mental noting may help you. Are you agitated? Note "agitation." Are you gripped in tension? Note "tension." Do you feel your pulse beating or your heart pounding? Just note it as such.

What else do you find?

Perhaps there is some clarity of purpose underlying your angry response. Perhaps inner forces are at work, percolating from the heat of anger. If so, how can this heat of the moment—an internal alchemical force—be used as an opportunity?

Perhaps there are other feelings that you uncover along with the anger, such as a sadness at being treated unfairly. If so, let them melt in the warmth of mindful awareness.

Or perhaps certain physical sensations are ignited by the smoldering heat of anger. If so, let the mindfulness be alert to physical sensations and how they change.

Or maybe an insight or message comes more clearly into focus that allows a shift or awakens a sense of clarity or confidence—a realization of a way you might take assertive action to remedy the cause of the anger, but with more awareness and less reactivity.

Whatever happens as you stay mindful with the anger, it awakens some possibility for transforming it.

9

Breaking the Chain

There's a saying in New England, "If you don't like the weather, just wait five minutes." ● I had been wanting to ride my horse, Bodhi, but I kept putting it off for one reason or another. Then on a sparkling early spring morning, one of my first thoughts on awakening was, "I'm riding today!" ● I went downstairs to morning coffee, meditated, and then sat cozily in my sunroom, the doors open to the spring day, appreciating the crispness of the air and the warm golden sunlight filtering through the plants. I found myself reflecting on what Buddhists call the Chain of Dependent Origination—that is, the way our thoughts and desires lead us to action. I noticed how easy it was to be carried along by the pleasantness of the weather and how that had led to the desire to be outside, experiencing the day, on horseback. ● Then a gray cloud floated by, blocking the sun for a while. It wasn't one of those wispy clouds you hardly notice, but the kind of heavy, dark storm cloud that so often creeps along and hovers over this neck of the woods just when we were looking forward to a warm, sunny day. ● With the appearance of this forbidding cloud, I noticed a radical shift in my outlook. As I became aware of the crisp air suddenly turning damp and cool and heard the whispering of the wind picking up, I noticed the stirrings of an unpleasant feeling and found thoughts of resistance floating through my mind: "Maybe it's going to get too cold to ride," "Maybe it will rain and get my saddle wet," "I really should write this morning, any-way." ● Then the gray clouds started to break up; rays of warm light spilled across the plants, making them come to life again. Now, on second thought, I imagined those same rays of light warming my back and my horse prancing along, delighting in the magical display of spring blossoms. With that the thought returned: "It's a perfect day to ride." And I ran off to get my riding boots.

And so it goes through the round of life. This tight connection between feeling, desire, and action keeps us chained to the cycle of conditioning. Without a moment's notice of how we got there, we're off—acting on a fleeting thought, a whim, dictated by one or another feeling of pleasantness or unpleasantness.

Repeating a self-defeating emotional habit carries an obvious cost. One of the brilliant insights of the Buddha was that the links of the chain between feeling, desire, and action offer a pathway on which to break free of the endless round of habit and conditioning—a kind of hidden door to freedom.

Breaking the Chain of Habit ● The Chain of Dependent Origination lies at the heart of Buddhist psychology. This ponderous-sounding analysis of mind articulates a simple principle: how our habitual patterns take shape and are reinforced. And it holds the secret of what we can do to break free of destructive habits.

The chain symbolizes the most basic cause-and-effect sequences in the mind in a way that offers remarkable parallels to modern cognitive science. The first links in the chain occur when the senses contact something—a sight, a sound, a taste. One link in the chain leads to another: From sensing comes contact, which in turn leads to feeling. Our feelings, when pleasant, give rise to craving more and then to clinging to the experience. Out of clinging we are led to action—usually the pursuit of more pleasure, or its obverse, the cessation of pain.

The Buddhist monk Achan Amaro describes how a feeling can turn into a desire—a "self-centered craving"—and how that desire then leads to grasping or clinging, and so to action. "If an interest arises, the mind latches on to it," says Achan Amaro. "We see something that produces a feeling of 'that's beautiful,' then the eye is attracted toward it and says 'I wouldn't mind having one of those,' then the absorption goes further, to grasping: 'Well, I *really* would like to have that, it's a *really* beautiful thing.' Then the decision to act on that, 'Well, no one is looking. . . .'"

Then, says Amaro, comes the thrill of getting what you want, which leads to "the point of no return—where, for instance, we realized, 'Oh, dear, this wasn't really mine to take,' and there is no going back. Once that situation has been born, we have to live through the whole life span of its legacy, whatever that entails"—even if that means grief, sorrow, and despair.

Cognitive scientists, from their studies of the workings of the mind, have reported much the same sequence. They see sensation as leading to cognition—a thought about what we sense—and to feeling, our emotional reaction to it. These thoughts and feelings in turn translate into intentions and plans to take action.

Neuroscience offers a parallel at another level in its analysis of how the brain processes information. It tells us that whenever we sense something, that information goes immediately from eye or ear to the thalamus, a relay station that translates raw physical waves into the language of the brain. From there the information is shunted to the neocortex, the thinking brain, as well as to the amygdala, that storehouse for negative emotional memories, such as the things we fear. If the amygdala recognizes an emotionally potent stimulus similar to something we reacted strongly to in the past, it unleashes a flood of emotion and a fitting action.

The amygdala acts as a repository for our repertoire of negative emotional habits, including our schemas. All our intense fears of abandonment and rejection, of unlovability or failure, lurk like demons in hiding, ready to rise up and attack at a moment's notice.

Our schemas are a screening system through which everything that happens to us must pass, like going through the security scanner in an airport. These emotional patterns spy on our lives, ever alert to anything that pertains to them, anything reminiscent of the focus of their fear or rage, or of the events that shaped them. If the schema gets a match, it immediately triggers whatever reaction we learned: we're flooded with fear and rage, want to run, fight, or freeze, have panicked thoughts about being helpless and unjustly treated. Whatever the emotional habit, it plays itself out all over again.

Schema Triggers ● Throughout evolution the amygdala's circuits

have been crucial to survival in the face of threat, triggering an instantaneous reaction that increases the odds of eluding the threat. Our brain's design primes the amygdala to react as though a threat were coming, even when the evidence is very slim. Better safe than sorry is the operating principle here.

But that can leave us sorry in another sense: our amygdala makes our schemas like hair triggers, ever ready to hurl us into an emotional reaction on sometimes questionable grounds. A schema reaction can be triggered by even mild cues—anything even subtly symbolic of what the schema reads as a threat can bring a rush of turmoil. A client tells me, for instance, that whenever her husband's snoring keeps her awake at night, she finds herself in a rage: his snoring triggers her deprivation schema. "I feel that he just doesn't care about my need for a good night's sleep. I know rationally that he can't help it, but somehow that doesn't matter. I just feel he's oblivious to my needs."

It doesn't matter that her reaction is illogical. The logic of the emotional brain, remember, operates through the rules of what Freud called primary process, where a mere resemblance or symbolic similarity gives two things the same identity, something like a hologram, where the least part stands for the whole. This means that a situation that is even vaguely reminiscent of those that created an emotional habit can act as a trigger.

For instance, some years ago I was called for jury duty. The juror's form asked, "Is there any reason you feel that you would be unfit as a juror?" I wrote that a good friend had been unjustly arrested some years ago, which made me question the universal fairness of the criminal justice system.

Ten minutes later I was told, as were several other people, "You can go now."

My reaction was an odd surge of relief and paranoia. Rationally, I knew I had probably been randomly selected to be sent home. But I couldn't help feeling left out; I had the gnawing feeling that I had been judged as "not belonging" on a jury because of my answer. I started having memories of having moved around so often as a child, and frequently being the new kid in class, feeling excluded, not fitting in. As I left the room, I was the new kid all over again, longing to be accepted into the social circles of the kids who had known one another for years.

The Crucial Choice ● Our emotional habits solidify around the repetition of a given sequence, from sensation to feeling to clinging to action. The unpleasant sensations we feel when a schema is triggered—say, the fear of abandonment when someone we care about seems to withdraw or reject us—leads us to try to calm our fears through maneuvers like a retaliatory withdrawal of our own.

In Buddhist psychology, such a habit is understood in terms of a cause-effect sequence: a stimulus (the rejection) triggers a specific feeling (fear), which in turn triggers a given action (withdrawal). Cognitive science understands habit in much the same terms. From the neuroscience perspective, emotional habit is stored in the amygdala and its extensions through a web of circuitry, where it grows stronger and stronger the more it repeats.

The force of such habits creates a kind of mental inertia—the classical terms are "sloth" and "torpor." The stronger the habit becomes, the less able we are to break out of these ruts. The brain takes the easy path, following the same sequence from sensation to feeling to action, over and over, leaving us prisoners of our own mind, unable to break free.

But the Chain of Dependent Origination also holds the key to freedom from habit. This key can be found in the link that connects feeling and action: how we react emotionally to what we experience, and what we do next. That moment is pivotal: it offers us a crucial choice point.

"A thought arose during a sitting," Lauren, one of my clients, told me. "I was feeling a distance from my boyfriend and having strong feelings that something had changed that would threaten our relationship. He'd been traveling, and we hadn't been in touch much. Immediately after I had this heavy thought, my abandonment fears took over. So I just noted the surge of emotion. Sad feelings arose—fear and sorrow around loss. I decided just to be with these feelings. Tears came lightly, and I let them flow. Then the feelings started to subside.

"After I finished meditating, I went about my daily tasks, but a while later the fear and sadness came back. Again I just stayed with the feelings and the thoughts that we might be splitting up and I would be alone. I decided I needed to accept whatever was happening inside me, even if it was sad. Again the feelings waned, but stayed faintly in the background of my awareness.

"I decided I needed to break out of my mental rut and do something invigorating, so I did some vigorous exercise for a while. Then I cleaned my office. As I did so, I felt a surge of energy. After a short time, I felt a subtle release of the background sadness—I could feel the grip of the schema loosening. There was a gentle lifting of the heaviness in my heart.

"Now I wasn't so worried about our connection. I was able to accept however the connection was unfolding. I could see that acting from fear, as I have usually done, would make me reach out too anxiously to my boyfriend—something I knew would make him uneasy and actually push him away. It was far better to leave things as they were, without anxiously clinging to him.

"I realize our relationship is somewhat like a trick candle a friend had on her birthday cake: no matter how much you blew it out, it would flare up once again. I knew in my heart that my relationship with my boyfriend was like that: even if there were periods when the connection seemed weak, it would always come back strong."

My client's ability to stay mindful of her fears, just watching the abandonment pattern blossom and then fade, exemplifies the point of craving on the Chain of Dependent Origination. There we have the all-important choice: to act on our impulses and emotions, or just to watch the thoughts and feelings as they bubble up and dissolve.

Even if we decide to act—to reach out when we fear abandonment—it's better to wait until the desperate neediness passes. Then we have more choice and can be more flexible. And if we can stay with those feelings without acting on them, we further weaken the link between the feeling and the impulse to act.

The Magic Quarter-Second ● Benjamin Libet, a neurosurgeon, made a dramatic discovery that points to the power of breaking the chain—and suggests just why mindfulness can be such a powerful method of bringing intelligence to our emotional lives. Because the brain has no nerve endings—and so feels no pain—and because neurosurgeons need to be sure they have not inadvertently strayed into the wrong area of the brain, patients do not get a full anesthesia during brain surgery, but remain awake and aware. This allows them to speak or move a part of the body to let the surgeon know that all is well.

Taking advantage of this unusual opportunity, Dr. Libet did a simple experiment: He would ask patients during surgery to move their finger. He used an ingenious clock face that tracked time in thousandths of a second, allowing the patients to note the time with extraordinary accuracy. This way they could report the precise moment when they became aware of the *urge* to move the finger.

Meanwhile Dr. Libet was also monitoring the electrical activity in the part of the patient's brain that regulated movement of the finger. This let him see when the brain actually began activity that would culminate in the movement. In short, it let him separate the moment of *intent* to move, from the moment of *awareness* of that intent, from the moment of actual *action*.

All this allowed the remarkable discovery that the part of the brain that regulates movement began its activity a quarter of a second *before* people became aware of the intent to move the finger. In other words, the brain begins to activate an impulse prior to the dawning in our awareness of the intent to make that very action.

Once the person is aware of the intent to move, Libet discovered, there is another quarter-second before the movement begins. This window is crucial: it is the moment when we have the capacity to go along with the impulse or to reject it. The will, one could say, resides here, in this quarter-second. This window offers us the chance to break the chain instead of blindly following our impulse.

In an automatic, mindless sequence, the impulse to act flows into the action without any conscious consideration of whether we want to go along with it or not. At the root of every emotion is the urge to act; impulse is inherent in emotion. And more often than not, we act these emotional impulses out without a moment of consideration: we feel, and we act accordingly, without pausing to think about it. Anger translates into lashing out; fear into withdrawal; hurt into tears.

This is where mindfulness can be emotionally freeing: it brings an active awareness to our otherwise automatic emotional patterns, interposing a reflecting consciousness between emotional impulse and action. And that breaks the chain of emotional habit.

The Power *Not* to Act ● Mindfulness offers us a way to access

that gap between intention and action, and to use the power of a veto to break the chain of habit. What ordinarily is an invisible chain of automatic sequences leading us onward through life comes onto the screen of awareness, suddenly giving us a choice point where before there was none. We do not have to go along with the impulse to act: we can just say no.

The most elementary example of how mindfulness gives us the power not to act on impulse is an itch: if you don't think about it, you automatically scratch. But if you become mindful of the impulse before you act on it, then you have the option not to scratch—and if, say, you have a poison ivy rash, that decision not to scratch is a wise option. So with emotions.

If we are able to notice the impulses that follow from our fears—of abandonment and disconnection, of not belonging, of catastrophizing and the like—we have the same option not to act on them. By bringing mindfulness to bear, we are able to notice the very first automatic thought that lies behind the impulse to act. And that gives us the freedom to break the chain of unthinking reaction right there.

Mindfulness shifts our attention from being immersed in an emotional reaction—say, anger—to becoming aware of the relationship between our mind state and what it is perceiving. Rather than being lost in anger and all the thoughts and feelings that go with it, we can see that what we feel is anger.

If we let go of the content—the specifics of what has made us angry and what we're going to do about it—and enlarge our awareness to encompass the entire process of anger, we can realize that this is anger. We can note the thoughts that go with it, can make a fine-grained observation of the mix of varied feeling that we lump under the broad label "anger," and can sense the impulses in our body to act—the clenching of fists, the furrowing of brow, the tension in the throat.

But we don't have to act on the anger. We now have the freedom to react or not. Though you do not have to act out the anger, you are not suppressing it. This is very different from repression, where you don't want to know, or don't let yourself know, that you are angry.

With mindfulness, the anger arrives firmly in your awareness. You know you're really angry. You may even want to yell at someone, so you notice that, too. There is tension in your throat, and you notice the hateful thoughts flowing through your mind. In other words, you experience the anger as fully and meticulously as you can, in great detail—quite the opposite of repression.

You don't suppress anger, but neither do you simply act from it. You now have the freedom to make a more skillful response. Perhaps you need to speak out firmly and assertively to point out an inequity or ask to be treated with fairness or thoughtfulness. But if you do it with mindfulness instead of out of rage, your response is likely to be more effective. You're better able to correct the situation, to get heard, or to come to the resolution that you really want, rather than simply triggering an emotional hijack in the other person.

You can convert anger from a destructive emotion to a constructive energy. As I once heard the Dalai Lama explain, when we transform anger constructively, we are left with a clarity about what needs to be done and an intense energy to achieve our goals.

The Mindful Shift ● Whenever our reaction to an emotionally charged situation emanates from a deeply ingrained habit, it narrows our freedom of choice in the moment. Even if that habitual reaction has shown itself to be ultimately self-defeating, resulting in the opposite of what we hoped for, we are doomed to repeat it—unless we can notice when it is about to capture us and dictate how we behave once again. That's the power of shifting into a mindful awareness.

With that awareness you simply let thoughts and feelings come and go naturally as you observe them with a steady attention. You neither react to those thoughts and feelings nor judge them in any way. You simply observe them with equanimity. This observing awareness changes our relationship to the thoughts and feelings. We aren't caught up in them or actively compounding them; we simply remain a witness to them.

For example, Lauren was prone to acute fears of abandonment, a reaction that could be triggered by the slightest sign that her boyfriend was losing interest in her. An unreturned phone call could send her into a fit of imagined scenarios, all revolving around his abandoning her: that he was having an affair, that he no longer found her attractive, that he was bored with her—without the slightest shred of evidence that any such thing was happening.

One day when she was obviously agitated, I urged her to describe the sensations she felt.

"I feel a quivering wash over my body, very unpleasant," Lauren reported. "A strong feeling of fearfulness seems to be feeding the quivering. It's hard to keep my attention on it—my mind would rather be distracted by something else."

I urged her to stay with the feelings, to let her attention rest there and ride the choppy waves of the sensations.

"My awareness wants to leap off—it feels like it's being creamed by waves of intensity."

But keeping her mindfulness steady, Lauren stayed with the swells of the sensations, like a small boat rising and bobbing along with the rhythm of the water moving beneath it. A warm feeling seeped through her body—and her mind—as she drew comfort from the steady awareness. With that comfort, warmth spread through her abdomen, calming the waves of fear and agitation. Her breathing slowed; her fear dissolved.

Along with that shift in her physical feelings came one in her mind. Rather than being afraid she would be abandoned, her spontaneous thought was "I'm free!" With that, a connected thought popped into her head: "It's okay to be left alone. I'll be fine." She said she sensed a reassuring inner connection that extended beyond the limiting sense of looming abandonment that her fears had been holding in place. As the fears—and the tightness in her body—softened, she had a new view of herself: What fear? Who was it that was afraid just moments ago? Where did the worried thoughts of disconnection and abandonment go?

Mindful awareness has this great capacity to free us from the self-imposed limitations of our fears and thoughts. This freedom through mindfulness does not come all at once, of course; it takes cultivating the ability of the mind to sustain an unwavering attention on the entire spectrum of feelings, pleasant as well as unpleasant. Lauren had been practicing mindfulness for several months by the time she applied it so successfully to her abandonment fears. If we put the effort into cultivating mindfulness, it gives us access to a set of remarkably beneficial qualities of mind.

Short-Circuiting Habitual Reactions ● In a sense, a habitual emotional reaction is akin to an itch, and an itch is a microcosm of desire. Try this sometime: When some desire arises, don't act on it, but just mindfully watch the tendency to take action and fulfill the desire. Simply be aware of that desire. Like an itch, desires will eventually fade.

You can do the same with examining the motivation behind your desire for something. See where the desire is coming from. Be aware of the motivation; notice, for example, if this desire springs from clinging or selflessness—from something you want for yourself or something you want mainly for someone else. Be aware, too, of any discomfort or distress that may be arising from your failure to act on the desire. Allow yourself to be okay with not getting what you want.

As you maintain this equanimity, see how the nature of the desire changes. Does it get stronger? Weaker? Do you feel that you'll be fine even if you don't get it? Do you still want what you thought you wanted?

Then, if it's not harmful, allow yourself the choice of acting on the desire. If you do so, stay mindful. Often a desire will change or wane if you observe it mindfully. After a while it doesn't have the same force, or it gives us less pleasure than we anticipated. The sense of grasping grows weaker as a lightness grows stronger. We can more easily see the nature of desire—and we may find that fewer desires need to be acted out.

That same strategy applies in handling the impulse to react when a schema is triggered. Once, while a client was on a meditation retreat, a friend of hers who was also on retreat did something my client felt was insensitive. This insensitive act came soon after my client had done something very caring for this friend. The client had been on retreat for some time, so she was able to bring mindfulness to the familiar feeling the incident evoked: the notion that no one cared about her needs and that she was always putting them aside to satisfy the needs of others.

Her mind, after weeks of intensive mindfulness, was buoyant and flexible. She immediately focused her attention on her reactions, observing them meticulously. She felt a constriction in her heart and some sadness, followed by hurt and disappointment. Then came the thought, "No one cares about me," accompanied by an angry impulse to hurt her friend's feelings by ignoring her. She stayed with this mix of reactions and feelings for a few long moments and was surprised to find herself moved to tears by the familiar sadness of feeling no one cared about her.

Then, in a moment, it was gone. The constricted sadness, the disappointment and hurt, the impulse to pull away. It had all come up, as it had done many times before. But this time she didn't let the reactions control her. She had used mindfulness to break the chain of thought-feeling-impulse. And with the breaking of the chain, something new emerged.

She didn't go through the long round of bitterness, self-pity, and sadness that she usually endured when her deprivation schema was triggered. Instead, now that she had been able to short-circuit her reaction, there was more space in her mind to consider other possibilities. Her next thought was a charitable one: maybe my friend wasn't aware of what she was doing—or didn't mean to hurt my feelings.

The whole reaction, from beginning to end, had taken just a few minutes. This is how a precise awareness can cut through even such strong habitual emotional reactions. When strong feelings are stirring, if we allow ourselves to feel them directly, just being with them instead of acting *from* them, they change. The key is to focus on them completely, without avoiding or resisting, without clinging or identifying—just *being* with them as they are, without judgment or blame.

Such a clean and direct cutting of the chain of habit will not happen right away; my client had been in an intensive retreat, strengthening her mindfulness to a high degree. But to the extent that we can muster a mindful stance while having a schema reaction, we will be able to weaken its power over us.

That pause between impulse and action offers a way to break the chain of habit. As Achan Amaro puts it, "If we can just live at the level of feeling, where we are mindfully responding to pleasure and pain, attraction and aversion, not just acting on desire, then we can live in a content, harmonious way."

Choosing Freedom ● In general, when we have a strong, intensely disturbing feeling about something—especially when the disturbance is out of proportion to what is happening—it's a signal that a blind emotional habit, more than likely a schema, is being triggered. Such feelings represent a moment of choice: we can let the reaction take us over in a trance of habit, or we can pay full attention to what's going on, getting even more in

touch with the discomfort and with whatever painful or even desperate feelings lie beneath it.

But if instead of examining the feeling with mindfulness, we simply act on it, then we reinforce the schema. That's what kept happening with Lauren, who has always been attracted to men who were sometimes warm and intimate but then drew back into emotional aloofness. Whenever she felt them draw away, Lauren would work herself into a frenzy wondering what she might have done to drive them away and trying to connect with them once again. The frenzy might be triggered by something as seemingly trivial as her boyfriend sounding too businesslike during a phone call.

I pointed out to Lauren that her frenzied attempts to reconnect were a way to avoid experiencing the painful fear of loss. The very fact that her feelings were so intense meant that there was a schema at play. But Lauren was distracting herself from learning more about what was involved in this emotional pattern through her desperate fixation on trying to save and repair the relationship, which was probably endangered only in her mind.

Such moments of intensity are an opportunity to learn, and to release the intensity itself. If you choose to confront the emotional habit—to become more attentive to the mix of racing thoughts and upsetting feelings instead of simply letting them propel you into action—a progression typically ensues that ends with the feelings just washing through you instead of controlling you. At first, as you turn your awareness to the experience itself, the feelings are likely to become even more intense and uncomfortable.

But if you stay with those feelings, they gradually diminish, becoming more bearable. Then, if you sustain your focus and rest in it as your mind goes through its changes, a psychological insight into the nature of the schema will often arise out of the confusion. When Lauren did this, for example, she realized that she gravitated to friendships with people—both men and women—who were ungiving and cold, and so triggered this schema over and over. She found herself reviewing her key relationships—a string of boyfriends, several of her closest friends—and realized they all shared the emotional distance she had always felt from her own mother.

A next step for Lauren, after this insight, was to change her own responses in those relationships—not just to calm her emotional reactions but also to try to change how others treated her. Once she was no longer in the grip of her feelings of deprivation, for instance, she resolved to express her need for emotional connection. And rather than doing it in a clinging way, she tried to be light, even playful, about it.

As we make these connections about the schema—why it has such a powerful hold over us and what we can do about it—these insights will lessen the power of that hold. It's as if the schema knows we're not afraid to feel it anymore and so gradually loosens its grip and fades from our mind—and our life. The next time it arises we're more familiar with it and more aware of what is actually going on, so we can see with greater clarity how the schema operates.

We know we don't have to be so afraid to experience the full force of the feelings that go with it, don't have to believe the accompanying thoughts, and don't have to compulsively enact the scenario it urges us to go through yet again. We're not as afraid to face all this because we've done it before and feel stronger now—the schema is more transparent, and we feel a little clearer, even wiser, about our emotional life.

If You Want to Break
the Chain of Habit

Try to tune in to the magic quarter-second—the gap between intention and action—by refining your awareness so that you can direct a mindful precision to becoming aware of your intentions. One way to cultivate this quality of attentive precision is through a subtle observation of the movements in walking meditation.

This can be done using the walking meditation instructions at the end of Chapter 3, but with a key change: bring mindfulness to the moment of *intention*. Before each step, before every turn, the mind forms an intention to make a movement. Mindfulness brings that moment—that quarter-second—into awareness.

Follow the instructions for the walking meditation on page 51. But in the lifting, moving, placing of each foot, be aware of the moment of intention before you make that movement. For example, as you turn to walk in another direction, focus your full attention on the intention to turn and then, after turning, on your intention to swing your foot forward. Before you stop, notice your intention to stop.

You can practice this very direct experience of observing intention in any other situation—even with your emotional reactions. Try practicing during the day to see how many moments of intention you can catch in that quarter-second before an action. For instance, if someone does something that annoys you, pause and bring awareness to your intentions before you make an overt response. Notice what your impulse is, what you feel like doing—perhaps making a curt or angry response. As you pause, consider other responses you might make—maybe a more direct communication about what you would prefer the person do differently.

It's amazing how quickly the brain can process information—a lot can fit into that quarter-second. As you practice, that pause can get longer. One person who tried this told me, "I didn't realize I had so much time in that quarter-second before I react!" Another said, "I'm catching more quarter-seconds in my life!"

10

Changing Habits

A client told me that in one of her favorite parks there were some delicate and beautiful flowers growing in a dirt path. Later, however, her heart sank when, visiting again, she saw that someone had paved over the path—and those graceful flowers—with concrete. ● But the next year as she was strolling down this same path, she noticed a section in the concrete where tiny buds were breaking through a crack. She was moved to see how these "tender heads of intention," as she put it, were more powerful than the dense hardness of the concrete. ● Changing schemas is like this. The tender heads of our intention are a powerful force that can, with sustained effort, break through the dense solidity of our schemas. The process of change starts with an intentional act—doing something different, something that alters an old habit. ● As an example, you might want to try this: Put this book down somewhere so you can still read it, but don't have to hold it in your hands. ● Okay, now cross your arms as you ordinarily would. Feels comfortable, right? ● Now cross your arms the other way: so that the arm ordinarily on the bottom is instead on the top. ● That's what it feels like to change a schema. At first it's awkward and unfamiliar. But if you continue repeating the new habit, it gradually starts to feel more familiar and comfortable—more like you. ● The word for "meditation" in Tibetan has as its stem the verb meaning "to become familiar with," says the teacher Chagdud Tulku. "We become familiar with other ways of being." ● Whenever we are trying to change a habitual pattern, the new habit will feel a bit strange at first. But the more we become familiar with it—the more we practice—the more natural it will feel. ● So with our emotional habits. With repetition, even what used to upset us can become something we can live with. A Caribbean woman was talking about the hurricanes that have swept through the islands each year since her childhood. Aren't you scared, I asked? "Ah, no. It happens so often down here you get used to it," she said with a laugh. "You just close up all the windows and tell yourself, 'Okay, whatever happens, just let it happen.'"

Her attitude—realistic preparation for an emergency, then acceptance of the inevitable—amounts to a remedy for the fearfulness typical of the vulnerability schema. That schema builds up the perception of danger by exaggerating any hint of a threat, so that small squalls become major hurricanes in the mind. The island woman had the opposite understanding: real danger may come, so you do everything you can to prepare, but once you've done what you can, just relax.

As the saying goes, she changed the things she could, accepted the things she could not, and had the wisdom to know the difference. For the vulnerability pattern, that philosophy offers a corrective for the distorted perception of the schema lens, which panics about everything, including what cannot be changed. People with this schema need to learn a basic lesson from sailing a boat: to go in the direction you want, find the balance between yielding to the wind and taking control of the sails.

Every schema has such antidotes, ways of thinking, feeling, or acting, that counter the maladaptive habits the schema perpetuates. We can change habits at any of four levels: our thoughts, our emotions, our behavior, and our relationships.

The 84,000 Antidotes ● The notion of applying antidotes has a

long history; Buddhist psychology holds that we can actively challenge and change our maladaptive emotional patterns—or afflictive emotions, as the Sanskrit term is sometimes translated. A classic Buddhist formulation holds that there are 84,000 afflictive emotions. But Buddhism assures us that there are also 84,000 antidotes!

One main strategy amounts to cultivating a state of mind that opposes the afflictive emotions. The basic principle: a positive mental state tends to stifle or suppress a corresponding afflictive emotion; where one is, the other cannot be in a given moment. Each afflictive emotion has a corresponding positive one that can supplant it in a healthy way. Anger, for instance, can be alleviated by reflecting on loving-kindness, arrogance by reflecting on humility, and equanimity offers an antidote to agitation as well as other disturbing emotions.

Buddhism measures well-being by the degree to which our mind is dominated by afflictive emotions or by the positive ones that are their antidotes.

Cultivating mindfulness is a main tool for altering this balance between healthy and unhealthy mental states. It's the universal antidote.

As another general antidote for distress, the Dalai Lama recommends caring for others despite our own problems. "The space of awareness is small, so our personal distress looms large," as he puts it. "But the moment you think of helping others, the mind expands, and our own problems seem smaller."

Ideal mental health in Buddhist psychology occurs when all the afflictive emotions are replaced with healthy ones, a mark of great spiritual advancement. In this transformation, mindfulness replaces grasping on the one hand and rejecting on the other, allowing for calm openness to whatever comes up in awareness.

From a Buddhist perspective, these antidotes are not absolute answers but rather relatively effective in transforming negative states to positive ones. The unfolding of insight through mindful investigation is what can actually free us from the hold of these tenacious habits. The ultimate antidote is, of course, full spiritual freedom—liberation. But even among those of us to whom that grand goal beckons, there remains the predicament of dealing with the pain created in our lives by the afflictive emotions and by our emotional habits.

So long as these emotional afflictions give rise to our suffering, applying antidotes to them is called for. Both Buddhism and schema therapy use antidotes as a way of neutralizing maladaptive emotional habits. The steps the Dalai Lama recommends for applying antidotes to afflictive emotions are remarkably parallel to those that work well with schemas. The first is to use mindfulness to bring the afflictive emotion into the clear light of full awareness. The second step is to apply an antidote, a positive alternative to the mental habit of the afflictive emotion.

Those steps were echoed in the earliest days of modern psychology by William James, one of its American founders. He saw clearly that to act on a negative habit was to give it sustaining life: "Everyone knows how panic is increased by flight, and how giving way to the symptoms of anger increase those passions themselves," James wrote. "In rage, it is notorious how we 'work ourselves up' to a climax by repeated outbreaks."

To change emotional patterns, like too hot a temper, James realized, the antidote was the purposeful practice of a better alternative: "Refuse to express a passion and it dies. Count ten before venting your anger and its occasion seems ridiculous."

In essence, James was describing a strategy akin to the principle in Buddhist psychology of intentionally acting in a way that opposes negative habits of mind. His recipe for change: "If we wish to conquer undesirable emotional tendencies in ourselves, we must assiduously, and in the first instance, cold-bloodedly, go through the outward movements of those contrary dispositions which we prefer to cultivate."

Bringing Awareness to Habit ● Early in my work as a therapist, another practical insight into methods for changing emotional habits came from Moshe Feldenkrais, a pioneer in body work. His way of working was through physical movement; many of his brilliant insights came from his struggle to regain control of his own body after it was paralyzed by polio. While my learning about Feldenkrais's work, which he called movement awareness, was limited, his system had a profound effect on how I think about working with schemas.

Feldenkrais proposed that the habitual ways we move our bodies are ingrained in the motor cortex, the part of the brain that controls motion. Most of us have a few habits of holding or moving that limit our potential or even cause us pain. To open people up to their full potential, Feldenkrais believed, requires breaking out of the rut of habit. And that, he said, means that changes need to occur within the motor cortex, so that new neuromuscular patterns can be formed that maximize rather than limit our ability to use our bodies.

Doing so, he proposed, could alter other habits, too, including emotional ones. He believed that making changes in the motor cortex would bring changes in the habitual conditioning controlled by other parts of the brain. "The only thing permanent about our behavior," Moshe used to say, "is the belief that it is so."

His attitude toward habit change was refreshing and encouraging: much is possible if we allow ourselves to climb out of our familiar mind-sets and routines and so gain access to a greater range of possibilities. Feldenkrais foresaw what neuroscience later confirmed: "neural plasticity," that the brain is "plastic," continuing to alter itself as repeated experiences shape it.

But such reshaping of the brain takes effort. Like learning to cross your arms in a new way, changing an emotional habit feels awkward at first, if only because the new way of doing things is so unfamiliar, even strange. But if you repeat the new habit over and over, the awkwardness eventually disappears, and the new habit starts to feel familiar and comfortable.

We need to work harder and longer at changing emotional habits, because the brain has to overcome the urge to follow the stronger, more familiar pathways for the old habit. The stronger the habits when originally learned, the more effort it takes to change them—and our maladaptive schemas are among the strongest. It takes sustained effort to build up weaker, less familiar alternatives to the point at which they finally become our spontaneous choice.

When changing a habit, though, people often stop too soon, failing to push themselves past the stage of awkward unfamiliarity. It feels unnatural at first, so we revert to the familiar habit, which feels more comfortable, even after we realize it no longer serves us. This is so often what keeps us bound to our emotional habits.

But if we are prepared to go through this period of unfamiliarity, not just expecting it but determined to persevere through it, we can eventually change the brain's automatic response to the new, improved habit. A clear understanding of the nature of habit lets us know what to expect along the way.

Intentional Change ● Feldenkrais saw that a powerful tool for breaking down our habitual conditioning comes from this simple exercise: First bring more awareness to some of the small activities of daily life that we perform so automatically we are tuned out as we do them, not thinking about them at all. Then intentionally change the habitual sequence. If you always brush your teeth and open the bathroom cabinet with your right hand, try to do it with your left. If you drive to work or school along the same route every day, intentionally vary the way you go, exploring different streets and unfamiliar territory.

This sounds simple, almost innocuous. But when we do a familiar task in a novel way, we stir a fresh awareness. The dull, automatic routine becomes an opportunity for a small awakening. In this sense, breaking free from a habit, no matter how seemingly trivial, can bring a shift in our awareness, inspiring a fresh attitude: beginner's mind, seeing things as if for the first time. And that fresh look gives us the option of doing things differently.

The same principle applies to our habits of mind. Bringing a fresh awareness to our mental habits can give us a new degree of freedom from them. As a gerontologist I know puts it, one of the biggest problems people have as they age is "psychosclerosis"—hardening of the attitudes!

Although Feldenkrais proposed his strategy for habit change decades ago, some recent discoveries in cognitive psychology support his notion. One of the more striking discoveries is about habits. As we've seen, once the brain masters a habit, the whole arc of its execution goes on outside our awareness. This rendering a sequence of action automatic and out of awareness occurs whenever we act in the same way repeatedly in a situation to execute a given goal. Once it is mastered, we need only see, hear, or fleetingly think something to stimulate that habit and set the whole sequence in motion.

For benign habits, like making coffee in the morning, this is fine. Just show up in the kitchen, and your brain and body, like nimble servants, will go through the motions of making the coffee, without your having to pay the least attention.

When our emotional habits are triggered, the results are not always so benign. And yet when the right cue comes along—say, a grating tone of voice reminiscent of the way a parent scolded us—we can overreact mindlessly, perhaps with an edgy retort, without any conscious choice in how we respond.

And the more we respond in the same old way, the stronger the power of the schema grows. Because our schemas are habits that operate largely outside of our awareness, we are often at a loss to change them. One predicament: these emotional habits unfold and are triggered by cues which, for the most part, register in our minds automatically.

Since these habits become stronger with repetition, their very strength means we are likely to repeat them. Under the spell of the schema, we were unaware of the choice at the moment when we began once again to follow the habitual response. Schemas tend to eliminate the possibility of choosing an alternative way of dealing with the same moment. The great protector of habits lies in their automatic, unconscious nature: we do not fully realize we are repeating the habit yet again.

But mindfulness can bring that unthinking repetition into awareness, where we can recognize the pattern and once again have real choice about how we react in that moment. By making an intentional choice to do it differently, rather than repeat the same old habit once more, we can begin to weaken the hold of the habit over us, and become more free. The antidote, then, works by bringing this process into awareness—that is, by making us mindful where before we were mindless.

Bringing an automatic habit into awareness in order to change it is a crucial step. As long as our emotional habits remain outside our awareness, we are powerless to do much about them. But once we realize what is actually happening—"There goes that schema again!"—we can take steps to change what happens next.

Two Simple Steps ● Exactly what steps to take has become clear from research on how to change automatic habits of feeling and thinking. The simple strategy: intentionally changing the *response* we make once we

recognize the habit has begun to unfold. This strategy acknowledges that the triggers for the habit now hold a certain inescapable power in initiating the automatic sequence—the initial reactions are much, much harder to change than is our final response. But once we become aware that the sequence is starting, we can consciously and intentionally initiate a different, more constructive response.

Say, for example, your social exclusion fears are stirred automatically on the first day of a new job as you meet the people you'll be working with. Your automatic schema response might be to feel uneasy and anxious, to tell yourself that no one is interested in talking to you, and to stay alone in your cubicle. But if you catch yourself starting to have that same old reaction, you can act to change the outcome by going up to one person you don't know, introducing yourself, and starting a conversation—and do so despite your anxiety.

The power of this simple strategy was shown in experiments on changing negative stereotypes in Germany, a nation where, historically, religious and racial stereotypes have had catastrophic consequences. A stereotype, of course, represents a mental habit. A malicious stereotype typically includes automatic disapproving thoughts about the target group, associated unpleasant feelings, and a propensity to act with hostility.

The German psychologists had people try to change a specific stereotype by purposely challenging their habitual response. For instance, to challenge their negative stereotypes of elderly people, volunteers resolved to themselves, "Whenever I see an elderly person, I will tell myself: Don't stereotype!"

After just a few weeks of this simple effort, there was a striking change in their formerly hostile attitudes: their automatic negative feelings were no longer activated by seeing an elderly person. Where before they might have avoided contact with elderly people, they now found themselves freer to engage with them in a friendly way. A conscious intervention into an automatic habit freed them from that mental rut.

A similar strategy has been used with success for years by people in Alcoholics Anonymous to fight a return to their old habit of drinking. Whenever they are tempted to drink, they intentionally alter their old response: they call up a friend in AA and talk instead of getting the drink. In a more mundane way we're using the same strategy when we're on a diet and we start to order the cheesecake in a restaurant, then catch the impulse and order the fruit plate instead. In all these instances the old habit was brought into attention as it started to play itself out. It was then given a new, better direction instead.

Consider how Miriam, one of my clients, used this strategy to change unhelpful reactions to her husband that were dictated by her vulnerability schema. Whenever he had to travel for business, which was fairly frequently, she would obsess over her fear that something dire would happen to him. In the first step she used mindfulness to put a helpful distance between her awareness and her turbulent feelings. She would catch herself as she was about to go through the same familiar routine, a kind of mental lockstep, for the hundredth time: yet again ruminating on dreadful scenarios of some disaster or other befalling her husband, particularly when he happened to be late with his nightly call to her while on the road. Those fears led her to lash out angrily at him whenever he was late in calling her.

Bringing mindfulness to the moment, she was able to step back enough to ask herself, "Do I want to make this real?" That gave her a chance to answer herself, "No"—and she would drop it. Opening up a space in her mind gave her more choice in the moment. Instead of lashing out at him, she would calmly ask why he was calling so late and request that he be more thoughtful about calling her next time.

It's a simple strategy with profound effects. There are, then, two steps to changing any unconscious habit, including schemas:

1. Become aware that the habit has been triggered.
2. Intentionally do something to change your habitual response.

What Changes in Psychotherapy ● That simple strategy

offers perhaps the most powerful pivot point for weakening the power of maladaptive schemas in our lives. Consider the bleak formula that sums up the dominant schema of a patient that psychologist Lester Luborsky calls Mr. Howard:

> I want closeness and affection from someone.
> I expect the other person to deny me that closeness and affection.
> I respond by feeling rejected, becoming angry and highly anxious, and blaming myself.

Mr. Howard was one of several dozen patients whose schemas have been analyzed by Luborsky's research team. As Mr. Howard and the others moved through psychotherapy to completion, Luborsky traced with exacting precision the changes in their schemas.

When therapy was successful, two kinds of changes showed up in person after person: the schemas' grip on their lives loosened, and the script

changed for the better its typical outcome. For Mr. Howard, this meant that
he was now, more often than not, able to enter into more satisfying relationships. In these relationships he felt closeness and affection from the other
person rather than the old rejection mixed with distress and self-loathing
that had once been all he could expect from relationships.

Things worked out better. But, as with Mr. Howard, what did *not* change
for the patients was the basic wish or need that was of such urgent importance to them. The improvements were in their own reactions and the
responses they got from other people. For Mr. Howard, much emotional
energy still centered on his need for closeness and affection, but now he had
learned how to get that need met: he had mastered a new way of reacting to
the same old thoughts and feelings.

The hidden ingredient in this transformation is awareness. As therapy
made Mr. Howard more familiar with his schema, he started to get better at
recognizing the signs it was acting up in some relationship. He could realize,
for instance, that he was seeing through a distorting lens that made him misinterpret what someone said to him, reading rejection and coldness where
none was intended. He could even see the humor in his predicament: "There
I go again!" And that allowed him to break the chain.

In short, by bringing awareness to our schemas, we can gain the
leverage that lets us change their story line. The basic fears and desires that
drive schema attacks do not change easily, if at all, but our reactions and
responses can. And that allows our schema reactions to lead to more satisfying outcomes.

Breaking Habits—and Changing Them ● Bringing these
invisible habits into awareness, then, is a first step to changing them. My
client Jake had gone through a painful divorce where the custody of his three
daughters was the main issue. Jake's joint custody arrangement meant he
saw them only on weekends. This new relationship with his daughters,
where he saw them just a few days a week, played into his unlovability
schema, and he became insecure about whether they still loved him.

This, in turn, made Jake too ready to acquiesce to their whims and re-
quests. He let down parental boundaries that before the divorce he had de-
fended. Where before, for example, he had been strict about not letting them
eat too much sugar, now on the days they spent at his house he let them eat as
much candy and drink as many sodas as they wanted. One of them would call
him up and ask if she could have a friend overnight on the weekend or if she

could go to movies back-to-back, and he'd immediately say, "Yes, sweetie pie"—even when he felt it cheated him of father-daughter time together.

When Jake became aware that his unlovability schema was driving his easy acquiescence, he resolved to change the pattern. As an aid to becoming mindful, he wrote a brief reminder on a Post-it, which he put next to his phone: "Stop, Think it Over, Talk it Over, Then Decide." This simple reminder helped him break the pattern of the immediate yes, and to give more measured parental replies.

A Timely Reminder ● Sometimes clients will make notes for

themselves or post reminders, like Jake's, to help them remember what to do differently when they recognize that they are in the grip of a schema. That technique was used by another client, Miriam, in her attempt to set limits for her self-absorbed, childish mother. Her mother had a long history of making constant demands and ignoring Miriam's wishes and needs. Now Miriam faced a difficult moment: she was about to have a baby, and the last thing she wanted was to have her mother around during the first few weeks. Her mother, of course, presumed she would be welcome there. Miriam knew she had to call and tell her mother that she and her husband wanted to spend time alone with their new baby before having visitors, including her mother, stay with them.

Miriam, anticipating that her mother would, as usual, put her own wishes first and make demands to get her way, knew it would not be an easy call. She was already feeling vulnerable because of the pregnancy, so she braced herself for the call and the inevitable guilt-provoking comments and complaints. She fortified herself with reminders of challenges to her schema thoughts. These had come up during therapy, and she had jotted them down in a notebook. She put that page in front of her, so she could consult the reminders during the call. Once the call began and the complaints started to come, Miriam could see that she had one of three ways to react: get angry, feel guilty, or stay neutral.

She looked down at her notebook, and read "Don't want anything from her. Don't give in to guilt. Remember your needs." Having these reminders allowed her to shift into neutral, and be clear and firm despite her mother's demands.

So when her mother said, in her best guilt-provoking voice, "But I *have* to see my grandchild being born," Miriam was able to stand her ground. She told her mother that she wanted only her husband with her at the birth, and that they needed a few weeks together with the baby before her mother came to visit.

Action Antidotes ● Putting into practice the opposite of a schema

tendency is a powerful antidote. My client Jake was telling me how gloomy he was feeling. Lots of emotionally upsetting things were coming up for him, and his girlfriend was getting impatient and angry with him. She was having difficulties herself, and had little emotional strength left to give to him. This made Jake feel overwhelmed: on top of feeling blue, he also felt that in this relationship he wasn't allowed to have such feelings—that he shouldn't "be a problem."

That was, in fact, the message he had gotten as a child. His mother was overwhelmed enough; he didn't want to add to her problems. It was assumed he wouldn't, and so he stuffed his worries inside. In effect, the message he got was "You can be part of this family only if you don't have any needs." As a child, he was accepted on certain conditions: that he not seem to have problems.

As Jake uncovered the truth of this pain he felt, he cried for a while. But as his tears passed and his face softened, he said, "So I've been trying intentionally to be a problem lately. If someone offers me something, even if it's just a polite offer and even if I don't really want it, I'll say yes!"

Then, as I was laughing with him at this, appreciating his imaginative application of action antidotes, I asked him if he wanted me to write down his next appointment on a card.

At first he said, "No, I'll remember it." Then he stopped himself, and said to me, "Yes, I do want a card. In fact, I'd like two!"

Prescribing a Break in the Pattern ● One prescription for

the symptoms of schemas lies in finding just such new ways of doing things. Of course, the old habit, the schema pattern—the brain's automatic response in the situations where it is triggered—will be very strong. Changing that pattern requires intention and effort—the new reaction needs to be rehearsed and practiced over and over if this better response is to make a real difference when it counts the most, in the moment the schema is triggered.

And, of course, the new response will seem awkward and unfamiliar at first. All the more reason to be conscientious about planning and even rehearsing that response.

At a workshop session on breaking schema patterns, two people came up with habits they wanted to change. We all worked together to help them think of the habit-breaking strategies they could apply.

One woman said, "I'm a perfectionist, a message I got from my father. He was hypercritical of everyone. At work I'm a manager, and whenever I see people doing things ineffectively, I get very impatient and irritated at them. What's worse, I'm the same way on the street. If someone is standing in my way when I'm rushing to get to the subway, I'll think, 'You idiot!' If a taxi driver goes down a street that turns out to be jammed with traffic, I'll get angry. I feel that people are intentionally doing stupid things to frustrate me. I'm angry all the time—it's very unpleasant for me."

As we talked it over, she began to see the distinction between times when her high standards were useful—at work, when she could give people performance advice to help them do better—and when they were futile, letting unavoidable difficulties get her upset. We came up with two antidotes for her: noticing the moment she started to have those angry, irritable thoughts, and talking back to those thoughts, giving other people the benefit of the doubt. That man standing in her way at the subway entrance has his own reasons for what he's doing; he's not doing it intentionally to ruin her day. That taxi driver could not control how much traffic he ran into down the block.

For another woman, the problem was subjugation. "I went out with my boyfriend the other night," she said. "All week I had been looking forward to going to a disco with him to dance. But he took me instead to a coffeehouse where there was a guitarist. It was awful music and a miserable night for me. But I didn't say a thing—I just quietly got angry.

"It's been like that all my life," she added. "It started with my older brother, who practically raised me. I used to do whatever he said. Now, in the back of my head, I have the sense that I can't just do what I want—I have to get someone's permission. I wanted to leave that coffeehouse and go to the disco with or without my boyfriend. But I'm too nice to do anything bad."

The group's advice for her was unanimous, light-hearted, and immediate. They said: "Do something bad."

In other words, the prescription for her, as for Jake, was to express her own needs. The antidote to her subjugation was to be uppity—the group's playful way of putting it—to practice asserting her own needs whenever she found herself going along yet again with something she really resented doing, to speak up and say how she felt about it and what she wanted to do. Of course, this assertiveness needed to be balanced by consideration for others—the group wasn't giving her a license to run roughshod over other people.

For these antidotes to work, I pointed out, they would have to make an intentional effort. It's helpful to rehearse the new response in your own mind, or even role-play with someone before you need to try it out. In this process, we can use mindfulness to help us stay calm and clear, so we can practice the new behavior. Whatever the action antidote may be, it will feel awkward and unnatural at first. But rather than let that initial awkwardness discourage us, if we can simply be mindful of these feelings without judging, there's a greater chance that the new behavior will finally settle in.

Catching the Subtle Signs ● In changing our automatic

schema responses, mindfulness acts as the crucial radar, alerting us to the fact that a schema has been stirred. That opens the crucial window that lets us change how we act.

This subtle mindfulness was at work for Lauren, one of my clients, whose deprivation schema was double-edged: on the one hand, she was extremely thoughtful and kind, attuned to when other people were in need of a caring gesture. That thoughtfulness reflected the positive qualities of the deprivation schema. But when this propensity is out of balance, it can become a maladaptive overeagerness to care.

She said, "I'm well aware of my boundary issues and how I can too easily drop something that I need to attend to, to meet the demands and pressing wishes of others. So I'd been planning to set aside a day with my business partner—we design Web pages—to go over my files on a major project for which we were facing a deadline. We chose to meet on a Sunday so we wouldn't be disturbed by business calls.

"A few days earlier I had told a friend that my partner and I would consult with her about her Web page design ideas. She had heard that a merger meant her division at a software company was about to be phased out, and she was feeling some desperation, trying to generate extra income from a project of her own.

"Then, the night before the meeting I'd planned with my business partner, I got an e-mail from my friend saying she would like to have a working lunch with us—she was leaving town the following day and felt an urgency to meet before her trip. My reaction to the e-mail was that I wanted to be supportive of her, but I was trying to protect this day to focus on my project. So I sent her an e-mail message saying, "Can we leave it open for now about the lunch? My partner just returned from a long trip, and we're feeling pressured by our own deadline. But we might be able to get through our work to meet with you, too."

Lauren said, "As I sent that e-mail I had some feelings of guilt. Somehow I felt I had to apologize for not immediately making time for her, for having my own priorities and needs. And I felt a building annoyance at having to rush through my own work so I could get to hers."

For Lauren, those background feelings and thoughts were a subtle clue that her own emotional deprivation and subjugation schemas were active. That clue was confirmed later that night, when she found herself wide awake at 3:00 A.M. "I found myself lying there thinking over and over about that e-mail. Something just did not feel right. I detected a quiet resentment tinging my thoughts about the possibility of my friend calling up to have lunch, right in the middle of our working time. I was puzzled: Why wasn't I feeling sympathy for her plight? Why this irritation instead?"

Since she couldn't sleep anyway, Lauren got up and did some walking meditation back and forth in her bedroom, aware of her mental agitation, and of the jittery feelings in her body. "Then it hit me: when I wrote to her, 'Can we leave it open for now about the lunch,' I had let down my own boundaries. I was leaving an opening for her needs to take priority over mine."

So in the middle of the night Lauren went on-line and saw that her friend had not yet read the e-mail. She pressed "unsend," a command that let her rewrite the e-mail before sending it again. This time she left out the part about leaving lunch open. Instead she wrote clearly, "It would be wonderful to see you, but we're not available until later in the afternoon or evening— depending on when we finish."

And, Lauren told me, "As soon as I pressed the 'send' key with the new message, I felt a great relief. My boundaries were intact, and I was clearly asserting that I would make myself available to help her, but only when it worked for me as well. I felt at peace with myself. I'd been tossing and turning for hours, but I fell asleep immediately after sending that e-mail."

Lauren had caught her deprivation and subjugation schemas in action, and did something positive to make her response more adaptive. Setting the boundaries she needs represents a major adjustment, countering her habit of ignoring her own needs to meet the wishes of others. Lauren did well this time by communicating clearly what was possible for her to do and by plugging the hole in her boundaries that "Can we leave it open" represented.

And what made this possible was her ability to read the subtle signs that her schemas had been triggered yet again.

This capacity to change our most basic emotional habits testifies to the remarkable fact that we can reeducate the emotional brain. Gandhi once said, "As human beings our greatness lies not so much in being able to remake the world . . . as being able to remake ourselves."

If You Want to Apply the Two Steps to Changing a Schema

Investigate your schema pattern to identify its key elements, so you can get better at spotting when a schema attack starts to build. This is a start for a two-step process of change. An analysis of your schema's patterns is a clarifying aid to mindfulness. It can help you recognize the early warning signs that a schema has been triggered. That signals you when there is an opportunity do something different—to change the outcome.

Then, given your automatic thoughts, feelings, and types of behavior, think of ways you can change their direction in the moment—find an antidote or, better, find several new options for yourself.

In short, whenever you notice the schema being triggered, become mindful and execute an antidote:

1. As soon as you detect a schema attack, intentionally make at least one positive response that blocks some part of the usual pattern.

2. Challenge your automatic thoughts. Do a reality check: Are you taking into account all the information available to you? Is there something you are ignoring or playing down that questions the validity of these assumptions? Can you remember times when these same sorts of thoughts proved unfounded? Or, if you can, ask someone else whose view you value if you're being realistic.

3. Take steps to remedy an unpleasant mood rather than letting that mood dictate how you act. Try shifting into a more mindful stance, noting your feelings instead of being swept away by them. Can you literally step away from what's upsetting you by taking a short walk or excusing yourself for a while? Can you step back in your mind, taking deep breaths or doing a calming meditation on your breath, if only for a few moments?

4. Do something constructive that changes the schema script for the better—like when Lauren changed the e-mail message. Be proactive, looking for positive ways to respond that will counter your old schema habits.

5. Practice making a more positive response at every opportunity. When you find yourself in the midst of, or on the verge of, a schema attack, find a positive change to make in your thoughts, feelings, or reactions.

11

Working with Emotions

One evening I was caring for a tired six-month-old baby whose gums had been made sensitive by teething. She was frustrated, sleepy, and squirming in her discomfort. Then she suddenly let out a loud yell. At first I was startled and not sure what she needed. Then, tuning in to how she must have been feeling and how much I cared about her, I lovingly asked her what she was trying to tell me. She immediately quieted down, and with a serious look in her eyes, began to list her complaints, one after another, in a clearly articulated gibberish, knowing that I would somehow understand. ● It was empathy that allowed her to calmly voice what she had felt a need to scream about a moment before. Empathy makes babies feel safe enough to express themselves. It's a tender message that we give one another whenever we care enough to give someone our full attention. Empathy is a reflex. This same warmhearted attention is a gift we can give ourselves as well, in those moments when we're squirming in our schema discomforts. ● We can turn our attention inward and with a warm sensitivity ask ourselves, "What do you need right now?" After all, behind the schemas that drive emotional habits are sensitized feelings that need care and compassion. ● Deep beneath unlovability and deprivation lies a pool of profound sadness; beneath mistrust and subjugation is a smoldering anger; beneath vulnerability, social exclusion, and abandonment lurks fear. An anxious self-doubt drives perfectionism and failure alike. And at the core of entitlement very often lies shame. ● But our schema habits—the strategies we've learned to use in coping with these feelings—tend to insulate us from the intense emotions buried below. Mindfulness gives us a way to burrow down, to connect with the raw emotions the schema protects us from.

Schema Avoidance ● At first we have to overcome the natural tendency to avoid connecting with the painful feelings that drive our schemas. Schemas are slippery; the mind naturally tends to avoid paying much attention to these zones of emotional turmoil. Schema avoidance is the tendency to shy away from looking squarely at these emotional habits.

Strong emotions are messages from the unconscious. Understanding why an emotion is so intense often yields an important insight into our psyche. Still, many people take the position that it's easier not to have these disturbing feelings, to cut them off as they come up. Closing off this way lets us delay facing what really is going on.

Someone with the abandonment schema, for instance, may feel like closing down as she starts to get close to someone, and schema thoughts—like, "I don't want to be abandoned again"—get primed. But it's important not to let the thought stop there, allowing the schema assumption to get reinforced once again.

Facing the fear, rather than cutting it off with the schema reflex of withdrawal, allows a further investigation: "If I stay aware of my vulnerability to being left, maybe I can see this more as a pattern of belief and emotional reactions—but not necessarily as true all the time."

The thought may come, "Why bother? Why open up if there's even a vague possibility that I might get hurt?"

But the opportunity to challenge and test that assumption hinges on our being able to stay with the painful emotions connected with it. Only then can we go ahead and test the assumptions in our lives—staying open to someone, for instance, and seeing if, in fact, the feared abandonment comes about.

Clients sometimes ask, "What if I don't know if I'm avoiding a feeling?" One way to use an investigative inquiry is to ask, "Am I being straight with myself?" Mindfulness is honest introspection, helping us see things as they actually are.

"Problems of all shapes and sizes come up all the time in life," says Jon Kabat-Zinn. "The challenge here is to meet them with inquiry, in the spirit of mindfulness. It would mean asking, 'What is this thought, this feeling, this dilemma? How am I going to deal with it?' Or even, 'Am I willing to deal with it or even acknowledge it?'"

Such investigation can make our feelings more accessible to an experiential understanding. Because mindfulness offers us attention with equanimity, it lets us enter that otherwise forbidden zone of painful emotion that lies hidden beneath a schema. Staying with our feelings mindfully allows us to penetrate into that forbidden zone, to get at the emotional source of a schema, and so release stored-up feelings.

The Antidote ● Mindfulness offers an effective antidote to schema avoidance. For example, Miriam, one of my clients, had a tortured relationship with her mother because she felt criticized by her as well as overly responsible for her mother's happiness, and resentful of that burden. In one session Miriam became very upset about their relationship. "My mother suffers so much," she said, caught in her own guilt.

"Might your mother suffer less than you think, but just complain about it more?" I asked.

"Yes," Miriam said. "But I take her complaining *very* seriously."

"Why do you think your mother complains to you so much?"

"To keep me close," Miriam said.

Her answer surprised me. "Close?"

After a silence, Miriam reconsidered: "It's how she controls me."

"That seems accurate," I said. "But do you think your mother really knows you?"

That question hit a tender spot. Miriam felt a surge of anger: "No, she doesn't know me. That's a perfect way to put it." The raw energy in her voice signaled a schema lurking.

At that, though, Miriam started to change the subject, to talk about something else. I brought her back to the topic and to feelings she was now trying to avoid. I asked her how she felt about what she had said: that her mother didn't really know her.

After a long, silent pause, she said, "I feel sad, real sad." Tears welled up in her eyes.

"I can imagine how sad that would make you," I told her. "Are you able to open up to the sadness and to the reason for the sadness? If you feel like crying, let it happen. But let yourself look at these feelings fully, without pushing them away."

This tactic applies mindfulness during an activated schema: getting in touch with the feelings, the thoughts, and the story that lead to them—getting in touch even with your resistance to experiencing the feelings. Sometimes the hardest part of working with a schema is getting beyond your resistance to the feelings. Because these emotional habits harbor or cover over such deeply painful feelings, we tend to find it difficult to focus on them. The mind tries to lure us away to something less disturbing. Miriam at first just skirted the sadness she felt about how little her mother really knew her and immediately changed the subject to avoid her sadness.

Often as we start to focus on a schema, our attention glides away. Like Miriam, we are distracted by some other thought—any other thought. That way we don't have to go near the pain. We do the equivalent of standing up from a meditation as soon as our knees hurt. We immediately turn our attention elsewhere to distract ourselves from emotional pain.

Mindfulness counters schema avoidance by keeping our attention focused on what we feel, even if those feelings are uncomfortable. We can let these emotions run their course instead of cutting them off before we have really connected with them.

The Emotional Charge behind Schemas ● "My neighbor

drives me nuts in exactly the way my mother does," Miriam complained to me another time. "He's always critical, there's always a negative, noodgy energy from him. I spin out for days in self-criticism after a run-in with him. What can I do?"

We talked about several strategies she might use. In Buddhist meditation, there are several approaches to working with disturbing emotions. One is to abandon the emotion; another is to transform it. From a spiritual vantage point—as well as a psychological one—closing ourselves off to our feelings obstructs a healthy openness in mind and heart, closing us also to the potential insights that emotion might offer.

Abandoning the emotion, for Miriam, might have meant avoiding the neighbor altogether or trying to keep their interactions superficial and at a distance. Miriam decided to take a transformative approach and dive into the thick of her schema reactions with an enhanced awareness next time her neighbor upset her so much, investigating the underlying emotions triggered by the bothersome neighbor who was so much like her mother.

When she investigated her schema reaction, she had a realization that connected her relationship with her mother to her reaction to her neighbor. At first, Miriam had been fixated on the neighbor as the problem. She was plunged into strategizing about how best to handle him: Should she avoid him? Confront him? Then she started to investigate her own reaction to him. What was it about him that was so upsetting for her? Why did he elicit such an intense reaction in her?

As she explored further, she saw that what unhinged her so about him was a hypercritical quality that was similar to the same quality in her own mother. Miriam had thought that moving a thousand miles away from her mother's relentless criticism would be enough of a boundary. But now she saw that her fear of being criticized was arising right next door and, even closer than that, in her own mind.

Miriam saw that this was not just about her neighbor, but about a larger pattern in her life. And now she realized she could use the reactions he triggered in her to gain access to the feelings underlying her schema. So she applied mindfulness, tracking the emotions connected with her reaction to him. When she did this, she felt a huge pool of anger and resentment—a lifetime of rage over being emotionally abused by her mother.

She found two approaches to making use of that rage. Sometimes simply being mindful of those feelings brought her a release from being fixated on them. She stayed connected to the raw experience of her angry feelings— the pulsing throughout her body, the agitation in her mind—with mindfulness. Though distraught, she did not get swept away by the thoughts themselves or by judging them or ruminating on them.

A few times, though, when her rage was particularly intense, she turned to a Gestalt technique, pounding a pillow while venting her anger at her mother. Then she returned to mindfulness, following those sessions of emotional release with meditation to let her mind calm down and further clarify its understanding. Once she did this, Miriam no longer felt helpless. Now that she understood what was behind her reaction, it no longer seemed to take her over so strongly. And when she did sense those old feelings being stirred up, she could focus on her own fear of being judged, a valuable opportunity in her internal exploration of her emotional patterns.

The investigative approach that Miriam used allows us to regard schema triggers as a useful way to understand the emotional charge behind a schema. Miriam used the moments her neighbor triggered her schema as opportunities to explore the deep feelings of anger underneath feeling criticized.

This attitude puts schema reactions in a new perspective: they become chances for transformation through discovery, with insights waiting for us just beneath the surface. When we see one of our reactive patterns as an opportunity to understand the workings of our minds, those very intense emotions we were once tempted to avoid become gateways to deeper understanding. As Tulku Thondup said, "Problems hold the key to their own healing if we bring our awareness to them."

Sorting It Out ● When people come to therapy, they often have already acknowledged that something is awry or out of balance—somehow not working in their lives. They don't always know what it is, but they are motivated to make the connection to their suffering and its causes. But it is not always clear how to find our way through the confusion and disorder.

Mindfulness practice cultivates an inner knowledge that can be of immense help in sorting through the confusing welter of our emotions. When this spotlight of awareness is directed toward the emotional chaos of our lives, or at our distorted thinking patterns, a recognition of the underlying causes can come more clearly into focus. Having a conceptual framework, like the schema model, can help clarify the process further.

Meditators often seek a clear place to rest calmly in the mind. But attention itself, even when directed toward the mental haze, offers a reliable refuge. When we can relax our tendency to grasp for a pat explanation, and just be present with whatever is happening without trying to alter it, we can bring to bear a deeper, more intuitive knowing. That in itself changes our reaction and our perspective.

We can use this intuitive knowing in the service of emotional alchemy in many ways. Whenever we are swept into an intense emotional state, like anger or sadness, we can bring mindfulness to bear in sorting out our confusion to find what might really be going on. Once we have some familiarity with our schemas, attention can take a precise focus: What was the trigger this time? What are the thoughts, the feelings, the impulse to act?

As we progress in schema work, our moments of emotional confusion will take on an entirely new significance, offering us a chance to probe deeper into our emotional habits. The alternative to avoiding the emotional discomfort of our schemas is to use the emotional pain as a beacon, a signal that something of significance is going on that we need to understand. We need to investigate the experience with mindfulness and stay open to it, particularly when it gets uncomfortable.

Two methods are particularly useful here. One is wise reflection, where we reflect on the emotional episode with mindfulness to let insights emerge. The other is sustained awareness, bringing the equanimity of mindfulness to bear during the episode itself, or during the lingering period while the schema stays primed, making us less reactive and more able to investigate our thoughts and feelings with greater clarity.

First, of course, we need to face the fact that the schema has been activated in the first place—that we have that familiar uncomfortable feeling. The tendency toward schema avoidance can make it harder to home in on the signals that can lead to emotional insights, or allowing the feeling to release itself naturally.

Jake was usually oblivious to his schema, and yet it would take him over again and again without his realizing it. Jake, remember, was divorced with three daughters in a joint-custody arrangement and would drop anything and anyone, including his girlfriend, to do whatever his daughters wanted. He used the method of wise reflection, sustaining his focus on his behavior until he broke through to its deeper meaning. As he was reflecting, he saw that he was trying to buy his children's love by fulfilling their every whim. He was being driven, he realized, by his irrational fear that if he didn't give his children whatever they wanted they would not love him.

With that realization, he suddenly felt a great sorrow well up inside; his sadness broadened into a steady flow. At first Jake had no idea what the sorrow was about. I encouraged him simply to be with the sadness, mindfully, and to use wise reflection to find an intuitive sense of what it meant. As he explored his sadness with mindfulness, he had a flashback to a time in fourth grade when he had desperately wanted to be liked by one of his schoolmates. His need for acceptance had been so great that he would spend his whole allowance buying candy and gum on the way to school to give to this schoolmate—a bribe. He now recognized the same desperation, the same overeagerness to please, in his behavior with his own children.

This recognition intensified his sadness: now Jake was sobbing quietly. Through his tears he told me he was also in touch with a feeling he'd had since childhood—that he always had to be a good boy to win the love and approval of his parents and everyone else. He remembered vividly the looks of disgust, even contempt, his parents would give him when he did something that displeased them, and how miserable he felt at those times. He came to believe he could never be himself—he was always trying to please other people to be sure they would like him.

That litany of associations and memories came slowly, as Jake reflected on his sadness and its sources. Jake left that session still feeling sorrow. He had finally connected with the deepest reservoir of emotion, the pool of grief his schema reactions had been keeping him from experiencing.

Resisting Our Suffering ● Since our schemas protect us from experiencing deeper underlying emotions that we find intensely disturbing, get-

ting to the layers of feeling behind a schema is like peeling an onion. Fear may be closest to the surface—as, say, with the abandonment schema—but beneath the fear there often lies a layer of sadness, and behind that may be anger.

Our schemas, however, make us behave and think in ways that keep us from going near these underground reservoirs of torment. The vulnerability schema, for example, protects people against panic by making them focus on repetitive, almost obsessive, thoughts about what may be wrong and what they might do to prevent that danger. The neurotic trade-off: by occupying the mind with worrisome thoughts and a milder anxiety, we avoid plunging into the more forbidding deep panic beneath. Worrying becomes a kind of magical ritual, warding off worse fears. In people with panic attack, the vulnerability schema no longer protects them from the compelling, morbid fear that they are about to die, but rather fans its intensity.

With the abandonment schema, the emotional trade-off goes along these lines: By clinging to those people I fear I might lose, or by not getting too close to them, I avoid the deeper dread and despair of being all alone. And for subjugation: By giving in to the other person, I avoid facing the explosive anger that my subjugation breeds.

Emotional deprivation propels people to act like caretakers rather than voicing their own needs. That way they do not feel the full force of their underlying anger or sadness. Socially isolated people shy away from others to avoid the fear or hurt that might come from a rebuff. And those with an unlovability pattern keep themselves at a distance so as not to face the sadness or fear of being rejected. (If you are wondering about the feelings underlying other schemas, turn back to Chapter 5 or 6.)

Using Wise Reflection ● Of course challenging habitual thoughts and changing our knee-jerk reactions are important dimensions in healing our schemas. And these remedies may come more easily than healing ourselves at the emotional level. But if we are to free ourselves from the grip of our schemas, then releasing the pent-up feelings that drive them represents an essential step, like lancing an infection to speed its healing.

My client Lauren used wise reflection to connect with the underlying feelings while she was struggling with her abandonment schema. One of her closest friends had gotten angry after Lauren candidly warned her that her fiancé seemed too narcissistic. The friend was so furious that she refused to talk to Lauren for weeks—although several months later, after the engagement was broken off, the friend thanked Lauren for her candor.

That angry withdrawal by one of her closest friends triggered Lauren's abandonment schema in full force. For days Lauren was swamped with fear, flooded with memories of all the times her jet-setting parents had left her for extended periods with a series of nannies before finally shipping her off to a boarding school. Those memories brought surges of great sadness and a poignant compassion for the little girl who had been so bewildered by these desertions. Ordinarily Lauren's schema would have driven her to desperate attempts to reestablish the connection with her friend, a way to calm her fears of abandonment. But this time Lauren used wise reflection to be with the feelings that were stirring so strongly inside her. On her own she experimented with letting herself experience the fear, the sadness, the troubling thoughts, and when they started to be overwhelming, she would intentionally focus on a calming meditation on her breath.

Coming back to the breath is like shifting into neutral; it can feel like a safe place to be—even in the midst of emotional turmoil. Then, after centering herself a bit, she would go back into the disturbing feeling for a more mindful investigation. In this process, she wove together a conceptual understanding, drawing on the schema model—aware of the dynamics behind her fear of abandonment—and a direct, sustained immersion in the pool of her feelings. She would feel the emotion, then go back to her breath, trying not to get lost either in the eddies of feeling or in the pull of a purely rational analysis. Then she would, as the monk Amaro puts it, "drop in" her reflections on her schema within this mindful space.

As she did this, a series of insights arose for her, allowing her to make connections she had not made before. The links got clearer and clearer between her sadness as a little girl at being left by her parents, her greatest fear back then—that they would stay away forever next time—and her reaction to her best friend's withdrawal.

At that point she broke down into uncontrollable sobs. She cried for that little girl, grieving for the loss she had felt. The intensity of her grief scared her, but she stayed with the feelings through it all rather than distracting herself or trying to do something, like desperately trying to reconnect with her friend, that would placate the schema. Instead, she immersed herself in the deep grief that she had been hiding from all these years. This allowed for a profound shift in her inner work, toward releasing the fears behind her abandonment schema.

Then, she later told me, "I realized, after facing my intense fear of being left, that if I lose this friend, that's okay. I'll be all right without her. I don't need to be controlled by these fears anymore."

Lauren found that mindfulness could help break through the defenses that keep us from noticing—let alone dealing with—the underlying feelings that empower the schemas at work in our lives. She discovered that turning to a meditation on her breath for a while when her abandonment fears became too intense had a calming effect. Then when she felt ready to open mindfully to her fears, she experienced her awareness as being more powerful than her fear.

Finally she immersed herself in the underlying pool of feelings—the abandonment fears—finding that they were not so terrifying after all. And that gave her more courage.

Connecting with Schema Origins ● Once Lauren had connected with her underlying fears, I urged her, the next time this schema was activated, to let herself be with the fear of losing a connection without letting her fear drive her to action. So when an episode with her unresponsive, aloof boyfriend next triggered those same feelings, this time she focused on them, without doing anything to try to make them go away. Lauren again found herself flooded with a vast pool of sadness. She had another series of vivid memories of being a little girl. This time she recalled her mother, an alcoholic who could sometimes be warm and affectionate, but would then suddenly become cold and aloof. And when her mother was so distant, that little girl was filled with the same sadness that the grown-up Lauren was feeling. Lauren then realized that she gravitated to friendships with people—both men and women—who were ungiving and cold, and so triggered this schema over and over.

Recognizing that you are caught once again in such a pattern and letting it go can be a small moment of awakening—So *that's* what's going on—as you acknowledge the pattern. And in such moments of recognition there can be a spontaneous increase in understanding and compassion for yourself, making you less likely to react impulsively from your schema fears.

If you can recognize the emotional roots of your schema, sensing the part of you that still identifies with the small child who first learned to feel this way, you can have more empathy for your schema. This recognition lets you feel less identified with your emotional patterns, less confined by them, because you can see clearly that it's not *you*, not your true nature, but rather a result of repeated conditioning, rooted in your early life, that you are acting out. But because all these years it has felt like the real you, you haven't seen it objectively.

Acknowledging the painful feelings locked all those years inside our coping strategies and bringing them into the light of awareness can release us from the vortex of emotional habit. The result can be more insight into how the mind operates and greater compassion for that part of ourselves that has been held captive by the schema. This stance of insight and compassion lets us step back enough to enter into an empathic inner dialogue.

Our Innate Wisdom ● This work involves cultivating an intuitive knowing, an inner wisdom. If we feel out of touch with this inner wisdom, mindfulness offers a way to cultivate this connection within. Just why this might be is suggested by some intriguing scientific findings.

The amygdala, a main source of our disturbing emotions, lies in the brain next to the hippocampus, which helps us remember what we know about a situation, including what responses are appropriate. Whenever we have a negative reaction to someone, that response reflects a conversation between the amygdala and the hippocampus, but exactly what they say stays largely out of reach of our awareness.

There are many other centers in the brain that store aspects of our memories of what has happened to us and what we have learned. When we face a decision or grapple with a troubling issue, the brain very quickly draws on all the relevant memories—many of which are stored beyond the reach of awareness—and offers us an answer.

But that answer does not come to us as a rational thought: Here's what I should do, and here's why I should do it. Instead, the brain gives us the answer as a sense of what is right or wrong in the situation. In other words, the answer comes in the form of an emotional certainty, not as a rational thought.

If we fail to tune in to that inner sense, or if we don't trust our intuitive insight, then we cut ourselves off from the potential wisdom we can bring to bear on the situation. Often, in the accelerating pace at which we live our lives, or in the confusion of turbulent feelings, we have too much internal static to attune to this subtler signal. But mindfulness gives us a way to tune in to these subtle feelings and hear the quiet voice of wisdom within. This intuitive knowing very often comes first as a quiet feeling. What the feeling means—putting it into words—comes to us later, with continued attention and reflection.

Accessing Memories ● Mindfulness practice, notes the monk Nyanaponika, strengthens intuition. One field for applying this intuition is in tracing subtle patterns that connect the episodes of our lives in a meaningful way. Mindfulness sharpens our cognitive apparatus, so that, for instance, per-

ceptions are clearer. So with memory, too. Very often when people go on long mindfulness retreats they find themselves gaining access to memories that had lain dormant for decades. These memories can have a special quality. "The intensity, clarity, and richness of memories gives a greater accessibility and provides fertile soil for the growth of intuition," Nyanaponika writes in *The Power of Mindfulness*. "Recollections of that type will have a more organic character than memories of vague, isolated facts, and they will more easily fall into new patterns of meaning and significance."

Reconnecting now with these memories, most of which will be from our childhood, allows us to understand what happened from a mature viewpoint. And once we have that understanding, we can go the next step in schema therapy, having an empathic dialogue with the part of our mind bound up in the child's view.

As my client Alexa immersed herself in the feelings surrounding her abandonment schema, a pivotal memory came back to her. She recalled how her father had been absent from her life for many years while she was young. He later rejoined the family, but he was volatile and unpredictable, prone to severe mood swings and angry outbursts. As a little girl, Alexa was often afraid of him, but he loved her and wanted to be there as her father. "One might think that was nice of him," Alexa said. "But for me as a twelve-year-old girl, it wasn't that easy."

Alexa had a powerful memory of a critical moment in their relationship: "I was walking through a park one day with my father, feeling uneasy and confused. He took off the Saint Francis medallion he always wore around his neck for protection, and gave it to me. Maybe the timing was off—I don't know. But I remember throwing the medallion on the ground." Alexa paused a moment, her eyes tearing up, as she told me what happened next: "He left it there on the ground and walked away."

Alexa and her father grew apart after that, and a few years later he died. Many years later she went back to the spot in the park where she had thrown away the medallion, not searching for it but to revisit the anguish and guilt she felt for not accepting such a meaningful gift from her father. She had nothing of his, and she longed for her father's medallion. For years she was plagued by remorse. Why had she acted so impetuously? She had no deep regrets in her life—save this one.

As she explored that memory now, as part of her schema investigation, she had a visceral sense of the twelve-year-old inside her. She suddenly heard a compassionate inner voice say to that twelve-year-old girl, "Of course you were angry with him. You had good reason to be. He abandoned you. He wasn't around for years, and when he finally returned, his violent outbursts frightened you."

Years of remorse melted away in that moment. Alexa wished that their relationship could have been different and that she had been more open to his love. And she still wished she had his medallion as a symbol of their connection, fragile as it was. But she now understood the reasons for her actions as a twelve-year-old. It all made sense to her.

Alexa's experience illustrates well how important it is to understand the deeper, symbolic meanings of events that can be locked away in our hearts for years. Her one moment of acting on impulse reverberated through a lifetime. And revisiting that impulsive moment let her have empathy for the twelve-year-old of years ago. Making such connections can sometimes release long held feelings and open us to compassion for how we acted in years past.

Empathizing with the Schema ● Once we are in touch with the pool of deep feeling that drives a schema, once we dive deep enough into it to find its origins, we need to take another step: we need to offer our empathy as caring adults to the part of us that is still thinking and feeling like the little girl or small boy who first started to have these schema reactions.

It was the Christmas holiday season, and Lauren was feeling a bit sad, as usual. "I know the holidays activate my deprivation schema," she told me.

From an objective perspective, it seemed that the holidays had gone well for her. She had spent Christmas at a gathering of loving and close friends and family. But one of her closest friends, to whom Lauren had sent an especially thoughtful gift, had not sent her a gift this year or even thanked her. And another had not returned Lauren's holiday call—part of a long-standing custom between them. Small matters in the broader scheme of the holidays, yet these were what Lauren's mind fixed on.

"I know it's not rational," she told me. "But I don't feel it's adequate just to say to myself, 'You know you are more vulnerable to deprivation feelings around the holidays. Just give it a rest.' That just feels like it's depriving me more. I feel my friend who never thanked me doesn't reciprocate in our relationship. And my friend who didn't return my call frustrates me by never taking the initiative to stay connected, especially since I've talked to her about this many times. It feels almost intentionally depriving."

For someone without Lauren's schema sensitivities, such minor acts might have gone by without a reaction. But for her, with her deprivation lens on life, they loomed large.

She continued, "If other people aren't going to come through for me, at least I should be able to take care of myself." Lauren decided to sit quietly with her feelings for a while, to get some calm and clarity, and then turn to her feelings and see what image came to mind. In her therapy she had started to create an inner dialogue between her hurt little girl and her nurturing adult.

"I see myself as a little girl, maybe five years old, wandering about looking for someone who would pay attention to me, someone to connect with," Lauren said. "This little girl says, 'Everyone is so busy, so caught up in themselves and distracted by their own problems. I can't find anyone to just be with me.' She tries to be very well behaved and affectionate, but no one seems to notice her."

"What would that little girl need to understand?" I asked. "If you were an inner caretaker, someone very nurturing who could be there for that little girl, what would you tell her?"

Lauren's answer was immediate: "I'd say, 'You're looking for love from people who can't give you what you need.'"

"And how does your conversation go?"

Lauren continued, in a sad, almost despairing voice: "The little girl responds, 'But they're my family—they're supposed to love me.' The nurturing voice says to her, 'They are too wrapped up in themselves, too deprived, to notice anything but their own needs. Turn instead to people who are already there for you.'

"Then the little girl looks for some quiet place to hide and be by herself, to be invisible, to have no needs. It's her habit when no one seems to care. But then she remembers what the nurturing voice said: that some people are there for her, and love her. She's just been looking to the wrong people."

Then, a new energy putting a lightness into her tone, Lauren adds: "So she goes to find those people whom she already feels loved by."

An Inner Dialogue ● At least metaphorically, there is a child within, a part of us that still feels like a child. This kind of inner dialogue, a conversation with the schema as embodied by the small child who first learned that particular emotional habit, offers a reparative experience from the inside. This approach is not recommended for everyone, but many people have found it helpful at some point in their emotional work.

When Lauren was speaking with the deprived little girl within her, she had an avenue for connecting with the part of her that harbors the underlying emotional needs of her deprivation schema: that frozen child inside needs to be heard and understood. Lauren was able to be with that sadness, but to keep the schema—personified in that little girl—from freezing around her unmet needs and slipping back into the familiar lonely isolation, not wanting to, or daring to, bother anyone.

Lauren's more mature and reasoned nurturing voice reminded the little girl that there *were* people to connect with. But she needed to look for love where love was being given freely in her life, instead of focusing solely on those people who were too wrapped up in themselves and their own needs to care enough for her—which is, of course, where the schema is compelled to look for those needs to be met.

That more positive response, coupled with empathizing with the little girl's pain and sadness, offers emotional healing. There was a dialogue between that hurt child who first embodied the pattern and the inner voice of a nurturing caretaker who represented what the schema craved. This inner relationship can make up to some degree for the initial deficiency that led to the schema—or it can at least reeducate the schema so that we learn a new response.

This wounded child within represents the schema reality locked in the amygdala. The healthy relationship with a nurturing, mature inner parent is, to some degree, reparative. The dialogue between them becomes part of the overall remaking of neural connections that goes along with healing a schema. It's as though we were re-parenting ourselves at a very deep level, making new connections between the emotional and the rational brain, creating the healthy response habits we failed to acquire in childhood.

We can engage in this reparative inner dialogue ourselves. However, if this inner re-parenting method occurs in therapy, the first dialogues can be between the therapist, acting as that nurturing voice, and the client giving voice to the small child that represents the schema reality, as in role-playing. This can then make it easier for the client to access the child in the schema, at which point she can work with the re-parenting dialogue technique on her own, giving voice to both parts of herself, as Lauren did.

In a sense, the child captured by the schema is like any other: she needs attention, has needs to be met. As one client put it, "Sometimes I feel like a little kid in an adult's life." It helps to have a way of checking in with these emotional needs. We can listen to these inner voices and respond, even if we can't always stop what we're doing to fully attend to these needs. We can show these feelings an inner empathy, being sure not to scold or repress—as when we talk to a small, hurt child. After empathizing with the inner child we can be more open to hearing a rational intervention, challenging the assumptions we cling to. In that interaction, the child can grow up in a matter of moments.

Releasing ● The cycle of pressure building and releasing is everywhere in the natural order. The body builds up dead cells and releases them in fighting an infection; tectonic plates scrape together creating immense pressure that is relieved during an earthquake; storms build in heavy gray clouds that release their weighty load of moisture in rain.

This natural process of releasing has a parallel in the psychological dimension. Often people who have done intense emotional work come to a place of readiness to awaken to how painfully an emotional pattern manifests in their life. They can see how their deep-seated belief in the underlying thoughts, the feelings that keep it in place, and the knee-jerk reactions that flow from them, hold it all in place. Despite the pain the pattern causes, it is all too familiar and, finally, too much to put up with any longer. An emotional pressure builds and ultimately demands relief.

One client told me about going through a cathartic crying session when such pressure had built up. She said she got in touch with immense pain and grief from realizing that her emotionally depriving parents would never meet her need for them to care about her. It built up and grew so intense that there was nowhere to go but through it. She found herself weeping and sobbing, gasping for air like a small child. It went on for a quite a while before slowly winding down. Afterward she felt there was nothing left to grieve; she experienced a profound letting go of a pain that has not returned.

Not everyone goes through this process, but when we reach this point of being unable to continue living under the weight of these distorted beliefs, an emotional unfolding and release can happen—often more than once. It is similar to the release of built-up pressure in nature, as the body and mind come together to produce a grieving that will release the pent-up emotional pain. It can be tremendously freeing to allow the mind to let go and the body to give itself up into the release, as though some inner force knows just how to release pain—as in the intense crying my client went through.

It's beneficial to let such a release happen the way it wants to, completely naturally. Seeing someone go through this process of release can be like watching a woman give birth, or seeing someone die. There is an inevitable momentum at work, a letting go into the greater flow of a natural force.

Mindful Grieving ● In nature, precipitation occurs when the droplets of water in a cloud become too large and heavy to remain suspended in air. Rain is nature's release. In the same way, tears are a wonderful release for the human organism. They can relieve the pain of our emotional wounds.

At the same time, a psychological principle holds that we have a built-in protective mechanism that keeps us from uncovering emotions that might be too overwhelming for us. Research with people mourning the death of a loved one, for instance, shows that ordinarily after such a loss, people go through periods of intense grief and sorrow that alternate with periods when they are not immersed in grieving. It's as though something inside gave them just the dose of sadness that they could handle, then stepped back to give them time to restore themselves before facing the next layer of grief.

Something like that typically seems to be at work when we open to our schemas. There is, oddly, a sense of loss as we start to give up the patterns associated with a schema, or as we review the early origins of the schema and reevaluate episodes from our lives. An old part of ourselves is dying off, and that leads to grieving.

Delving into the details of a schema seems to set this process in action. Larry Rosenberg, a teacher of mindfulness meditation, puts it well: "True insight means seeing things as they really are, not as we want them to be. Coming to this acceptance is the work of mourning."

Simply putting aside the lens of a schema, seeing more clearly, means giving up the old way of defining ourselves and looking at the world. We surrender our maladaptive habits, our desperate clinging to the schema's reality and reactions.

When Jake got in touch with his unlovability schema, he found that it made up a large part of his basic identity and stance in the world. Too eager to please, always trying to be the person he thought others wanted, Jake lived in a false self, a facade. He said despairingly that he wasn't sure who he was anymore if he wasn't the person who was always pleasing others.

Not knowing who we really are is common when we begin to challenge our schema beliefs. Our emotional habits are familiar ways we define ourselves, and so it can feel unsettling for a while to dismantle this sense of self, even if it's a distorted and painful self.

Of course, seeing that we need to let these habits go and actually surrendering them are two distinct steps. First we need to become clear in our minds about how our schemas do not work for us, and so build the resolve to change them. The next step is actually going through the work of changing, of letting go of the old ways.

As we do so, we leave part of ourselves behind. This means, at some level, we have to accept that loss. We're witnessing a small death: of core beliefs, of a certain image of ourselves, of misplaced hopes or fears, or just of familiar habits or comforting assumptions. As we let go of these entrenched habits and cherished ways of seeing ourselves, we need to mourn their loss. When we grieve, we are less likely to once again seek to avoid that pain out of the kind of fear that has driven our schema reactions.

"So," says Rosenberg, "insight and mourning go hand in hand. We can't give up what we don't understand. We have to come to know something for what it is before we can let go of it."

The Power of Opening Up ● At Stanford University, women with advanced breast cancer that was spreading through their bodies were put in support groups with others like them. At this point in the cancer, there was little or nothing doctors could do to save them. Everything had been tried, and now it was only a matter of time until each of them would die. These women found that the group was the only place in their lives where they did not have to hide their feelings. Their families and friends often had such dread of talking about the cancer that there was no chance at all for the women to open up about how they were feeling. With other women who faced the same harsh reality, however, they were able to cry and weep, to rage against the unfairness of it all, to be utterly free to let their feelings out. And they were free, too, to be caring with one another, to offer emotional support, to hug one another through their tears.

To the surprise of the physicians who had set up the groups, there was a powerful medical effect from the groups. The women who went to them lived *twice* as long as comparable breast cancer patients who, though they received conventional medical treatments, did not go to such a group: an average of thirty-seven months for those in the groups versus just nineteen months for the others.

There's an important word missing from the English language. It's the equivalent of *antarayame,* a Hindi word meaning "knower of the heart," someone who sees clearly every corner of our interior world and accepts us just as we are. This quality of feeling known and empathized with, understood deeply for who you are, is a powerful healing force. In the Dalai Lama's words, "One of the deepest human desires is to be known and understood."

Those who work with a skilled psychotherapist, one with whom they feel trust and rapport, can experience this sense of being deeply understood and accepted. A therapist can be a mirror for the client, creating a container where the client feels safe to open up, be seen, and be reflected back with acceptance. This is one way therapy can serve a re-parenting function, giving clients the dependable, caring attention they may not have received in childhood.

That sense of being known and accepted can also come from friends. We all experience some form of suffering at one point or another. It can be a powerful vehicle for connecting with other people. Sometimes the connection happens around everyday forms of suffering—the loss of a loved one, a setback in life—bonding us to others who share our grief. Empathy naturally springs from a heart in pain; it's a great gift we can give to one another.

I've seen this empathic support in my workshops when people are exploring their schemas together. It can be very bonding. At one point in this self-exploration, a woman said half-jokingly, "I feel I'm a little crazy."

So I asked, "How many people here feel that they're a little crazy?"

Every hand shot up, including mine.

The healing power of empathic support is true, too, for emotional wounds, even when the source of the empathy is ourselves. In an experiment, people wrote in a private journal their thoughts and feelings about the most traumatic experience of their lives—or even just about some pressing worry—for about fifteen minutes a day over five days or so.

Just getting these feelings out had surprisingly beneficial effects. For one thing, their health improved; they had fewer illnesses over the following six months. There was a significant relationship between the feelings they expressed and their health: the more turbulent the emotions expressed on paper, the greater the improvement in their immune function.

The greatest benefit of all was for people who in their early writings expressed the strongest feelings, like deep sadness and hurt, or intense anger and frustration. At first, they just gave a voice to their emotional pain. But then, over the next few days, their writings showed they were reflecting on the meaning of the events that gave them so much distress—they were able to find a pattern or meaningful narrative. I find that this progression happens naturally in this work as we give voice to our schemas.

If You Want to Voice the Feelings Connected with a Schema

*W*rite about the thoughts and feelings stirred up in you by reading about the schemas that seem most relevant to you. You don't have to put huge amounts of time into writing—just ten to twenty minutes at a stretch, whenever a compelling thought or feeling comes up and you have a chance to jot it down in a private journal.

1. Don't censor your thoughts. Be completely open, saying things you might not tell anyone else. Remember, this journal is for your eyes only. The more honest you are with yourself, the better. This is your chance to say whatever you'd like to tell someone else, but feel inhibited about saying to them. Put it all in your journal.

2. Write whenever and wherever you have the inspiration and are free to do so. Don't feel you have to write every day, but keep the momentum going by writing when you feel moved. It may help to do your writing in a private place where you feel secure and undistracted.

3. Write about both the objective facts and your feelings about them. As your emotions well up, really let go, putting it all down on paper. Free-associate—just let it all pour out.

4. Don't worry about how it sounds or looks. No one is grading you; you don't have to be careful about spelling or grammar. If you hit a block, just write over again whatever you've just written.

5. Keep this journal for yourself. Don't write with someone else in mind whom you might want to show this to someday. If you do that, you'll start editing it with that person in mind, or you'll try to justify what you say.

6. Keep at writing over the course of several days, weeks, or even months, if you find it helpful. Your thoughts, feelings, and insights will change as you delve deeper into working with your schemas.

7. As you remember the events in your early life that seem to have shaped your schema, consider writing a letter—which you don't need to send—to the people or person in your life who was most involved. It might be a self-absorbed parent who made you feel emotionally deprived or a group of kids at school who made you feel

left out. Vent your feelings about their behavior in the letter. Make it part of your journal. This can be an extremely effective way to give the frozen little child at the core of a schema a way to express feelings, disappointments, and needs.

There is another reason to keep a private journal if you are going to embark on this inner journey. If you start early on, it becomes a way of tracking your progress along this path if you note what triggers your most troublesome schemas, the thoughts, feelings, and actions that go with them, and how often they come up.

Writing in the journal will give you a place to pull together your insights on the sources and origins of your schema, the situations that trigger it, and to gradually piece together a fuller picture of your typical emotions, thoughts, and reactions.

The journal also gives you a way to reflect on your deeper feelings about the relevant issues in your life as well as on the early experiences that seem to have shaped the schema. And it gives you a chance to vent your feelings without having to confront people in your life.

Over several months of doing this work, your journal should help you track changes in the thoughts and feelings that come up, in how you react. If your work with schemas is having an effect, you will notice a gradual decrease in the number of times in a given week or month you have schema attacks, or a lessening of their intensity, or how long they last.

12

You Don't Have to Believe Your Thoughts

When I was a child, my grandmother had a wondrous old Oriental cabinet in her living room. On its front there was a carved and painted tableau of a woman in a kimono carrying a parasol as she walked down a path from a pagoda. Gazing down on her from a distance was a bearded, kimono-clad man in the window of what looked like a teahouse. ● The scene was an alluring glimpse into an exotic landscape. Everything in that scene was fascinating: the buildings, the people, their clothes, the gnarled trunks of the trees, the huge flowers. ● As a young girl I daydreamed about that scene for hours, and it remains a pleasant, vivid memory of visits to my grandmother's house. I've wondered if that cabinet was a seed of my own journeys in life: the trips I've made to Asia; becoming a student of the Japanese tea ceremony, flower arranging, Indian dance, and Asian spiritual practices. ● When my grandmother died, my mother, knowing how much I loved the cabinet, suggested to other family members that it be given to me. But others decided that my grandmother's furniture should be sold and that the proceeds should go into the estate. The cabinet had been just one of many pieces of furniture in her estate, but once I expressed an interest in it, the cabinet took on a special mystique. A relative who hadn't paid any special attention to it until then suddenly became convinced it was extremely valuable. ● So we arranged to have a certified appraiser examine the cabinet and determine its value, which I would pay to the estate. A couple of family members anticipated its worth would be great, an essential asset of the estate. As some relatives talked, the price ballooned—a fine old Asian antique like that might be worth a hundred thousand dollars or more! ● Finally came the day when the appraiser looked at the cabinet. Her conclusion: the cabinet was not from Asia at all, but an American imitation—

Japonaiserie, as it's called—and not very old. Besides, she pointed out, the paint was chipped, and the veneer had begun to flake off. Her assessment: it might be worth three hundred dollars, at most!

My family's heated, overblown view of that humble cabinet was much like the distorted thinking typical of schemas. It's so easy to see something the way our wishes would have it be, and then convince ourselves that our assumptions are the truth. What we lack is the corrective reality that the appraiser brought to bear.

The power of schemas to impose their reality on our perception—to re-create our world on their own terms—has a basis in brain function. The amygdala, the center for emotions, sends long branches into most parts of the neocortex, the area where signals from the senses are analyzed for their meaning. When the amygdala is hot—for instance, during a schema attack—these branches also become more active, influencing how the neocortex analyzes what we perceive, how we interpret what we see or hear, and how we think.

This can distort how the brain interprets what we see, shifting the likelihood that an emotionally loaded interpretation rather than a realistic one will be applied. When the amygdala heats up with intense activity, emotionally loaded thoughts loom larger in our field of attention. This would explain how our schemas shape so powerfully the way things seem, almost as though they cast a spell over us.

Tibetan Buddhism speaks of such distorted thoughts as "cognitive obscurations," a powerful variety of mental affliction, and a basic cause of psychological suffering. Fortunately, even if we can't control the circumstances that lead to such thoughts, we have the ability to free our minds from their hold.

Breaking the Spell ● Sara had an understandably ambivalent relationship with her former husband. They got along in many ways, sharing custody of their children, and—after a tumultuous breakup—gradually reconnected with each other as friends.

Before the divorce, as she and her husband were growing apart, Sara had assumed that he was highly critical of many things about her. While he was very plodding in the things he did, she was impulsive, spontaneously throwing herself into each new passion, like learning to make watercolors or a psychology class, then deciding after a while to move on to something else. Sara was sure he disapproved of this chaotic pattern of fits and starts—that he thought she was ditsy.

But one day as they were talking, long after they had divorced, she decided to ask him about it—after all, what did she have to lose? So she confided in him that she had always assumed he had this opinion about her.

To her surprise, his response was, "That's one of the things I always loved about you!"

When we are under the sway of our schemas, we assume that our distorted beliefs are the truth. But if we challenge the assumptions that go with a schema, mindfulness can act like an inner appraiser, bringing an unbiased perspective. This lets us see our hidden assumptions afresh, and so call them into question rather than simply let them guide our perceptions.

Thoughts have no power except the power we give them. Questioning our mental habits and challenging the assumptions that justify them has been a mainstay of cognitive therapy. The first step in this challenge is to observe our schemas carefully, becoming more aware of how they are triggered in our life, and of the habitual thoughts, feelings, and knee-jerk reactions that go with them.

By bringing the details of a schema into awareness, we gain a larger perspective on what's happening, and this allows us more choice in how we respond. If we can recognize the schema as it is being activated, we can challenge it on any of three levels: cognitive—our thoughts and how we interpret the situation; emotional—the feelings these thoughts arouse; and behavior—the acts those thoughts and feelings lead to.

We've explored what mindfulness can bring to working with the emotions of a schema and what it can bring to changing our habitual reactions. In this chapter we explore how mindfulness can help us challenge the thoughts that schemas generate in us.

Empathic Reframing ● But first, a reminder about empathy. When

we work with our maladaptive schemas, it's especially important to nod to our emotional reality even as we challenge our habitual thoughts. Many of our schema habits of thought and feeling were learned early in life, before we had developed the rational thinking abilities we have as adults. This makes it especially important to relate to our schema reality in the preverbal mode of our early feelings.

We must empathize with the schema before a rational shift can occur. As we saw in Chapter 11, the process of empathizing can sometimes lead to a period of grieving as we open up to the painful truths encrusted in the schema and begin to let it go. That emotional work is parallel to the rational effort of challenging the thoughts and assumptions of the schema.

Any time we tune in to a schema's thoughts, it's helpful also to be attuned to the accompanying feelings with empathy. That empathy can take the form of a mental nod acknowledging the feelings behind the schema, a quick mental note like "abandonment" or "exclusion," or a more articulated thought process such as, "Of course I'm anxious now—my schema fears are making me assume I'm going to be abandoned or left out."

Once you've connected to the schema with empathy, it's important to take the next steps in changing these tenacious emotional habits. But if we get too rational too soon, the little child locked in our schema may not feel the empathy with its emotional reality and so may rebel. If we offer such care and sensitivity to our emotional wounds, they will more readily respond to the medicine of emotional work, particularly the rational labor of challenging the distorted assumptions that fuel them. But without empathy such purely rational challenges may be a bit like covering an infected sore with a Band-Aid without treating the wound itself.

What Troubles Us ● "It is not things themselves that trouble us," wrote Epictetus, a first-century Greek philosopher, "but our *thoughts* about those things." The ancients recognized the power of our thoughts to make us miserable, and they knew that this insight pointed to the remedy for our misery. Buddhist teachers have long urged us to examine and challenge the thoughts and assumptions that mislead us into taking actions we later regret.

These ancient recipes for inner work are contained, for example, in some suggestions from the Dalai Lama, offering practical steps for dealing with afflictive emotions. One is to develop a clear understanding of why the emotion is destructive—in other words, to step far enough back from it to see that the reaction is self-defeating. Another is to examine the unfounded or distorted assumptions that give rise to the emotion. Realizing that these thoughts are just projections of the mind helps counter the disturbing emotions they provoke.

He also recommends one crucial method: "Cultivate mindfulness right from the beginning," the Dalai Lama teaches. "Without mindfulness, you give the afflictions free rein." And once they take hold and gather strength, it becomes harder and harder to counter them. But with mindfulness, we can keep the tendency toward afflictive emotions from developing into a full-blown eruption. Acquiring the habit of bringing a sustained, mindful awareness to our confused thinking as often as possible offers an inoculation of sorts against emotional turmoil.

Mindfulness provides a means of ferreting out the automatic thoughts that silently trigger our schemas. Nyanaponika says that mindfulness "identifies and pursues the single threads of that closely interwoven tissue of our habits. It sorts out carefully the subsequent justifications of passionate impulses and the pretended motives of our prejudices . . . mental habits that are no longer unquestioned."

Our emotional conditioning can result in tunnel vision, the feeling of being trapped in a confining, uncomfortable, almost claustrophobic space built from repetitive thoughts, assumptions, and beliefs. Mindfulness offers a spaciousness in the mind that illuminates this darkness, expanding our vision beyond these limits, creating a space of clarity around compulsive reactions and thoughts.

Mindfulness gives us some breathing space from automatic distorted thinking patterns, so we can reperceive them more clearly and put them into a more realistic perspective. This spacious clarity lets us investigate those reactions so we can open to the feelings and thoughts connected with them and gain insight into the schemas that power them. It brings a possibility of freedom where there had been only the hopeless heaviness of compulsive repetition.

For example, the lens of a schema like emotional deprivation tends to lead us to interpretations like "See? He really doesn't care about me." But mindfulness lets you see this lens itself—that these thoughts are skewed by the schema—rather than simply having your reality limited by the schema's view.

Mindfulness of Thoughts ● "When you are practicing Zazen, do not try to stop your thinking," the Zen teacher Suzuki Roshi advises. "If something comes into your mind, let it come in and let it go out. . . . It appears that the something comes from outside your mind, but actually it is only the waves of your mind and if you are not bothered by the waves, gradually they will become calmer and calmer."

As we saw in the instructions on mindfulness, thoughts in themselves are one of the classical objects of attention in this practice. One method— mental noting, where we label familiar thoughts as such without getting pulled into them—is quite helpful in working with our schemas. Noting gives us a way to track the habitual thoughts of a schema. Instead of going along with those thoughts, we can step back and recognize them for what they are: mental habits. We can say to ourselves, "exclusion" or "mistrust" or whatever schema the thoughts represent. This gives us an added anchor in the mind to resist the tide of those thoughts and to help us determine how active the schema seems to be.

Mindfulness teacher Joseph Goldstein points out that one reason it is so important to make our thoughts the object of mindfulness is that "if we remain unaware of thoughts as they arise, it is difficult to develop insight" into them.

Meditating on thoughts—being mindful of them—as he defines it, means "simply to be aware, as thoughts arise, that the mind is thinking, without getting involved in the content: not going off on a train of association, not analyzing the thought and why it came, but merely to be aware at the particular moment [that] 'thinking' is happening. If we fail to do this, to see our thoughts as such, they remain the unconscious filters on our perception."

While these instructions are for meditation practice, they offer a way to cultivate and strengthen a habit of mind that proves invaluable in working with schemas: the ability to step outside a thought that has taken over the mind, to see it as simply another thought.

One aim of Buddhist practice is to help us know when our mind is deluded by distorted thoughts and when we are seeing clearly. This act of mindfulness is the first step toward challenging that thought rather than letting it define our reality at that moment. The thoughts that come up during a schema distort our reality—if we let them. Stepping back from our thoughts through mindfulness gives us the freedom to question the thoughts and so be less controlled by them.

Challenge the Assumption ● Once you have used mindfulness

to catch a schema in action, you can seize on the automatic thoughts that empower it and then challenge them on the spot. If you persist in this tactic, the thoughts will eventually lose much of their power, especially as you realize you don't have to believe these schema-driven ideas.

One of my clients, Kathy, a professional musician, came up with an all-purpose counterstrike for her perfectionism schema and its constant self-judgment. Kathy calls it her "universal automatic thought antidote." Automatic thoughts are the slippery initial defining thoughts of a schema, the ones that prime the flood of feelings and lead to a schema attack.

One example starts with a typical scenario that would trigger her schema, but it then goes on to prescribe an antidote:

> I'm sitting in an audience listening to a great musician who practiced six hours for this performance—the same six hours that I spent making a pot of soup for my houseguests.
>
> An automatic thought comes to me: "What am I doing with my life, making soup when I should be practicing for six hours like this person?"
>
> And the musician performing after his six-hour practice session is thinking, "I should be like this great musician who's performing tonight at Carnegie Hall and who needs only three hours of practice."
>
> And the musician at Carnegie Hall is thinking, "I hate this—I've got to get a life."

This antidote to her perfectionistic thoughts captures a playful spirit that Kathy was often able to bring to this work. The ability to bring a lightheartedness and humor to our schemas is a powerful way to reframe these weighty thoughts. Woody Allen's self-deprecating humor often has this effect; we can all relate to the comic absurdity of his neuroses. One of the schemas he's made himself famous for is vulnerability. "The most wonderful phrase in the English language," Allen, a notorious hypochondriac, once said, "isn't 'I love you,' but rather, 'It's benign.'"

Helpful Comparisons ● Kathy told me that she once heard a
woman perform extremely well and was fascinated with the performance. Instead of her inner voice criticizing herself in comparison, Kathy was genuinely happy for this woman. But the woman, after playing, started crying, saying, "I'm so sorry you had to listen to that—it was awful." Kathy couldn't believe the woman was being so self-critical after the lovely performance. It helped her to see her own perfectionism schema all the more clearly.

Comparisons can be helpful in countering schema thoughts, particularly with perfectionism. There are two ways you can compare yourself to others, one that makes you feel better, and one that makes you feel worse. The automatic thoughts, unfortunately, go in the direction of the one that makes you feel bad.

Upward comparisons, where you think of yourself compared to someone who is much better, can lead to putting yourself down, to self-blame, even to guilt. Medical patients who constantly think of themselves only in comparison to people who are well are quite likely to get depressed about their own condition. That's the effect Kathy's put-down thoughts—"I'll never be that good a musician"—had on her.

Downward comparisons, where you see how you match up to someone who is worse off than you, make you see how well you are doing relative to how bad things could be; they cheer us up a bit. For example, when patients with serious diseases think about someone with a far more advanced case, they end up feeling a bit better about how they themselves are doing. After all, they realize, things could be worse.

Kathy countered her self-critical thought with thoughts of how much she enjoyed her life and how the onerous routine of top-level musicians could deprive them of such simple pleasures as making a delicious bowl of soup for dear friends. In doing so, she turned an upward comparison—"I'll never be as good a musician as she is"—into a downward one: "at least *I* have a life."

Counter-Thoughts ● I was talking to Jake, a client who has a strong emotional deprivation schema, about how empathic people with this pattern can be and what natural caretakers they are: "One positive side of deprivation is that you learn to be very nurturing. It's when the nurturing gets out of balance and your own needs go unmet that you feel deprived. Nurturing others can be very healing and nurturing for you, too—if you're not feeling deprived. Then there's more than enough caring to go around."

Jake made a significant internal connection: "It's just like Chi-kung! There's an exercise where you rub your hands together and then play with a ball of energy between your hands, moving them apart and together in a circular motion. You're tapping into Chi, universal energy that connects everyone. It's the energy you tap into to heal. You are a part of it, and so is the person you are healing. This is shared energy that everyone taps into, and so it is beyond giving and receiving. Everyone is nurtured; no one feels deprived."

The notion that there's more than enough to share poses a direct challenge to the emotionally impoverished thinking of the deprivation schema, that there will never be enough caring to go around. When we examine the thoughts that empower a schema—like looking at a lab specimen under a microscope—their irrationality becomes fairly obvious.

You don't have to look very deep to see the absurdity of a schema thought the next time you catch it crossing your mind. But it helps to have rehearsed in your mind the challenges to those thoughts, so you will be able to bring them to bear when you need them the most: when a schema attack is about to unfold—or when it has you in its grip.

Just as each schema gives rise to typical thoughts, so there are specific counter-thoughts that oppose them. Having counter-thoughts ready makes it easier to challenge them, once mindfulness has brought them to your attention.

Not Believing Our Thoughts ● I often suggest that my clients
use an inner dialogue with their schemas, talking back to the thoughts rather than remaining passive. For instance, whenever the thought came to mind, "I'm a failure—nothing I've ever done has ever amounted to anything," one client would purposely bring to mind times she had succeeded and done well—a memory that undermined the validity of the schema's view.

This inner dialogue itself demands a measure of mindfulness: staying active and mentally alert, with your inner radar attuned to—detecting and challenging—such thoughts rather than simply letting them run on and on. That radar hinges on a special reflective perspective called meta-cognition, the ability to step back and notice the nature of thoughts rather than simply thinking them.

In applying this observing power of mindfulness, we should remember, as therapist Marsha Linehan puts it, to "step back *within* yourself, not outside yourself, to observe. Observing is not dissociating," where we experience ourselves as though at a distance. Mindful observation of thoughts involves connecting with the thoughts but not getting lost in them or running away from them.

Mindfulness allows us to create just enough mental distance from thoughts to see them as such. This stance shifts our perspective on our thoughts, letting us see that they are just thoughts, not reality. And with that insight we can realize that *we do not have to believe our thoughts*.

That realization is liberating. It lets us disengage from what otherwise would be emotionally compelling notions. Old mental habits—like "I'm worthless; it's hopeless; my life is futile"—can run on and on, but if we hold to a mindful stance we can recognize them as mere thoughts, seeing them as well-worn ruts in the mind: "Oh, I'm having *those* thoughts again." As we recognize them for what they are, we break their tyranny in the mind.

Mindful recognition sidetracks what might otherwise become a cycle that spirals downward into a schema muddle.

In short, mindfulness not only makes us more aware of our thinking but also lets us redirect the process so we are no longer compelled to go down such well-worn grooves. Many of my clients find it effective in such moments to engage in an active inner dialogue with their schema, as though it is a small child and they are the inner parent.

For instance, one client had realized that her deprivation schema triggered a habit of bingeing that had caused her to put on weight. So she decided to go on a diet and to talk back to her deprivation schema when she found herself going through emotionally triggered food cravings. When she caught herself in such moments, she'd talk back to her deprivation schema, saying, "I'm not depriving you if I don't eat this ice cream."

The second way mindfulness disempowers schema thoughts has to do with the nature of attention itself. Schema-driven thoughts are most powerful when they preoccupy us, taking front and center of the mind's stage where they fill us with their drama of angst, or trumpet desperation. But mindfulness edges those thoughts to one side of the mind's stage, reducing them to minor players, muting their shouts to mere whispers.

Wrathful Compassion ● The fierce-looking deities in some Tibetan art represent the spirit of wrathful compassion, an attitude of uncompromising battle with the forces of ignorance. The compassion in this fight lies in its goal: to free people from ignorance.

While challenging our thoughts may seem quite dry—so rational and unemotional—the process often takes on juice when people get fed up with those nagging voices. The act of challenging schemas can take on the warrior spirit of wrathful compassion.

For Olivia, wrathful compassion was a battle cry. She saw her perfectionism—with its oppressive self-critical thoughts—as the enemy, her struggle with these thoughts as an inner crusade. In the process of girding for the battle, she sharpened her mental weapons, the counter-thoughts she would unleash to vanquish the oppressive voice of inner criticism.

She wrote me a note:

It's time to do battle with this poisonous snake that has taken up residence inside me.

When it tells me to be guilty, I will say, "No, I am not going to be guilty. There is no reason to be guilty."

When it tells me that I'm unworthy, I will say, "No, I'm valuable and am loved unconditionally."

When it tells me that I'm incompetent, I will say, "Just leave me alone. Stop bugging me. Get out of my life."

When it tells me that I haven't accomplished anything, I will say, "You are trying to make me believe these untruths with your insidious, hissing voice. You're the one who's hateful and miserable and incompetent and loathsome. Now get out!"

I'm wringing this out of my system. I don't care how long it takes. But I'm mad.

Her passion made her all the more determined to catch these thoughts as they started to arise in her mind, and immediately counter them with an antidote.

Acknowledge What Is Valuable ● As we challenge our schemas, we need to sort out the adaptive from the maladaptive part. To the extent that our assumptions or reactions are realistic or effective, no problem. We challenge only what does not work. In some ways, as we saw in Chapter 5, our schemas are partially adaptive attempts to get basic needs met. They are semi-adaptive answers, partial solutions, that can drive us in positive as well as negative ways.

I recall how one client with strong perfectionism took on too much. She had long thought of adopting a child. But she didn't just take in any child—she took into her home a severely troubled teenage boy from an institution on a trial run for possible adoption. He was angry and impulsive, destroying some of her most valued possessions, picking so many fights at school that he was expelled, even getting in trouble with the police. My client was a working single mother, and the added demands were overwhelming for her. She had health problems, including hypertension and asthma, that were worsened by strain.

Adopting a child in itself was fine—a compassionate act that would have been nurturing for her as well. But her unrelenting standards—the inner voice of her perfectionism—told her she wasn't doing enough unless she took in the most challenging and demanding child. She thought that was a virtuous decision, when in fact, compelled by her schema, she had taken on way too much.

But these patterns aren't always negative. Perfectionism can help motivate people to perform their work at a high level. It becomes dangerous only when it drives them in ways that put their lives out of balance, as it did with my client, who was endangering her own health. When challenging a schema, we need to ask, for instance, how it might put our life out of balance, whether it seems to distort our perceptions, and how we feel about things and about the choices or responses we make.

Bringing Mindfulness to Depression ● "I'm a failure. Nothing I've ever done has amounted to anything. It's hopeless. And it will always be hopeless." Those dispiriting ideas and others like them constitute the depression schema, a mental lens on reality guaranteed to turn any sunny day into gloom. Ruminating on such thoughts over and over, in endless mental tape loops, is a recipe for depression.

But the power of mindfulness in challenging distorted thoughts has been demonstrated dramatically in treating people with chronic depression. John Teasdale, a cognitive scientist at Cambridge University who is also a meditator, has been teaching mindfulness—along with using cognitive therapy—to groups of patients being treated for depression. What he's found has lessons for working with our maladaptive schemas, too.

He works with the toughest cases—people whose depression keeps recurring. In such people, thoughts alone can become triggers for the schemas that activate depression. While a person's first few episodes of depression typically are triggered by an adverse event like the loss of a job or the death of a loved one, in later episodes the person's negative thoughts themselves increasingly become triggers for the descent into depression.

Teasdale finds that among those who become severely depressed for the first time, about 50 percent of cases are triggered by an upsetting or traumatic life event. Only 20 percent of second episodes of severe depression are triggered by an upsetting event. And just 10 percent of third episodes have triggering events.

Life's provocations are the cause in progressively fewer relapses, Teasdale says, because depressing thoughts increasingly take on the power of actual setbacks and upsets in setting off relapses into depression. Such a relapse can begin innocently enough, when a bad mood reactivates the thought patterns that typified a previous episode of depression. Those thoughts trigger more foul moods, in a downward spiral.

What for others might be only a mild bout of the blues holds a special risk for those with a history of depression, as though those moods and thoughts were viruses to which they were especially susceptible. They are particularly vulnerable to thoughts which, if allowed to reverberate, can eventually lead to another descent into despair.

The thoughts themselves become the trigger for the depressed feelings. For this reason, depression has sometimes been called a thinking disorder. Cognitive therapy and mindfulness both offer direct antidotes to the thoughts that can fuel depression.

The Mindful Antidote ● Mindfulness brings relief from despair in two ways: it allows us to perceive our thoughts as mere ideas rather than as overwhelming truths, and it makes them loom less large in the mind.

The power of mindfulness in fighting our maladaptive thoughts has a basis in the mechanics of attention. The numerous tracks by which information runs through the mind are akin to the parallel interconnecting freeways across the United States. This web of roads means there are dozens of different ways to get from, say, New York to San Francisco, even though a handful of superhighways are the main thoroughfares.

Likewise, in the mind, different kinds of information run along a multitude of connected paths. For instance, the basic features of what we hear—like pitch, timbre, volume—run along one set of paths, while the literal meaning of those words runs along another. The emotional implication of the meaning runs along still another.

Most of these paths run outside the stage of our attention. Teasdale points out that the mind's capacity for such out-of-awareness processing of information is seemingly endless, but that its capacity for knowing what occupies awareness at any one moment is quite restricted. Our attention can fasten on just a single coherent stream of thought at any given moment.

This limit on attention amounts to a kind of bottleneck in the mind. Within that narrow space, thoughts compete to capture the center of our mental stage, like actors jostling with each other to seize the spotlight.

Since only one thought can be in stage center at a given moment, as one thought dominates, others wane. Mindfulness itself joins this competition. When we consciously reflect on what is going on in our own mind, that act takes up the limited resources of our attention.

As the monk Nyanaponika observes, since attention has a limited capacity, "if the clear light of mindfulness is present, there is no room for mental twilight." For people prone to depression, this makes mindfulness a kind of inoculation against their more pernicious thoughts. But this is true for any maladaptive thoughts: mindfulness fills much of our attention with something other than the mental tape loops that activate our schemas. By becoming mindful, we set up an alternative mental act that competes with the thoughts of any schema.

Stopping the Train ●
Mindfulness helps to derail schema thoughts by focusing our awareness on the here and now, simply noting what we experience without getting caught up in our thoughts or our reactions to them. By contrast, the state of mind that gets lost in schema rumination is mindless, with the train of thoughts running on and on, as though set on automatic pilot.

"Stop That Train" is the title of a reggae ballad. Mindfulness stops the train. While mindless rumination lets us drift away into the fog of depression, mindfulness reminds us not to float off but rather to be keenly aware of the fact that we have begun to drift—and to come back to the vivid present.

At the same time, a mindful stance allows us to step back from a thought and see it as such. Instead of being immersed in the idea that "I'm utterly worthless," you can recognize what its presence means: that you're caught up in a mental state in which you view yourself as utterly worthless.

That mindful labeling of a gloomy self-judgment is a mental act that further competes with the depressing thought itself for the meager resources of attention. And now what was a dire judgment—the schema thought—once examined through the lens of mindfulness, is transformed into a mere thought. This simple act derails the schema-bound train of thought. There are again two steps: use mindfulness to spot the schema thought, and then challenge it, redirecting the train of thought in a more positive direction.

The Schema Inoculation ●
Teasdale says the aim of mindfulness in treating depression should not be to prevent occasional bad moods—they're part of life. Instead, the focus should be on preventing such negative moods from escalating into the kind of mental gridlock that leads to major depression. Let the moods come and go. Allowing them to come is the easy part, but how can you make sure they'll go?

The answer lies in preempting any train of thought that would lead down into a valley of depression—or to a schema. One strategy for hijacking a train of thought is to change the course of the tracks themselves so that what starts out as a schema-bound train is switched toward a different emotional destination.

This redirection occurs in cognitive therapy when people are coached to challenge their thoughts. Using mindfulness to spot our schema thoughts, we then challenge them on the spot, changing their course as they run through our mind. For depressed people, this means seeing gloomy thoughts about the hopelessness of their predicament as simply signaling a normal, passing bad mood—something they can deal with—rather than as a dire, irrefutable truth. A thought train like "I'm feeling down," which typically leads to the conclusion "I'm no good," gets rerouted to "I'm feeling down, but that's normal from time to time."

The more someone can perform this mental morphing of schema-bound thoughts into neutral ones, the less likely a schema attack becomes. The best results come when a person does this inner homework over and over again, in all kinds of situations and on all sorts of occasions, in many, many different circumstances. In other words, the more often this is practiced, the better the effects. The mental habit that once led inexorably to a schema attack becomes transformed.

The power of this method of inoculating ourselves against depression was demonstrated in a five-year follow-up study of people prone to recurring depression who were treated using Teasdale's mindfulness approach. For people who were caught in a bout of depression, the combination of mindfulness and challenging thoughts persistently led to a recovery. But even more important, those who *continued* to do this homework as needed after they recovered had far fewer recurrences of depression as the years went by. So with any schema: the more often we stop a train headed toward a schema attack, the less often we have to make that stop.

A daily session of mindfulness meditation cultivates and strengthens precisely the kind of attention that needs to be applied when a schema thought comes to mind. A mindfulness meditator is, in effect, practicing the attention strategy that offers protection against being hijacked by a schema, but doesn't have to wait for schema thoughts to happen by. Therein lies a great capability that mindfulness adds to psychotherapy. It offers a daily opportunity to prepare for a moment that is otherwise unpredictable, like the fearful or angry thoughts of emotional deprivation, or the sadness of an episode of depression. Such a moment might not occur for weeks or months—until the next brush with a schema attack.

For people prone to depression, this skill makes them more able to confront their next onslaught of depression-bound thoughts with a remedial reaction at an early stage in their emergence—exactly the strategy for resisting the full-bore onset of gloom. And for working with any of the maladaptive schemas, this all-purpose radar makes us more alert for the next moment when these emotional habits are being primed, so we can head off a hijacking as it is building.

Stormy Thoughts ● The sky was darkening and getting cloudy; storms loomed. I sat in my writing room after meditating, reflecting on the similarity between the inner and outer elements of the weather and my state of mind. Someone I was counting on to fulfill an obligation hadn't come through on our agreement. I had helped her recently when she was in need, so I felt especially disappointed when she let me down.

Thunderstorms were predicted, but then there was a pause in the wind, as the thick clouds parted, allowing streaks of sunlight to filter through. In the same way, the dense emotional clouds opened up to allow the light of awareness through, creating the space for a wiser reflection: I saw that I had a choice—to act on these impulses of irritation and anger, or to investigate the deeper layers of my state of mind.

The wind had calmed down considerably now, and birds were chirping again, no longer bracing for the storm. An attentive awareness of my anger began to dissolve the mental agitation that had been building toward an outburst. I started to explore the irritation that had taken me over.

We typically assume that dark clouds have to release their built-up moisture in a storm before things can clear up. But change can come in another way: I watched the gentle wind move the dark clouds to the south—and clear away the threatening storm, widening the blue space of clear sky.

So with our inner storms. As I reflected on my thoughts about being disappointed by someone I counted on, I realized it was the feeling of not being cared for that had fed my irritation. I recognized these thoughts as having a familiar ring, so typical of other times when this schema was activated.

I started to challenge my own thoughts: Maybe there was a good reason she couldn't help. Anyway, this was just a minor thing. Our friendship was what really mattered to me.

Taking the time to reflect, instead of just reacting, left my mind clearer, not consumed by stormy thoughts or befogged by confusion. I could act more wisely.

Begin by noticing that you are having them.

1. Become mindful. A mindful awareness can tune you in to the signs—perhaps a familiar feeling or typical thoughts—that a schema has been activated. As soon as you realize a schema may be primed, pause mentally and focus on the thoughts running through your mind, on your emotions, and on the sensations in your body. These are clues to *which* schema has activated. By pausing and waiting until the dust settles in your mind, you can also test whether you are over-reacting at that moment—that is, to confirm that indeed a schema has been activated.

2. Notice your schema thoughts as such. Realize they may be distortions. Remember: you don't have to believe your thoughts.

3. Challenge those thoughts. Remind yourself that they distort the way things really are. Bring to mind what you have learned about how your schema thoughts embody false assumptions, and what the corrective thoughts have to say. Gather evidence to refute the thoughts, perhaps by talking with someone who has a more realistic perspective on the subject.

4. Use empathic reframing to acknowledge the schema reality while you put into words a more accurate picture of things. Empathic reframing allows you to nod to the way the schema sees the world, even as you correct that flawed perception. Be patient, as you would with a small child who simply misunderstands how things are.

One of my clients, a children's dance teacher, found it particularly hard whenever a child didn't want to come to her class. She would get harshly self-critical, taking the child's decision as a judgment of her own ineptness. One day the parent of a child who often misbehaved called to say that her daughter didn't want to come to class. That was the schema trigger.

1. My client became mindful. "I had just been meditating," she told me later, "and I observed how I responded to her comment. I felt my muscles clench, my stomach tense. I felt fear flooding through

my body as I imagined that other parents would see me as inept and withdraw their children from my class. I contracted around these reactions, as the feelings built."

2. She recognized the schema thoughts: the telltale signs of her perfectionism schema, the fearful thought of being criticized for doing a less than perfect job.

3. She challenged those thoughts. Pausing mindfully, she tested the assumptions behind her thoughts by first asking herself if anything about her teaching style was in great need of improvement. Her reflection put her in touch with the praise her work had been getting from other parents. So then she told herself, "Let me go back to the original information: this is not about *me;* this is about a problem child. She has trouble in groups. She doesn't get along with other children. The mother already understands that her child misbehaves. It's not a reflection on me that this girl doesn't want to come to my class."

4. She used empathic reframing. She reminded herself, "I know I'm vulnerable to criticism, and I know that sensitivity comes from how critical my parents were when I was little. But I don't need to feel that way anymore. These thoughts don't do me any good."

13

Relationships

In the tale "The Lion King," Simba, a lion cub, is to become king of the pride one day. From his noble father he learns about the interconnectedness of life. In this grand circle, all beings are connected in a symbiotic way, sustaining one another as prey and predator: the lions feed on gazelles, but when the lions die, they feed the grass on which the gazelles graze. ● But Simba's father is killed by an evil uncle, who usurps the throne. Fleeing, Simba feels abandoned and alone. He is too young to survive on his own in the jungle, confused and frightened by everything he sees. In the throes of overwhelming feelings of abandonment, he feels helpless, despairing that he will always be alone. ● But fortunately he is taken under the wing of two older pals, a warthog and a meerkat, who befriend and protect him. They teach him the ways of the jungle, filling the role of parents for him. He no longer feels alone—he has a surrogate family. He feels protected, nurtured. From them he gets an even stronger sense of connectedness to the circle of life, a sensibility he brings to his reign when he later regains the throne and becomes king. ● This story can be read in many ways, but I see it as a tale of the transformation of fear into courage and of suffering into compassion—a metaphor for how the deep passions of emotions can be transmuted. And at the schema level, the tale offers an example of how relationships later in life can be reparative for the emotional wounds of a schema like abandonment. ● So many of our schemas surface in the cauldron of our closest relationships, whether with a romantic partner, a parent or child, a friend—anyone with whom we have a strong emotional connection. That fact makes relationships double-edged when it comes to schemas. On the one hand, they can make any relationship an emotional battleground, but on the other hand, relationships themselves offer an especially ripe opportunity to let us do the inner work that will free us from the grasp of our schemas.

An added benefit of breaking the chain of habit inside ourselves comes from how it reverberates through our relationships. Any relationship is a system, a web of causal interactions, so that how one person acts elicits a given reaction in the other person. Systems theorists and family therapists tell us that one way to alter a system is to change how one part of it acts, thus altering how other parts react. Changing ourselves, then, offers a way to break our relationships out of destructive ruts.

Schema Chemistry ● A great paradox of our most maladaptive schemas is their power to draw us to partners who will trigger them. This propensity is especially strong for patterns like deprivation, abandonment, mistrust, and unlovability. Indeed, we sometimes have the most intense romantic chemistry with someone who pushes these emotional buttons. The most alluring lover very often has an emotional fingerprint similar to that of the parent who was the very root of the schema.

The patterns are well recognized. People with the deprivation schema can be drawn to lovers who are ungiving, narcissistic, aloof, or cold. For people with the abandonment schema, chemistry often occurs with partners who are unavailable or unreliable. The partner's abandonment can take the form of living far away, traveling constantly, working into all hours of the night, or being in another relationship.

Those with the subjugation schema can gravitate to a passive relationship with entitled partners who assert their own needs and ways of doing things. In the mistrust schema, people are all too often drawn to a partner who is untrustworthy, manipulative, or emotionally, physically, or sexually abusive.

And for those who have the unlovability schema, a relationship with someone who is distant or unavailable prevents the intimacy that might lead to the discovery of their own imagined flaw. A relationship with a partner who is critical and rejecting would also have a familiar, almost comforting, feeling.

Why these strange chemical reactions? Schemas drive something akin to what Freud called repetition compulsion, where people are drawn into re-creating in adult relationships the childhood patterns that shaped the schema in the first place. There are several reasons for this paradox. For one, these relationships feel familiar, like home, despite the pain; the hope is that this time we can change the story. For another, they repeat ways the person learned in childhood to stay connected, and so they seem reassuring.

Finally, there may be the hope that this time things will be different and the relationship will be reparative. For once, the deprived person will receive the care and attention she craves; this time the abused woman will find a man who can be trusted. At least that's the primal hope.

Indeed, couples therapists point out that this is precisely what can happen in a healthy relationship. Each partner, to some extent, acts in ways that are reparative of the schemas of the other. As these primitive needs are met, the passion of the original schema chemistry may fade to a glow as the bond of love and understanding grows. The potential in a relationship, then, is for both partners to help heal the emotional wounds from their pasts.

Small wonder, then, that of all the parts of our lives, schemas seem hyperactive in our most intimate relationships. Since so many of us bring our schemas to relationships—in fact, seem drawn to a particular person in part because he or she triggers a schema or two—such relationships are especially rich arenas for recognizing and altering our schema reactions.

When Things Can—and Can't—Be Worked Out •

When schemas are activated, it is as though they come out of hiding to reveal themselves in vivid detail. If partners are motivated and willing to do the work, these times can be seen as an opportunity to get access to the inner workings of the schemas—access that might be unavailable while they are safely hidden away, untriggered.

From this perspective, a degree of schema activation in close relationships can be seen in a positive light. But it all depends on how we use these schema triggers: to investigate the schema in order to challenge them, or to reinforce them by turning away from the schema as such, and instead let their distorted beliefs dictate how we react. The first approach opens a door to great freedom, the second simply reinforces and maintains their destructive patterns, keeping them in place.

Certain relationship patterns tend to perpetuate schemas. For example, when both people have the same schema, and neither has done any work on the pattern, it is very difficult for them even to see that the schema has taken them over. Both partners fall prey to the same distorted thinking.

Say both partners are prone to the emotional deprivation pattern. If one misinterprets something the other does as thoughtless disregard for her own needs, she may pull away in hurt or anger, in a way that triggers the same deprivation schema in her partner, who also then feels hurt or angry. One may sulk while the other becomes demanding. They share a blind spot—the lens of the schema—and so neither is likely to see that there is any other way to react or to interpret what's happening.

Another common obstacle to freeing a relationship from schema battles is when neither partner wants to make the effort to become aware or to change. Highly complementary schemas—particularly when one partner feels entitled and the other subjugated—can create a glue-like complacency, an inertia that prevents both partners from rocking the boat.

A special case involves the deep suspicions fostered by the mistrust schema among people who were abused in childhood. A feeling of safety and security will elude a partner who has this schema. When one partner feels unsafe, the other partner may be at a loss to create the reassuring emotional container that would make mutual schema work possible. In such cases, outside help may be called for—either a therapist who specializes in treating people who have been abused or an appropriate support group. Needless to say, if abuse is occurring, an intervention is essential to end it before schema work can possibly begin.

The Schema Tango ● When a couple fights, a kind of schema tango ensues, in which a schema attack in one partner can set off a reciprocal attack in the other. So many of the emotionally loaded moments in a relationship arise because one person's schemas have triggered schema reactions in her partner. Those moments of crisis offer an opportunity for the anguish to open a door to healing. It all depends on what the partners do with that moment.

Of course, the schemas will not disappear entirely. You are still likely to have the thoughts and feelings that come up when the schema is triggered. But as time goes on, with work the intensity of those schema reactions should wane. You can break the chain by finding new ways to act when the schema does get aroused.

For example, my client Janet wanted more attention from her husband. Feeling especially needy, she became demanding, which made her husband pull back. So she felt frustrated, thinking that his pulling back meant he didn't care. Gradually Janet was able to investigate this pattern, which repeated itself time and again in their relationship. From talks they had, she realized that her husband was reacting that way because of a schema of his own. He had been bossed around by domineering parents early in life and had a dread of being controlled yet again. When she approached him for attention, he was reacting not to her need but to what he saw as her control-ling demands.

She had been misinterpreting his pulling back as a lack of caring. Understanding this dynamic helped her take his reaction less personally. Then she could turn her attention to observing her own schemas in the situ-ation. Deprivation—the fear that she would never get enough love or atten-tion—was one. When these fears started to take her over and make her demanding and clingy, she reminded herself, "I'm particularly vulnerable to feeling that people don't care about my feelings. I tend to overreact, taking things too personally."

Remembering this, she was better able to disengage from her habitual reaction and consider an alternative, which let her open up communication with her husband. She was able to tell him that she sometimes felt uncared for and so became demanding, and that she realized this made him pull back. "I understand why you might withdraw if you feel that someone is being controlling," she told him. "It's not my intention to be demanding or controlling—I'm just blinded by my need in that moment. Can you help me find a way to say what I'm feeling without putting you off or making you feel like running away?"

When she told him that, her husband understood what had been going on between them. He started to feel more empathy for her, and he remem-bered how much he enjoyed feeling close to her. He agreed to work with her to catch his own reactions as they happened—in other words, Janet and her husband made a mutual mindfulness pact.

Interpersonal Mindfulness ● Willing partners can work to-gether to identify and dismantle the schemas that can cloud a relationship. Mindfulness can be interpersonal: we can bring a mindful awareness to someone else's schema reactions. If you have a relationship with someone where mindfulness could become a natural part of things, then you each double the potential amount of awareness that can be brought to your own schemas.

Some of my clients do this in their own relationships. One woman told me that she talked to her husband about a close friend, with whom she felt an impaired connection. As she was talking, she said, "Even though I feel deeply connected to her, I realize that our friendship could end at any moment."

Her husband looked puzzled and became reflective. "She's an old friend and your connection goes deep. It's unlikely your relationship would end so easily," he said, challenging her fear.

Knowing that they could communicate in schema terms, my client impishly blurted out, "Yeah, but the abandoned little girl in me needs to know that I'd still be fine without having her in my life!"

He picked up on her schema language and slipped into that frame of reference. He nodded in agreement, playfully colluding with her: "That's right—that's exactly what that abandoned little girl needs to understand so she won't have these fears."

When you are familiar with schema reality, you can more easily empathize with what someone else is going through emotionally, even if you don't rationally agree. You see how the schema beliefs are working; at the same time you realize what the schema needs in order to change. That gives you not just more understanding but also more compassion—and sometimes a bit of humor.

When both partners in a relationship understand how schemas are shaping and skewing their reactions to each other, the relationship itself can become a powerful arena for emotional alchemy. If the cortex symbolizes clear awareness and the amygdala stands for the reactivity of schemas, in a sense, each partner can bring a mindful "cortical" awareness to the other's moments of "amygdala" mindlessness.

To some extent, raw emotions arise from a part of the brain without words. Helping put those emotions into words by talking them over with someone we trust can bring clarity. It's as though the other person's cortex is soothing our amygdala. If one partner is confused about an amorphous emotional reaction, talking it out may allow her to get clearer. If one partner is losing it, the other might help him realize that a schema reaction has begun, and so recover from it more quickly.

This approach is perhaps most challenging in those moments when *both* partners have simultaneous schema attacks—that is, when they have an argument. In that case, the first step is for at least one of the partners to calm down or de-escalate. This may mean physically separating for a time to cool down before resuming the discussion. Then, as the heat of the moment begins to pass, one partner or the other can begin to shift levels, going from the schema reality—the terms of the argument—to the level of reflective awareness, beginning to ask, "What really was just going on?"

Be careful, of course, not to use the shift in levels as another round in the battle, to dismiss your partner's reactions as merely their schema acting up. Saying something like "You're just caught in your deprivation schema again"—especially if that utterance is motivated by your *own* schema attack—will simply trigger more schema reaction.

Instead, the most useful ways to de-escalate are to calm down yourself and to empathize with the feelings your partner is having, even if you don't rationally agree with his point of view. Then, after you've both calmed down, you can use the argument as material for a mutual investigation of what schemas were triggered and why.

When it comes to dealing with someone who is in the heat of a schema attack, it is generally a good idea first to empathize with the schema—and the person. Empathy disempowers schemas. Acknowledge the way the schema sees things and the feelings that go along with that reality. Then the other person can begin to disengage from the schema and think more objectively.

Such empathy in a relationship can have a reparative effect. When the person gets caught up in the schema, he is in the throes of the reality spawned by the little child at its core. But if he feels that he is being heard, cared about, and accepted, that realization can have a re-parenting effect on the schema. If partners routinely do that in such moments, it can be very bonding—and they can have a beneficial corrective effect on each other.

Dissecting a Schema Fight ● When a husband and wife go to

a couples therapist to seek help, each tells a quite different story about what's going on. A seasoned therapist will not buy either story completely. Much of what's being said is usually distorted by each partner's schema lens. The truth is usually somewhere in between, in an account that acknowledges the truth of both views.

It's much like those experiments in physics where two different kinds of instruments are used to measure light. The first kind shows that light travels in waves. The second shows that it travels as discrete particles. The truth is somewhere in between, in an account that recognizes the truth in both views.

Over the years that I have been working with this approach to therapy, my husband and I have often used this mutual investigation to deconstruct arguments we've had—after we've cooled down, of course. Early in our relationship we had arguments fairly frequently, usually about the same things. As time went on, we used this mutual mindfulness to understand what schemas were being activated.

Once we had both learned the schema model, we could deconstruct our argument. When we reviewed it through the schema lens we realized that, no matter the supposed issue, at the schema level more often than not it was some version of the same schemas acting up over and over again!

For instance, once my husband and I were getting ready to give a workshop together. I was concentrating on my notes, when my husband came bustling in, interrupting me, and said, "Let's do it this way!" and started to tell me how he thought we should do the workshop.

I said, somewhat coolly, "I'm not ready."

He didn't say anything—he left the room.

That wasn't much of an argument on the surface, but underneath it was a microcosm of a dance of schemas that we had seen over and over, triggered by all kinds of ostensible causes. When we looked at it later, here's how we deconstructed the schema-level conversation:

His "Let's do it this way!" triggered anger in me—from my subjugation schema. I felt that he wasn't letting me do things in my own way and was ignoring my need in the moment to buckle down and prepare.

My "I'm not ready!" triggered in him a touch of unlovability. That schema interpreted my icy reply as a rejection, which triggered in him feelings of not being appreciated. His silence and withdrawal expressed hurt feelings.

As time has gone on, and the schemas that trigger these reactions between us have become increasingly clear to us, the number of arguments between us has declined greatly, along with their intensity and length. We've become much lighter in that realm, more able to witness these emotional habits start to arise in our minds than to let them take us over for a contentious quarrel. We've been able to reframe disagreements from being just an unpleasant episode to avoid, to a fascinating mutual discovery of how distorted thinking patterns interact. And we've seen that the truth lies somewhere in between, in an account that recognizes both views.

Schema Play ● My two horses, Yeshe and Bodhi, spend all day together. Although they adore each other, as is natural in the domain of horses, Yeshe is the dominant partner in their two-horse herd, Bodhi the submissive follower. Yeshe spends much of the day bossing Bodhi around, pinning his ears back in a threat to herd Bodhi where he wants him to go. Sometimes they remind me of a couple where one partner feels entitled, the other subjugated.

But to the degree that horses have something akin to schemas, I notice that Yeshe and Bodhi have a way of working them out: they play-fight, rearing up on their hind legs, baring their teeth, nipping at each other. And during these play-fights, Bodhi becomes very bold, even aggressive, with Yeshe, who doesn't seem to mind relinquishing his place as the dominant horse for a while in the spirit of play.

That playful spirit can be brought to working on our relationships, though not during the heat of a schema attack. But playfulness can work especially well when you've already begun to disengage from your schema-driven patterns of interaction. As you've done some schema work together with your partner and get more aware of each other's patterns, a lighthearted attitude can help greatly as an antidote to the heaviness of schemas.

One example comes from my marriage. Early in our relationship, my husband was driven by a perfectionism that kept him locked away in his home office for hours longer than he really needed to be working. As a result I sometimes felt neglected. My abandonment schema caused me to be especially troubled by that closed door.

As we worked on what schemas were being triggered in each of us by the situation, my husband had a revelation. He saw that he himself did not really want to spend all those needless hours at work. His work life was so out of balance with the rest of his day that he was cheating himself of life's pleasures.

After years of working on this, one day as he was reflecting on the early roots of this pattern that propelled him to spend so much of his life hard at work, he told me a story. He had a memory from around age four of playing house with the girl across the street. She would stay home and do household chores like cooking, and he would go to work (this was the 1950s).

But being only four years old, he hadn't the least idea what work was. So he'd go over to a corner of the room they were playing in, squat down, and say, "Work, work, work," over and over again.

By that time, after years of working together on our schema patterns, we had gotten to the point where a playful spirit would spontaneously emerge in our conversations. That playfulness, of course, has to occur with some sensitivity and the right timing, so that neither person makes light of the other's feelings.

But now sometimes when my husband is working late when he could be out enjoying other things, I'll stick my head into his office, see him so serious poring over what he's doing, and I'll playfully say, "Work, work, work."

Works every time.

Tough Love: Schema Work with Friends ● A standard

model of compassion is a benevolent, sympathetic, caring love. But compassion can come in many forms; sometimes tough love is preferable to the conventional package. Some spiritual traditions, like Tibetan Buddhism and Hinduism, have wrathful representations of compassion, which symbolize cutting through tenacious attachments and forms of ignorance. When the mind is so clouded by self-deception that it can only see with distortion, forceful action is the antidote, jolting us out of the sleep of ignorance.

For many years the pain of Eliza's addictive relationship patterns caused her great confusion. She had a long series of failed relationships with men, and each failure triggered her abandonment and deprivation schemas. Her fears that a man would leave her drove her to become so clinging and reactive that, more often than not, her own impulse to hold on to the men drove them away. Whenever this happened she would be overcome by an obsessive litany of whining complaints about each disappointment and the men who let her down. She would recite her woes to anyone who would listen. In fact, over the years her conversations with friends and family came to revolve around little else.

For years her circle of loved ones put up with this tendency because they loved and cared about her and she clearly needed to have them listen. But after many years two of her closest friends finally talked the situation over between them, and then told her they couldn't listen to her endless complaints anymore. It was not healthy for her to be consumed by this hysteria, they said. It only reinforced her belief, fed by her deep emotional habits, that she was a helpless victim.

They encouraged her to examine her complaints and the feelings that went with them and to challenge her tendency to give in to them. From then on, her two closest friends made a deal with Eliza: whenever they talked, they would remind her if she started to fall back into the old whining and complaining. Eliza had already joined a therapy group and so was receptive to this new arrangement—though she confessed that she still felt abandoned and uncared for when her friends refused to go along with her need to complain.

In refusing to accept Eliza's habit, her friends were challenging her underlying patterns of emotional deprivation and abandonment. When we go along with someone's schema-driven habit, we are, in a sense, colluding to maintain that schema. We can help other people challenge their schemas by doing so ourselves. But the tough love approach demands caution and empathy. It's important to stay neutral behind what we are sensing to be true for the other person, and to say how we see it in the noncontrolling, conditional language of "possibly," "perhaps," and "maybe." If the other person senses our ego involvement or feels that we are controlling her, presuming to see what's best for her, she may get defensive, feel judged and hurt, or be resentful.

But if we approach them with their best interests at heart—but not presuming we know the answers—then they're more likely to be receptive. And in the best case, we may find an ally in the warrior spirit within them—and find them grateful to us for being straight with them.

Empathy for Your Partner ● Just as you've done for yourself, you can do a schema profile of your partner. You can start to keep track of the times when your partner blows up or has some other extreme and self-defeating emotional reaction. You can try to see what the triggers are that set off schema attacks in your partner, try to get a sense of how he or she typically starts thinking and feeling during the heat of the attack, and observe any typical habits that play themselves out during the attack.

This greater familiarity can make you better at empathizing with your partner's schemas. Such empathy does not mean pandering to the schema, colluding with its view of things, but rather challenging those assumptions about people and the world. It also allows you to be more sensitive to the other person's schema vulnerabilities, so that you trigger the schemas less often.

Compassion converts empathy into action. Once you know the thoughts and feelings that typify another person's schemas, you can use that empathic understanding to guide how you act with them. This, of course, applies not just in couples but in any relationship where you have such an insight. Understanding another person's schema patterns can help you avoid acting in a way that would trigger the schema.

For instance, if you know someone has unrelenting standards, praising his accomplishments when appropriate gives him something he doesn't do—or do often enough—for himself. It challenges that inner voice of self-criticism that continually prods him to strive harder and harder. But you can also be a voice urging him to put his life more in balance, to counter the extent to which his perfectionism makes him drive himself too hard. And you can also let him know you accept and appreciate him the way he is, not just for what he can accomplish.

If someone has the deprivation schema, showing that you care about her needs, that you make an effort to take her feelings into account, can have a similar ameliorative impact. Likewise, if subjugation counts among the schemas that drive her, be careful not to tell her what to do, and avoid language that would make her feel controlled. Being provisional in how you put a request will let her feel that she has a choice. For instance, instead of saying, "Let's go see that new movie tonight," you could say, "There's a new movie in town. Are you interested in seeing it?"

These seem like small gestures to make, but in terms of their impact on the other person's schemas, they are reparative moments. You give the person an opportunity to experience the world and other people as different from the expectations her schemas dictate. Each such moment offers just one more experience strengthening an alternative view that is counter to how the distorting lens of the schema would make things seem.

Schema Compassion ● Getting as familiar with your partner's

schemas as you are with your own has several other benefits. For one, understanding that your partner's angry attack signifies that a particular schema has been triggered again helps you not take the reaction personally—it's not you that's at fault; it's the schema. This realization can help you keep your own schemas from being triggered in reaction to your partner's flare-up.

A Buddhist principle holds that awareness leads to empathy. Compassion is the natural expression of clear awareness. At the level of working with schemas, this means your own mindfulness of your partner's schema engenders empathy for him. Realizing that what's happening stems from your partner's schemas, for instance, can let you see him as vulnerable, like a hurt child, rather than as a jerk. Step back from things as they seem and try to realize how the schema is seeing them. This way you will not take his response so personally, and you can feel not just understanding but compassion.

Say he starts sulking, getting distant and withdrawn. If you have the defectiveness schema, his withdrawal might trigger your own feelings that he is not interested in you. But if you can use mindfulness at that moment to recognize what's happening, then instead of falling under the spell of some schema of your own, you can stay clear enough to be more empathic toward your partner.

Empathy at such a moment might help you recognize a familiar pattern and find a healthier response. You might realize, for instance, that when he withdraws into a sulk, his deprivation schema is at work again, and what he really needs is for you to show you care about him. If you make a caring gesture, he is very likely to come out of his shell.

This approach—understanding what is actually behind someone's actions—can be useful in any relationship in which the other person's schema attacks have been a problem—with your in-laws, your grown children, your friends, or anyone else. But it has particularly powerful applications within a couple, as relationship therapists have long told us.

For instance, one of the natural rhythms of a couple revolves around the tension between the need for intimacy and the desire for autonomy. As we've seen, many of the core issues for certain schemas—notably deprivation, abandonment, and unlovability—revolve around this dimension of connectedness. As the two partners go through their own orbits of moving away to be autonomous, then returning to unite once again, they can encourage each other to fulfill their individual needs and so enrich the relationship—or they can let this natural cycle build a sense of separateness.

Understanding that your partner may need to go away for a time can be important, especially if any of the connectedness schemas are active in you. It's good to remember an observation by the family therapist Carl Whitaker: "The more you can be apart, the more you can be together." This is as important as learning, for someone who has an unlovability schema, that your partner can be angry with you and still love you; or, for someone with the abandonment schema, that a temporary separation is not a loss.

The mutual realization that each of you has schemas at play in your relationship marks an opening for joint growth. "Once you see your partner as a wounded person," the couples therapist Harville Hendrix says, "you are beginning the process of a conscious relationship." That process requires, though, that you jointly make your relationship a safe place in which to explore your schemas rather than using that exploration to collect ammunition for the next battle.

One extremely helpful tool in the interpersonal mindfulness this process requires is what Hendrix calls mirroring. In mirroring, you make sure you hear and understand your partner's point of view before you give your own. It might take the form of listening and then saying, "What I hear you saying is . . ." In other words, you feed back to your partner in your own words what you understood. You give voice to your empathy and give your partner a chance to verify that you have actually empathized with accuracy.

If your partner has the abandonment schema, for example, and blows up at you when you come home late from work, the mirroring might be "When I didn't call and you got upset, you thought I had been hurt or was dead, and so you were afraid." That states the facts—you didn't call and your partner got upset—as well as the feelings and thoughts that went with it. That empathy validates the symbolic reality of the schema and makes it easier to straighten out what happened.

Breaking the Chain in Relationships ● It was Christmas Day and Whitney, one of my clients, was at her kitchen sink washing dishes while her husband and children played together with their presents. Whitney had made breakfast, cleaned up, made lunch, and now was cleaning up after that. She had been up very late on Christmas Eve getting everything ready, and she was on the verge of exhaustion, which made it all the harder to be working away.

As she labored at the sink, Whitney felt a buildup of resentment. Her mind started to dwell on the fact that *she* wanted to have some playtime, too. "Why isn't my husband helping me? I feel taken advantage of. . . ." The thoughts rolled on.

Then she paused and asked herself: "You're having a problem with this, aren't you?"

Another voice inside answered, "Yeah."

So the inner dialogue began as she investigated her reactions. As she reflected on her resentful thoughts and feelings, she saw how she herself was creating more of a problem by reacting to her resentment with even more irritated thoughts, and reacting with even more intense resentment to these added thoughts.

Driving all this, she understood, was a sense of deprivation—an all-too-familiar feeling that she knew she was susceptible to. She realized, too, that her husband didn't really know what she was feeling, and that if she simply let him know and asked for help he would pitch in right away.

With that insight, she saw her resentment dissolve, and let it go. What then welled up in her was the overflow of exhaustion she had been feeling. She stopped what she was doing, and gave herself what she really needed most at that moment: she told her husband she was exhausted, and then she collapsed on the couch and took a nap.

When she woke up, Whitney saw that the kitchen had been cleaned and the house straightened up from the Christmas morning mess. Her husband had figured it out himself (he may be one in a million!).

That simple incident signaled a turning point for Whitney in dealing with the relationship patterns her deprivation schema had so often created:

feeling overwhelmed, put-upon, and taken advantage of, she would get angry and resentful or sulk, and her husband would respond with anger or hurt of his own.

Now, as she worked with her schema reactions, she was gradually able to become mindful of them and to change her usual response: she would communicate her need to her husband. He usually responded well when she was able to tell him what she really needed without snapping at him.

But now Whitney had taken her schema work to a new level. As she saw her resentment come up, and detected the reactions and thoughts that drove it, she could empathize with herself, challenge her assumptions, and watch the resentment dissolve. And her husband, by then, had become more attuned to the kinds of situations that triggered her reactions, and was more often able spontaneously to take responsibility without her having to say a thing.

Of course real issues—not driven by schemas—inevitably come up in our relationships. But as we change our own habitual reactions, the habits of interaction built up between us can dissolve, and new, more positive ones take their place. And we can handle the inevitable issues with less heat and more light.

Sometimes you can do this work directly with your partner. Other times it may be enough to deal internally with your own emotional reactions. Or you can use a combination of internal and partner work, first running it through in your own mind, and then directly with your partner. By that time reactions should have cooled down a bit so you can think and react more clearly.

Of course, not all partners are cooperative, and few are well motivated and aware of the dynamics in a relationship. If your partner is so rigid that he has little awareness of or interest in this process, the frustrating patterns will keep playing out. If your partner will not work with you, you can still do your inner work and so change your patterns of interacting; that in itself will improve things.

Unless the relationship is destructive, I usually encourage people to stick it out and do the schema work on their own. Chances are, doing schema work on your own will either benefit the relationship or—if it doesn't work out even after these efforts—help you in a future relationship.

Reparative Relationships ● While still in grade school, Mary was molested repeatedly by a relative. When she finally told her mother about the abuse, her mother shrugged it off. One result, understandably, was

that Mary viewed her relationships with men through the lens of the mistrust schema. But later, as a grown-up, she was drawn to abusive men.

That troubling legacy of childhood maltreatment has long been remarked on by those who work with survivors of abuse. In seeking out romantic partners who are prone to violence, for instance, someone who was the victim of violence may harbor the hope of having a reparative experience: "For once, just this time," the wish goes, "it will have a happy ending." These people are, as the song says, looking for love in all the wrong places. Of course, when there is violence—or the threat of it—in a relationship, the remedy sometimes includes leaving.

The poignant hope that "this time it will be different" is behind the repetitive cycle of all schema-driven relationships. People realize at some level that their adult relationships may offer them a corrective emotional experience, one that harbors the antidote to the very schema that drives them into the relationship in the first place.

In short, we sometimes *can* help heal the emotional wounds of the people we love the most—*if* we make our relationship with them a reparative one. And in the same way, they can help heal our wounds.

In creating a relationship that might become reparative, you don't have to find someone who embodies the perfect antidote. But if your partner is willing, you can start by making the relationship itself an arena for mutually heightening mindfulness and applying that awareness to the schemas that are at work in each of you.

As you and your partner become aware of the schema needs that drive your relationship, you can recognize the signs that a familiar schema has been activated once again, and you can use those signs to devise an antidote. For example, if your partner feels insecure and unlovable, you can be especially affectionate; if your partner feels that her needs are not being noticed, you can be particularly attentive. Such small gestures of understanding and compassion can strengthen the foundation of trust and closeness in a relationship.

If You Want to Apply Mindfulness with Your Partner

Try to unearth the schemas that are buried behind your arguments.

Most fights are, in part, symbolic of some larger issue. It's not just showing up late or not sharing household responsibilities that triggers schema rage. It's the underlying feeling that our own needs are not being considered or that we're being subjugated. Or perhaps some other schema is giving emotional intensity to how we react.

If you and your partner can tune in with mindfulness and discover that a schema is at work, you can use your arguments as an opportunity to identify and disarm that schema. If you do this more or less regularly, your schemas will gradually lose their power to set you off. You'll be better able to deal with your partner about the dirty dishes or the bills next time around.

Next time you and your partner have a fight, wait until the dust settles a bit, when the heat of anger has cooled somewhat and you can begin to think more clearly about what just happened. You can speed the cooling-out process by going off alone for a while and doing the basic calming practice of meditating on your breath.

Once you feel calmer, apply the wise reflection method, where you alternate between mindfulness practice and letting the thoughts and feelings of the fight come back. But this time bring wise reflection to those thoughts and feelings: instead of letting them take you over, so that you are immersed in the reality they create, watch them with mindfulness. If you're still too upset, take a few minutes to create a more calm and clear space in your mind by following your breath, using the calming practice. Then, when you feel quieter, turn your attention to your feelings and thoughts about the fight itself. Notice the situation at the three levels:

1. What are you feeling? Note where in your body the sensations of your emotions are most intense. Is there a knot in your stomach? Trembling in your legs and arms? Tension in your neck and shoulders? Was a chain reaction of emotions at play—for instance, did hurt trigger anger? Is there a mixture of feelings—not just anger, perhaps, but sadness, too? Do these feelings remind you of other times in your life when you've been upset the same way? Are they a clue to an emotional pattern that this fight is part of?

2. What are your thoughts? Not just the most obvious thoughts—the voice of your anger—but the more subtle thoughts that are fueling that anger. Are you telling yourself, for instance, "He never takes my feelings into account"? Why did this particular event trigger those thoughts?

3. What are your actions? What do your thoughts and feelings make you want to do—or what did you do?

Finally, putting it all together, does this give you a clue to the underlying schemas that primed the fight? If so, you can go on to the next steps:

1. Get together with your partner again, and this time review the fight from the perspective of what schemas were at play. Explain how your partner's actions triggered the schema. If you can, give your partner an idea of the origins of that schema in your life and why you have learned to respond in certain ways to the trigger. In other words, let your partner understand why you reacted so strongly from the perspective of your schema reality. But do so with empathy both for your partner and for your schema.

2. Revisit the specifics of the issue, setting aside the schema part of your reaction, and settle things more clearly. You can also get a sense of how to avoid triggering your partner's schema, what your partner really needs in such moments—for example, to feel cared for—and what to do when your own schema starts to trigger in the future.

3. If you have conflicting needs, try to negotiate so that you make an effort to be more sensitive and aware of each other's needs, and gradually work at changing how each of you reacts.

4. When the same patterns get triggered again, try to be patient. These patterns take some time to change, and you will probably have repeated opportunities to try out new ways to relate and behave with each other. All this relearning takes a while.

14

The Circle of Life

The restaurant was packed and the people at the next table were talking so loud that I couldn't avoid hearing the drama unfolding between the parents and their college-age son, who apparently was on a visit home from school. ● The son was telling them how interested he'd become in acting and how excited he was to find something he loved so much. ● The father interrupted. "But what about your grades? I just heard that the Williamses' son is on the dean's list at Yale. You haven't been doing that well." ● "I'll work on them," the son said. "I just feel very focused on this new direction. I want to explore it further." ● "Is that all you're going to do with your life— flounder about?" the father said, his contempt all too clear in his tone. ● The son's voice dropped an octave. "I'm not just floundering, and I have some great friends who like theater, too. We've enjoyed working on plays together." ● "Your friends are going nowhere," the father responded, his voice dripping with disgust. ● At that, the mother spoke up for the first time: "Fred . . ." Dad had crossed the line, but she said nothing more, returning to her passive role. ● But it was too late. The son abruptly got up from the table, threw his napkin over his half-eaten meal, and walked away. ● I heard the father say to the mother, perplexed, "What's gotten into him?" ● We had just paid our bill, and I got up to leave with a heavy heart. As we went up the stairs to leave the restaurant, we passed the son sitting there, his head resting on his hands, looking very sad and frustrated and tapping nervously with his foot. ● I wanted to say something to help him as I walked past: "They probably see this as their way of caring for you. They don't see that they are driving you away. Maybe you can tell them that you know they're trying to help you, but their criticism is too harsh, and could they find a way to put it differently." ● But was it my place to intervene? I hesitated as I walked by, but I said nothing. The moment passed. To this day I wonder what became of that young man.

If what I overheard was typical of his interactions with his parents, I was witnessing the creation of the failure schema in him.

The Intergeneration Chain ● During a meeting with a group of psychotherapists, the Dalai Lama was intrigued to hear about the problems of Westerners' low self-esteem and resentment toward their parents. These notions were novel to him; he couldn't imagine that people would not love themselves and their parents. Another new idea for him was that, at least during phases of therapy, it might be useful to encourage and allow anger to emerge as part of a larger healing process that could end in compassion.

He caught on. Later I heard him giving a talk where he said that, from a Buddhist perspective, anger is harmful. But he also acknowledged that at times there might be a therapeutic advantage to getting in touch with angry feelings to become able to let go of them—for instance, when one has low self-esteem from having been abused. When someone goes through therapy, for instance, "maybe a little anger for a little while can be useful."

Still, in general, this is a point on which Buddhism and Western psychotherapy may differ. Yet even if we grant the need for a selective therapeutic anger, it's not enough just to feel resentment over childhood hurts and to blame parents. That may be useful to a point, while we are exploring the conditioning that has molded our emotional habits. But we can also empathize with the parents, siblings, or whoever else was involved in the conditioning, to see that they themselves were acting because of their own conditioning, and on and on through the generations.

That realization can eventually—when the time is right—elicit compassion toward our parents or others involved as the anger heals. From the perspective of this intergenerational chain, you may wonder if there is any one place to put the blame.

But by seeing our parents' role in our own childhood conditioning, we can understand our own reactions as learned habits from the past, not as who we truly are. A schema represents an outmoded holdover from earlier learning. In other words, remind yourself, "I'm having this reaction because of what I learned to do back then, not because of what's actually happening right now."

Breaking the Chain with Parents ● A woman in a workshop

was lamenting her relationship with her grown daughter. "My daughter attacks me, saying I ignore her, that I don't listen to her," she said. "I feel so hurt that I end up in tears. I dread the times we get together now."

We talked over what might be going on, starting to see what schemas might be at work. The woman decided that her own tears could well stem from an underlying pattern of unlovability, with her daughter's rejection triggering a schema attack. Then we turned to her daughter's complaint. When I suggested that her daughter's words seemed symptomatic of the emotional deprivation schema, the woman nodded in agreement. And then, after a thoughtful silence, she blurted out in astonishment, "My God—my daughter's got a schema!"

It was a revelation to her. She had never seen that her own habit of tuning out and chattering on without paying much attention to what her daughter was feeling or needing could have led to the emotional patterns that now erupted in strife. She was shocked.

Her reaction bespeaks an important truth: parents, and anyone else whose behavior may have led to our own schemas, generally did not intend to do us any harm. More often than not they are blindly acting out the patterns they learned in their own early years.

Schemas can be passed down in families over generations, with parents unwittingly spreading them to a new generation like a social gene. Entitlement in a parent can lead to a self-absorption that creates emotional deprivation in a child; that child's emotional deprivation, once she becomes a parent, can lead to an overly solicitous, too generous parenting style that in turn fosters entitlement in the next generation. The particular form the schema takes depends in part on the coping style—avoiding or overcompensating—that gets chosen.

Once you realize that your own parents have been victims of schemas, too, you may be able to see that in a sense they are not to blame. This is not to excuse those cases where parents intentionally perpetrated harmful acts. But as the Dalai Lama has said, the problem is the person's afflictive emotions, not the person.

In a sense, breaking free from the grip of schemas that involve our parents represents much of what psychologists call individuation—becoming an autonomous, mature person. To the extent that we are adults enmeshed with our parents at the schema level, bound by the dictates of schemas we've internalized from our early relationships, we have not yet become fully autonomous, particularly at the emotional level. A psychodynamic view would see us as arrested in a developmental stage, with a need for emotional healing to close the gap.

Some clients find it useful to minimize contact with a key person in their life—usually a parent—for a time, while they work internally on disengaging from schema patterns that are still alive in their interactions. Getting some actual space from a person with whom you're enmeshed can give you time to heal, so that you can come back into the relationship later on with greater ability to be yourself, freer of those patterns.

Relationships that are heavily bound by schemas have a built-in inertia that resists change. When one of the people in the relationship starts to behave differently, the change can trigger a counterreaction in the other person. But it's not necessarily the other person who doesn't want to change; it's his schemas. Some say you can't change people. That may be true, but you *can* change patterns.

Schemas, in a sense, have a life of their own; the work of repairing them entails draining them of their vital force. As we saw with changing our own schema patterns, in a relationship, too, it takes a period of adjustment to get comfortable with new ways of interacting that are free of old schema-driven patterns.

As we change our own schema responses, we naturally start to focus on altering the dysfunctional patterns in our close relationships. Here, of course, we meet resistance: other people often don't like it, particularly when the closeness in the relationships is in part neurotic, when the two individuals are feeding on each other's schema needs. In such cases the schemas are a cornerstone of the relationship itself, a way of maintaining the bond.

In relationships like these, as we change we may find that the relationship loses some of its intensity for us. To the degree that our own schema was a basis for the emotional bond, the relationship may seem threatened. But what really may be happening is that the intense connection we interpreted as closeness no longer feels as comfortable because we now can see its schema basis more clearly.

When Therapy Can Be Reparative
● In psychotherapy, the client's relationship with her therapist can be a partial re-parenting. The psychotherapist serves as a surrogate for the "good parent," or at least a "good enough" parent, creating an arena for unlearning our old schema reactions.

In many ways a therapist, and often a good spiritual teacher, can be a source of strength, clarity, emotional connection, and guidance, especially when we can't see clearly ourselves. It's very important for people to trust this connection, especially in ways they could not trust their earliest relationships. With a therapist, there needs to be a dependable certainty of connection and attentive caring. That alone can, to a degree, repair the emotional wounds of childhood.

When these ingredients are in place, the therapist can become a source of connection and caring that allows a reparative relearning of what to expect in a close relationship. It can be equally reparative when a therapist or a respected teacher acknowledges that the way we see ourselves has real meaning and is to be taken seriously. So can their not seeing us in the negative ways we may see ourselves.

Clarifying Schemas with Parents ● When the woman in my workshop realized that her own habit of tuning out had contributed to her daughter's deprivation schema, she was able to understand why her daughter so often seemed angry with her. As we explored their interaction patterns more deeply, she came to a realization: "My daughter feels that I don't listen to her or understand her. No wonder she gets so angry at me."

I asked her if she thought it was true that she did not listen. "Yes," she said, "I can see it more clearly now. And to further complicate the breakdown in our communicating, I often get too defensive when she expresses her anger toward me. My reactions make it harder for me to understand the dynamics between us. I'll make more of an effort now that I see what's going on."

Was there anything else she might do, I asked, to change the pattern between them? She thought for a while, then said, "This would be easier if she didn't get so angry. Her hostility makes me freeze up."

I suggested that she ask her daughter if she could try to communicate her needs without angrily attacking her. That very act, if the mother followed through to make the effort, might in itself be partly reparative, if indeed the daughter had been feeling her mother was depriving her of a caring attention.

So often when people are sorting out their schemas they assume that their parents have in the past, or still do, intentionally hurt them. While that is often true in cases of abuse and extreme neglect, most parents are not even aware that their actions shaped a schema in their child. When and if they do become aware of it, they typically don't know what to do about it. Except in some severe cases, that does not mean they don't care enough to try, though some people are just not interested in making an effort, or are too defensive or self-absorbed to bother.

If our parents are still in our lives, and if these schema patterns still control too many of our interactions, it can be helpful to try to work on them with the parent. The degree to which we can do this varies greatly, requiring, for one thing, a willing, open parent. There are no easy solutions when it comes to relationships with our parents. Each situation is unique, with its own possibilities or limitations.

But if working with the parent is not a possibility, or if it's far too early even to try, healing can still occur. It is not a necessary step in changing our schemas. The essential work is internal, as we work on breaking the chain of emotional habit.

And as with couples, if only one person in the relationship changes, that inevitably alters the interactions. All of our relationships, including with our parents, are systems in which how one part acts affects all the others.

An Emotional Wet Suit ● Then there are the relationships with parents where schema patterns are continually sparked. My client Miriam had a mother who had been emotionally abusive and who continued that abuse into their present-day interactions. She had been harshly critical of Miriam, and now, when she visited, she was critical not just with Miriam but with her husband and children as well. Her visits were emotionally toxic.

When Miriam timidly brought up the possibility of discussing her emotional patterns with her mother, the response was cuttingly dismissive: "I have enough problems of my own. I can't be bothered with yours."

"That remark was like a knife in an open wound," Miriam told me.

For her, a first step in freeing herself from the resulting schemas was to erect a wall, a firm boundary, between her mother and herself. "You need an emotional wet suit," I told her, "a barrier with no holes that will protect you."

So Miriam limited her contact with her mother for months, permitting no visits, talking to her on the phone only a certain number of times a month, and firmly ending the conversation whenever her mother started to get abusive. And Miriam did her schema work internally, in the safe area behind these boundaries.

Only when she had won a degree of freedom from her schema reactions, and when her boundaries were intact, did Miriam feel safe once again to engage with her mother in their normal routines.

As people disengage from their schema interactions with parents and gradually heal, such barriers may dissolve on their own, as they are no longer needed. But with parents who continue to perpetuate the schema patterns in the relationship, it may be useful to keep a mind-set that maintains a boundary. To do this, it is essential that you be clear about that boundary yourself and remember that it no longer works for you to be treated this way.

Inner Dialogue with a Parent's Voice ● My client Jesse can be talking along, telling a story in his entertaining way, when out of the blue his demeanor and tone of voice will change slightly and he'll go into an angry, critical tirade about someone for several minutes. Then he'll just as suddenly go back to his normal, engaging manner.

A thought pops into my mind: He just channeled his mother!

She had been a strict disciplinarian with highly critical judgments, and Jesse by then knew well how she had shaped his own perfectionism schema. But he was still unaware of what seemed to be a momentary trance when it was as if his mother spoke through him.

Jesse was gradually able to make the connection between these moments of being "possessed" by his mother's voice, and the inner voice of self-criticism that drove his perfectionism.

Jesse was expressing voices that usually reverberated only through his mind. In a sense, the parent who inhabits our schema reality is not the one we know now as adults but the one we remember from childhood. This was true for Jesse.

This offers a therapeutic opportunity: If we can't talk to our actual parent about the hurts and feelings of a schema our mother or father has helped shape, we can still engage that inner parent in a dialogue. Just as we found a voice for the child part of us who believes the schema reality and dialogue, we can do the same with the representations of the parent frozen inside our mind.

Consider how Miriam did this. One day she called me in agony. For two hours straight she had been hounded by an inner voice judging, badgering, and belittling her.

I suggested she take the same passion behind her agony of judgmental thoughts and the pain she was feeling, and channel that passion into yearning to be free from that pain and suffering. She had been on several mindfulness meditation retreats, so I suggested she reflect in her meditation on the nature of suffering and the path to freedom from suffering—a basic Buddhist concept—but directed toward her schema suffering. "You know it's possible to be free from this pain. Yearn for that freedom for yourself. Wish it for yourself as in the loving-kindness practice you've done," I suggested.

"But when I do that, I hear a voice answering back, 'I don't want you to be free. I want you to be miserable.'"

I was struck by her tone of voice as she spoke those words. "Just then, as I listened to your voice saying those words—'I want you to be miserable'—I heard you sound exactly the way you do when you mimic the voice of your mother. She still has such power over you, and you still get sucked into it. You let yourself get enmeshed in her misery."

"She keeps her misery going in me," Miriam said, "as if she's planted and watered it. And I've let her keep it going. I've put up with her perfectionistic, critical standards, her put-downs. I have to be very watchful that I'm not seeing the world through her schema lenses, which make everyone critical, negative, and unloving."

As we talked it over, Miriam decided to find a tone of voice within herself to talk back fiercely to her internalized critical mother—perhaps one she had used in an actual confrontation with her. She would experiment with different voices until she found one that works, one that let her feel more powerful than that inner voice of her mother.

She practiced that inner dialogue with an attitude of mindfulness, staying open to whatever felt most natural, not judging at all and not feeling guilty for getting angry if she needed to. She marshaled equanimity, trying not to let herself get sucked into the pull of her mother's guilt tripping.

With that resolve, Miriam began an inner process of fighting back to her mother's voice. She would tell her, with conviction, "You can't treat me this way. You can't get away with this emotional abuse." When she felt she needed to, she would go off alone and scream out her feelings at her mother. She found this helped her feel powerful and stand up to her mother.

With time, that inner dialogue became fairly automatic. Whenever Miriam heard her mother's voice putting her down, she would immediately come back with a mental challenge.

Eventually, the response became both more positive and more automatic. "As I was driving home from work," she reported one day, "the old voice said, 'You did a terrible job.' But then another voice butted in out of nowhere and said, 'You did a great job!'"

These powerful voices that get in touch with the rage from, in this case, emotional abuse, can help a person feel more powerful than the voice of the schema—and in Miriam's case, more powerful than her mother's emotional abuse.

Changing those inner dialogues can take many forms. I asked one client, whose overly critical father had led to her perfectionism schema, if she still wanted her father's approval, either internally or externally. "In actuality," she said, "I rarely see him, and now I recognize his limitations. But internally, I think I still want his approval." Challenging that inner voice, I suggested, was the next step.

There are many messages, many healing scripts, that we can give to the inner voices of parents. This kind of battle or challenge to the schema is just an example. At some point, many people in schema therapy write letters to their parents (rarely sent to them, though) in which they pour out their feelings about the way they felt they were treated, saying what they would like to tell the parents in real life, but feel they cannot.

Forgiveness: All In Good Time ● I've had several clients who got to a stage in working with a schema where they were able to bring it up with a parent whose behavior had been instrumental in shaping the pattern in the first place. While this is not a necessary or always even a possible step, it can be helpful in getting past blame to forgiveness.

The mother of one client, who had always been hypercritical of her daughter, made a candid confession: "I treat people this way because I'm so unhappy myself."

Likewise, another client had a mother who often treated the daughter in a childish, self-absorbed, and reactive way. It became clear to my client that her mother's behavior was due to the form of entitlement that stems from deprivation. When my client finally confronted her mother, the mother confided, "Normally my outrageous comments roll right off people. They ignore me; I feel they're not even hearing me. I feel I have to shock people with a demanding remark to get their attention."

Once they were able to talk it over and the daughter told her mother how hurtful this treatment had been for her, the mother apologized: "I can understand why you would feel that way—you're really very sensitive, more so than most of the people in our family. I'm used to people ignoring me. I didn't realize I was hurting your feelings."

When you see that such behavior is itself schema-driven, you can have more understanding, even compassion, for the other person. On the other hand, schemas don't follow rational logic. In the emotional reality of the schema, the people in our lives whose actions led us to develop a schema are "to blame"—at least that's the way it feels to the schema.

As I mentioned before, we need to empathize with these feelings in the schema before rushing to try to change our emotional reactions. This means that while forgiveness may come in time, it might be best for it to come only after we have acknowledged and expressed (if only to ourselves) the truth and feelings of the schema reality.

There is a natural timing to forgiveness, preceded by gradual stages of readiness. That process begins with first acknowledging the schema, and having empathy for the feelings and perspective it embodies. Later, as we get more distance on the schema perspective, we may direct our anger at the schema itself. And with time the emotional charge of the schema will start to release itself.

We need to connect with our schema feelings, but not get stuck there. Buddhism and psychotherapy disagree on one point about forgiveness. From the Buddhist point of view, compassion and forgiveness can start immediately. From a psychotherapeutic perspective, forgiveness comes only after we have acknowledged the symbolic meanings of our emotions. Another consideration is that some schemas, particularly those that stem from severe neglect or abuse, are harder to forgive.

You may want to investigate your own inner timetable to find out where you stand. Since every person and every relationship is unique, there is no one correct response when it comes to forgiveness.

Empathizing with a Parent's Schema ● As we work within ourselves to win more freedom from our emotional templates, our knee-jerk reactions start to lose their hold over us and let us respond differently.

Lauren felt intensely angry whenever her mother once again tuned her out. But after she did some deep work on the deprivation schema, which she traced in part to her mother's narcissistic self-absorption, that reaction started to weaken.

After coming back from a meditation retreat, Lauren called her mother. "I started to tell her about the retreat," Lauren said. "Then, true to form, she cut me off after a few words and went off on a long digression about herself."

But Lauren noticed a change. Instead of feeling the sadness behind her deprivation, and then the angry thoughts toward her mother that usually flooded her at that point, "I watched the whole thing with a new kind of fascination. Having just been on retreat helped. I said to myself, 'So this is clearly where my sense of deprivation comes from.'

"Noticing my silence, my mother asked a couple of questions about me, then turned the conversation right back to herself at the first possible moment. I said to myself, 'I don't have to do this. I don't have to feel sad or angry. I don't have to let her do this, but I don't feel like getting into a big discussion about it with her.'"

So Lauren handled the moment differently. "I said to my mother, 'I'm going to hang up now,' and I told her why—not in anger, just very straightforwardly. Just an explanation of how I was feeling, what bothered me about what she was doing, and why I felt the need to stop. And then I hung up. No fight this time."

As Lauren reflected on the phone call, her thoughts were not, for once, consumed with anger toward her mother. Now clear in her mind that she didn't have to continue to put up with her mother's self-absorption, she could reflect on why her mother was so self-absorbed. She remembered hearing about her mother's childhood as an orphan adopted by an alcoholic couple who were lackadaisical about attending to the emotional and practical needs of their daughter. Her own mother, she realized, probably had a deep deprivation schema. "No wonder she's so self-absorbed," Lauren said.

But as we start to see things as they are rather than as the schema sees them, we can see our parents and others just as people, with human frailties and problems of their own. We can see that, in most cases, they were acting unconsciously rather than intentionally trying to hurt us. (An important exception here is in cases of abuse or neglect, and even then it may be possible to empathize with an abuser who was himself abused.)

Then, as we get more in touch with our feelings about those people and their behavior, we can start to empathize with *them*—that is, understand the forces in their lives that led them to act as they did. And finally, in time, that understanding can give us more compassion for the circle of schema life as these patterns are passed through the generations.

Expressing Forgiveness ● Forgiveness can take very ordinary

forms. Instead of saying, "I forgive you," you can express forgiveness as a change in how you relate to the person. Understanding, too, can be a form of forgiveness.

People find creative ways to get the message across. Lilly and her mother had a tormented relationship, and Lilly felt deeply deprived. But as she worked on her deprivation schema, her long-standing anger toward her mother faded and she started to appreciate her mother more.

She used an eggbeater her mother had given her fifteen years before.

One day the thought entered her mind, "I wonder if I ever thanked my mother for this eggbeater." So Lilly called her. "This may sound strange," she said to her mother, "but have I ever thanked you for that eggbeater you gave me a long time ago?"

Her mother thought that Lilly had thanked her.

But Lilly said, "Well, I just wanted to thank you for all you've given me over the years. And I want you to know that I love you."

It was a moment of tenderness between them, a kind of feeling that had grown rare.

When Lilly told me about it, I asked her if she felt that healing past wounds had changed anything for her in this relationship, if she felt different about anything. She said it had: "There's no more struggle. I just feel this spontaneous forgiveness."

As I mentioned earlier, a practice taught at many mindfulness retreats is a short meditation on loving-kindness and equanimity. This meditation is typically done at the end of a session, to wish for others the well-being that one has experienced. For one of my clients, this practice had particular power. "I come from a highly dysfunctional family in which everyone overreacted," she told me. "Everyone was always attacking, blaming, or criticizing the others. This behavior was accepted and passed down in my family. I thought this was how it was between people; this was how it was for me.

"Once I started therapy, I could see that this just fed into my schema reactivity, especially deprivation and abandonment. I overreact by getting very angry when these schemas are triggered. I felt that expressing my feelings was what mattered, so I ended up either shouting at people or withdrawing in a sulk. These reactions cost me a lot in my relationships with men, driving them away.

"I don't want to be the kind of person who screams and yells and loses it. I want to be able to pause, to count to ten, to be gentle with myself, and to project that gentleness outward. I tried to work on it for years, with several different methods, but nothing seemed to help. I used to think I needed to be medicated to control my reactions.

"It wasn't until I did a mindfulness retreat that I found that ability inside myself. That was where it needed to come from. The loving-kindness practice was especially helpful for me. For one thing, it got me to think about the perspective of others and to see them with equanimity. And I realized the power of wishing well-being to other people. Seeing them from a place of equanimity, finding the balance from the inside, is what finally helped me temper my reactions."

A Family Saga ● Just before the First World War a young girl was traveling with her father on a ship from Italy to the United States. Her father, to avoid a custody battle, had abducted the little girl and was taking her far away, so her mother would never find her.

With sad green eyes the girl gazed out at the endless sea. Perhaps she sensed that she would never see her mother again. Then, in an angry act of protest, without a moment's hesitation she threw her favorite doll into the ocean.

That girl later married while still in her teens and had three children. Still young herself, she tried to mother them, to give them some semblance of a stable life, while she ran her husband's dance studio in New York City. But she was so young and so deeply troubled that she ran away, abandoning her husband and three young daughters. Eventually she did come back into her daughters' lives, but while there was affection, their relationships were often stormy.

One of her daughters, in turn, had two children when she was very young. She tried to mother her children and give them some semblance of a stable life, but as a young single mother she felt overwhelmed by the relentless responsibility. So for years she would leave her children with nannies or with relatives for several weeks at a time while she went off to cope with her own life. She always returned, though, and eventually devoted herself to mothering the children she loved.

This is the story of my own mother and grandmother. It wasn't until my grandmother's funeral that I heard the story of her as a little girl on the boat from Italy.

At her funeral I listened to the heartfelt eulogies of my generation, her grandchildren. Each in our own way, we described the genuine love that we felt for our grandmother. Given the legacy of abandonment over the generations in my family, I was struck by how we seemed to feel no anger toward her.

Even so, I sensed some emotional holding patterns in myself being brought out into the open air as the truths of my grandmother's life were told. One question kept circulating in my mind: if my grandmother contributed so greatly to the intergenerational schema patterns in my family, why do I have no feelings of resentment toward her?

I saw how I clearly understood my grandmother's emotional legacy. But when it came to my mother, understanding and forgiveness were harder to come to. After several years of intense inner work—and sometimes outer work directly with my mother—I had let go of many of my schema-based relationship patterns with her. They had begun shifting, even healing themselves. Needless to say, this was not easy.

I realized I had come to a new place of readiness, especially when I felt she was making an effort to change the patterns in our relationship. I felt a genuine willingness to accept and forgive my mother. There was a poignancy in watching her lose her mother. When she first visited my grandmother in the hospital before she died, they cried in each other's arms. It was as if a lifetime of hard feelings melted away in those few moments, healing decades of tormented feelings. It was their final embrace.

After my grandmother died, my mother said to me, "My mother had so much love to give. I really saw that at the end. I only wish I had realized that while she was alive."

I feel fortunate to have come to this same realization about my own mother while she is still alive. And while I still feel a need to stay clear about the potential for the old patterns to resurface, I also feel free to express and accept a love that has always been there.

By healing our schemas we melt the walls that separate family members, allowing us to experience the underlying love and connection undistorted by the lens of these emotional habits. It's almost as though these emotional imprints are passed down through generations like a virus mutating to adjust to changing environments. As schemas begin to heal we can more easily see the impersonal nature of our emotional conditioning—so much is passed on unwittingly.

If You Want to Work with Feelings about Your Childhood

Try this guided meditation. Read through it, then try it as you remember it, with your eyes closed:

First, for a few minutes just be with your breath mindfully, letting it quiet your mind and soothe you.

Now bring to mind a place where you feel perfectly safe—perhaps with a person you trust and love, or in a warm, comfy bed under a cozy quilt, or maybe on a beautiful beach with the sun warming and relaxing you—someplace where you feel secure, protected, and nurtured, a place where you feel secure enough to be yourself.

Have the accepting attitude of mindfulness, just letting thoughts and feelings come up without judging them, and know that at any point you can return to your safe place, comforted by the natural rhythm of your breathing.

Perhaps you have gotten in touch with something from your childhood, making a connection between an emotional pattern and how it originated. Choose something you feel ready to work on mindfully. If something comes to mind that is too upsetting, that you don't yet feel ready to be with, save it for another time and choose a simpler issue that you feel more ready to be with.

If a person comes to mind who is somehow connected to this pattern, someone from whom you feel you have not received what you needed, invite that person into this mindful presence. If, for example, it's your mother, see her as open and attentive, as she listens to you.

Allow yourself to be very honest, telling this person something you've needed to say. Take the time now to go into your heart and think of what you need to say to her, and say it now. Tell her openly, honestly, and mindfully some ways that you would wish her to be—perhaps more present or more sensitive or caring, whatever feels right for you. Use whatever words work best for you.

Let yourself feel protected and safe as you talk, and let yourself be genuinely heard and cared for by this person as you tell her. She is genuinely listening to you, and she appreciates your honesty in connecting with her. She has an open acceptance while you are saying what she needs most to hear and understand from you.

Now let her say to you what you have needed to hear: "I'll be caring and sensitive to you," or whatever it may be, whatever feels appropriate for you.

Now allow yourself also to see her humanness. Notice how her actions have mostly to do with her own schemas or her inability to see clearly, rather than her ill intentions. Revisit your safe place where you imagined feeling comforted.

As you finish, know that you can return to this place of mindful honesty within yourself whenever you need to, feeling perfectly safe and protected by your own mindful awareness.

Trust that on some level you have been genuinely heard and accepted for yourself. Even if you don't directly engage in this kind of dialogue with the actual person, a healing will have begun internally.

You can be in touch with your own truth, and you can express that truth. This mindful presence is who we really are, beyond our thoughts, our reactivity, or our schemas. The clear sky is becoming visible behind the changing clouds.

15

Stages of Healing

After three or four weeks in therapy, a client complained to me that she was making too little progress. "I can see how my abandonment fears have kept me from having the kind of relationship with a man I've wanted, and it's really clear to me how my subjugation pattern draws me into relationships with narcissistic men. But I still react to my boyfriend in the same destructive ways. Shouldn't I be much better by now?" ● The question is telling. Our culture encourages the quick fix and the instant answer. But this work has its own organic rate of change; it won't be hurried. ● For one thing, simply learning about our destructive emotional patterns and the power of bringing awareness to them will not produce some magical improvement. What's required is a deeper kind of learning—not just comprehending the concepts but changing the habits themselves. ● These two kinds of learning involve different parts of the brain, each of which learns in a different way. Intellectual understanding is centered in the neocortex, the thinking centers in the topmost layers of the brain. This part of the brain learns very quickly, connecting new ideas and information to its existing webs of knowledge. Just reading about something is sufficient for intellectual learning. ● But changing emotional habits also involves the more ancient limbic centers deep inside the brain. This part of the brain learns differently. It has taken years and years, starting early in childhood, for the emotional brain to acquire its repertoire of habit. Schemas like perfectionism and deprivation become ingrained through innumerable repeated episodes. It naturally takes time to undo these emotional habits and to master a healthier response.

An Organic Rate of Change ● As we've seen, the task of
changing a schema is two-fold: we have to unlearn the self-defeating old

habit and replace it with a new, healthier one. That change is very different from mere intellectual understanding—it involves the emotional brain. It takes much persistent practice, cultivation of the ability to bring awareness to what had been unconscious behavior, and sustained effort to try out the new way of thinking and acting despite its initial awkwardness and relapses into old habit.

The whole process of healing deep schema patterns can take years. You will read this book, no doubt, much faster than a schema is able to change. It is crucial not to try to rush the healing process, even though you know how the story should end. Give it time.

People typically go through several phases and stages in this process. The first revolves around learning to bring mindfulness to emotional habits that have long been busily enacted outside the daylight of awareness. But that simply initiates a series of organic changes that seems to have its own natural course and timetable.

Some of these phases can be emotionally trying. I remember advice given by one of my meditation teachers, U Pandita, to a group on retreat. He was urging us on, especially through those moments when we were suffering through upheavals. He likened the yogis, as he called us, to babies going through stages of development, like teething: "They cry and wail at odd times," he said. "An inexperienced mother may worry about her baby during periods like this. But truly, if infants don't go through this suffering they will never mature and grow up." For a yogi those periods of distress, he pointed out, are actually signs of developmental progress.

So too in working with schemas. As we go through periods of intense emotional catharsis, we need to stay with the emotion rather than pulling back. A calmer and clearer destination lies ahead. When sometimes we relapse into our old maladaptive habits, we need to take the relapses as opportunities to better handle the same triggers when they come up the next time.

A classical Buddhist text in the *vipassana* tradition on the stages of insight that lead to liberation speaks of one phase where people feel a disgust with the habits of mind that keep them from being free. When clients show a similar disgust for their schemas—telling me, "I'm sick of this pattern, I can't stand letting it continue"—I quietly rejoice. That is a landmark along the path to freedom.

One purpose of schema work is to recognize and gradually disengage from the patterns that interfere with a more genuine connection with ourselves and with others. This happens in stages, some of them repeated many times in a cycle of continual relearning.

As we continue to disengage from our schemas, to see them afresh, we may wonder at some point how we have carried these burdens for so long. Our schema-driven motivations shift, fall away, or simply no longer hold the same compelling importance. We may find, for example, that we no longer have the same need for a certain kind of interaction or treatment from our parents, as those needs get released in the emotional grieving of schema work. Reparative experiences can mend the wounds left over from our early years. As a bumper sticker wryly put it, "It's never too late to have a happy childhood."

We may find, as people often do, that as schemas heal they no longer pull at us with the same emotional intensity. But emotional alchemy does not wrap our afflictive emotions in a neat little package and dispose of them once and for all. This work is an ongoing process, deepening the insights, discoveries, and adjustments that we make.

But as schemas drop away from their position of dominance in the mind, we become more free to devote our attention to other dimensions of life: work and creative pursuits, family and relationships, social concerns or action, spiritual practice. This enhanced range of choices emerges gradually but becomes an increasing reward for walking this path.

Last Gasps ● One of the puzzles of schema work for many who

begin it is the fits and starts that seem to create an unsteady rhythm in making progress. We have small successes, then startling setbacks. These habits resist change; they seem to struggle to retain their hold.

In terms of brain function, there is an intriguing parallel between emotional habits and addictions. All addictions, researchers have discovered, create the same imbalance in the brain's circuitry for pleasure. Those circuits exchange a chemical called dopamine; the more dopamine, the more pleasure we feel.

Every addictive substance contains molecules that mimic dopamine in the brain. In the brain's natural state, the dopamine circuits carry only very small amounts of the chemical. But addictive substances, whether nicotine or heroin, flood the brain with vast amounts, hundreds or thousands of times more than is natural. The intense high that people feel comes from this flooding of the dopamine circuits.

But after the high passes, the brain is fooled: it thinks there are now vastly greater amounts of dopamine in its circuitry—an imbalance. To reach a state of equilibrium, the brain drastically reduces the number of dopamine receptors, the part of the brain cell that receives and reacts to the chemical.

This, in turn, means the brain now has too little dopamine and so loses much of its capacity for pleasure. The result: the discomfort and distress of someone who is going through withdrawal—and has the desperate urge for a fix all over again. But if the addicted person can go through this stage and resist the urge, the brain will eventually normalize its levels of dopamine receptors and we will feel like ourselves once again.

So with emotional habits. Each schema has its own underlying neural circuitry, made strong through the countless repetitions of the pattern over the course of our lives. Every time the schema is triggered, we replay its familiar sequence of thought, feeling, and reaction. When someone with the abandonment pattern, for instance, perceives a person pulling away from him, he panics and clings to her.

But when we begin to change that pattern, we deprive the schema of the habitual sequence. If instead of panicking, the person can remain cool and calm, reminding himself that this is the abandonment schema, then he doesn't have to believe its panicked thoughts of loss and loneliness, nor must he act from the fear. The schema will resist this change, trying to maintain the familiar patterns.

We experience this as the schema acting up, exerting its pull through its typical thoughts and feelings with added urgency, much like the dopamine circuits sending their desperate messages, frenzied thoughts of where to get the drug, how good it would feel, trying to drive us to seek another fix. So as we give up the habits of a schema, the deep fears and other stormy feelings the schema ordinarily keeps at bay now well up in a kind of last gasp.

As the hold of the schema weakens, however, and as we exert the force of our will by not acting on it, it gets more frantic. We go through an almost inevitable period of strong waves of the old familiar feelings. But if we continue to hold the line and don't give in, the waves will recede, just as the brain goes back to its natural equilibrium when someone kicks an addiction.

As we get better at breaking the chain, those same familiar surges of feelings no longer compel us to play out the old sequence. What we do when we have those feelings can be more adaptive. The schema thoughts may arise in our minds, perhaps just as bare whispers of their old roar, but we no longer have to do their bidding.

Weakening the Hold ● As we become more aware of how our schemas are pushing us around, we're more able to push back, to intentionally resist the habitual impulse dictated by the schema and instead go in a more productive direction.

Here's what Caroline did to fight back against her deprivation schema: "My friend always waited for me to put the energy into our relationship, to be the one who called, who planned what to do when we got together, to make things happen. I felt if I wasn't the one sustaining the friendship, it would fall apart. During this period my friend was an intern and really busy, so I went along. But after she finished her internship and had more time, nothing changed. We were already growing apart. So I got fed up and told her I didn't want to play that role anymore—I wanted a more equal relationship.

"I've got the deprivation pattern, so it was really hard for me to have that straight talk with her. But it felt like an important step in changing my patterns.

"After that talk, however, I never heard from her again. If that had happened a few years ago, I would have been devastated. But I was all right with the end of this friendship. I didn't feel willing to keep it going any longer on those old terms. I felt *really* good about being clear about my own needs."

Moments like Caroline's serve as benchmarks in our progress in freeing ourselves from old emotional habits. As we do more of the work of freeing ourselves from a schema, its hold on us gradually gets weaker. Finally the pattern comes up as a mere thought in the mind that holds little or no special power over us—or it doesn't arise at all.

Miriam had been working with me for a while on changing a pattern in her relationship with her mother, whose constant criticism had taken a toll on Miriam. Whenever Miriam talked to her mother—a few times a week by phone—she ended up overwhelmed by feelings of self-loathing. Miriam's perfectionism meant her mother's harpoon-like critiques and put-downs triggered a flood of self-criticism in Miriam.

On top of that, her mother's neediness and self-absorption resonated perfectly with Miriam's subjugation and deprivation patterns. Miriam had always felt that she could never do enough to help her mother, and she never dreamed of voicing her own needs or feelings. The net result was that after a phone conversation with her mother she felt waves of self-criticism and guilt.

At least that was the way things were before Miriam worked on the pattern. Now she tells me, "It's hard to believe that my mother had such a powerful negative effect on me. Now when I'm talking with her, I'm aware of the moment when a schema starts to take hold in me. I can hear my mind start to tell me things in its self-hating mode. But when I say to myself, 'What's going on here?' I immediately realize I don't believe the things the schema is telling me—that I'm not good enough, that I should feel guilty, all of it."

Miriam sees the schema's distorted reality much more clearly now: what she knows to be true is becoming stronger than what the schema tells her is so. After much effort, she exemplifies a stage of healing where the schemas begin to lose their power. Their iron grip is weakening, though they still rise up to try to impose their tyranny once again. But since Miriam's belief in their version of things is so much weaker, they have become more transparent.

One sign of this is that the people in Miriam's life who once held so much power over her by triggering the schemas—especially her mother—no longer exert that control. When she listens to her mother now, Miriam says, "It's comical to see what a caricature of the nagging mother she is."

She no longer expects her mother to change into the kind of mother she always wanted. This has been freeing for Miriam, who now finds she can have that kind of love with her children and husband, and with the children she teaches.

But Miriam is experiencing more anger toward the small daily injustices in her life—another sign of schema transformation. Where before she would have been nice to people, not letting her feelings well up or show, she now feels more rebellious. With her inconsiderate neighbors, with the dismissive attitude of the woman at the phone company, with the punk kid who cuts her off in traffic, she's now free to express her displeasure.

That expression may at times be a bit aggressive. Of course her assertiveness needs to include a sensitivity to others—we can stand up for ourselves without being inconsiderate. But she is shouting to the world—and to herself—that she's not to be treated unfairly anymore.

The Power of Letting Go ● Isabel called me in crisis, breaking down on the phone in tears, telling me she didn't know where to turn. A graduate student in architecture, she had gone to a class and made a presentation, along with two other students. Her adviser had praised the work of the other two, but had been very critical of hers.

For hours after the class Isabel was immersed in a sea of self-loathing and self-criticism so intense that nothing she could tell herself made her feel any better about her ability. She was lost in the torment that unrelenting standards can create. Nothing seemed to help. Mindfulness failed her; she couldn't bring to mind a single thought that might challenge the accusations whirling in her head.

As we talked, I asked how she had been before this episode. Had she been able to watch her self-critical thoughts with mindfulness, to be aware of them as they arose in her mind. She said yes, that actually she had been more self-accepting lately.

But now, she kept saying, she was deeply afraid. What was that deep fear? That she didn't know who she was if she was not perfect at her work. Without perfection, she was nothing, nobody.

Aware that Isabel had made great progress working with this schema in recent months, it felt to me that after all the inner work she had done, she had broken through to a deeper layer, to the primal fears and intense feelings that hold the perfectionism schema in place. She needed to grieve for these feelings and the personal history that contributed to them—and then let go.

I asked her to stay fully aware of her feelings and to listen and see if there was anything she needed to hear underneath those feelings.

She said that she didn't know if she would be accepted if she wasn't perfect at what she did. She felt she had failed at life.

I asked if she could just allow that feeling to be there without running away from it. What if you *weren't* perfect—would that be okay?

With surprising calm, considering her deep distress moments before, she said softly, "I wouldn't be loved or accepted if I wasn't perfect."

Then I asked Isabel simply to be with the feeling of facing the truth of that fear. We sat in silence for a few minutes.

"It feels like a relief," she finally said, her voice a whisper. "I think I'd be okay if I wasn't perfect."

"You probably would find it tremendously freeing," I said.

"I'm amazed at how much power these feelings have over me."

"These fears are the fuel that has kept the schema in place," I observed. "The schema doesn't have much power if these fears aren't alive in you."

"I feel this relief, but there's also this empty hole: who am I if I'm not the perfect person this schema says I should be?"

"That's how schemas work," I explained. "They take up a lot of space in your mind, so it feels as if there's a hole when they shrink. Changing them feels unfamiliar; it's not how you're used to knowing yourself. Of course you're not sure who you are if you're not the schema—you're not used to the feeling of being free of it yet. But just think—now you get to discover who you really are without this schema distorting your view of yourself."

Now Isabel was excited: "Yeah! It's amazing how much control that schema had over me, and it's good to know that I don't have to keep putting up with that fear."

"These schemas die hard. It's almost as if the schema has sensed that you've been getting free and it doesn't like that. Even schemas are afraid to die. So it made a powerful stand, and it consumed you for a while."

"I'm glad you were there to talk to. What shall I do if it comes back so strong again?" Isabel asked.

"Try not to get locked into your conceptual mind—it interferes with what's happening naturally. Just let go of the schema thoughts with a mindful presence. Just stay connected to awareness and try to be mindful whenever the schema appears. Try not to be concerned about what needs to happen; healing happens by itself, if you let it, with the soothing effect of awareness."

Then I suggested she do something to let the schema go: "See if it helps to have an inner dialogue between the nurturing, compassionate part of yourself and the sad little wounded schema that is dying out. You've been grieving the loss of that part of you."

"I feel sad for that little girl in me who tried so hard to be loved," Isabel said.

"It is very sad. You can feel sorry for her—but in a compassionate way. With your compassion and nurturance, tell the other part of yourself that it doesn't need to be perfect anymore to be loved. Reassure it. Be kind to yourself and give yourself a lot of space and time for this to readjust and settle into a new place. This has been a significant shift."

If we can be with our sadness, loss, or regret without trying to make it better by reassuring ourselves or trying to escape it through distracting ourselves, then something else becomes possible: grieving for the cause of the painful emotion.

Mindfully grieving means allowing the feeling to be felt, to build or change, and finally to dissolve, on its own. There's no clinging, resisting, avoiding, or pushing away. Just be with the feeling of whatever comes up—and let it connect to its natural ending.

Feeling Freer ● It would be misleading to look for a final cure in emotional alchemy; this is an ongoing process, and improvement looks different for each person. For Sara, it meant the divorce she had dreaded so

much turned out to be liberating. Her worst fear had been being abandoned and alone, and she had endured years of subjugation to her husband for fear that he would leave if everything wasn't just right. But once he *did* leave, Sara, having worked intensely on her fear of abandonment, was fine on her own. She is now leading the life she wants to, and she has begun dating a man who seems nurturing and caring and who makes her a priority. She's taking it slow, but feels that she has found someone she can be herself with.

For Miriam progress meant freeing herself enough from the hold of her perfectionism that she could set firm boundaries to protect herself from her intrusive, hypercritical mother. And Miriam was able to find in a nurturing marriage and family life the love and acceptance she always longed for.

For Jake, the improvement came in no longer giving in to the whims of his children for fear they would not love him.

While each person is unique, there is still a gradual increase in freedom, as can be seen in my client Julian. He first came up to me after a workshop, and asked if he could continue this work as a client. He had just gone through a distressing repetitive pattern.

In his forties and single, he would meet a woman he was interested in and start dating her. Things would go along well for a while. Then, at one point, he would sense her becoming cold and distancing herself. He'd feel rejected, and the relationship would end with his feeling abandoned.

One incident was significant: he had dated a woman who soon stopped returning his calls. When they first got together he was mildly interested in her. But when she stopped returning his calls, he suddenly became infatuated, feeling she was someone he wanted to marry—though he hardly knew her. It was all too clear that his schema chemistry drew him to women who triggered his feelings of abandonment.

Over the time we worked together, I saw Julian go through this cycle several times: he'd be drawn to a woman somehow just beyond his reach—not really done with her own past relationship, or about to move to another city—and emotionally remote. The relationships usually lasted a few months, then ended in heartbreak for him.

The schema fuel driving this pattern for Julian revolves around a reparative fantasy. The tantalizing chemistry comes from the unattainability of the woman and the hope that this time the outcome will be different, that the "lonely little boy inside me," as he describes it, will be rescued by one of these emotionally unavailable women. He sees that they are much like his cold and distant mother, whose love he continually felt deprived of, as though she had abandoned him.

Stages of Healing

That connection came home most clearly with the woman who stopped returning his calls. He started waiting for her to call, then brought his awareness to bear on the feelings stirring as he waited. That soon led to a vivid memory: "I'm in my crib, maybe two, crying out to my mother. She doesn't ever answer. It's as though this has gone on for forty years. It's not just in my past; that two-year-old is crying out now, crying so hard he's afraid he won't be able to breathe. He knows why he's crying—all those years of neglect, all those lonely moments in his crib, in my life."

That began a process of grieving his pain as he made the connection to his pattern of being drawn to rejecting women, feeling so strongly attracted that he is certain he can't live without them. So when he feels rejected, as he usually does at some point, he is devastated. At times he has been in the grip of his abandonment fears for days at a time, crying and grieving the loss of the love that he never really had—now or back then in his childhood.

Julian has gone though many repetitions of this cycle. He's all too familiar with the pattern. He spent months grieving his loss, going through a catharsis. Having done that, he says, seems to have freed up something inside him so that he now can take a more mindful stance, applying a cognitive challenge to the old thoughts as the pattern arises, without resisting or giving in to the underlying feelings of deprivation that fuel it.

Julian now knows specifically that it's the feeling of rejection—the feeling that he doesn't matter to someone he deeply cares about—that triggers his fears of emotional abandonment. He uses the schema's signs and symptoms as a reminder to become mindful. When he senses the approach of rejection, instead of going into the panicked fears of that lonely little boy, he now reminds himself that his abandonment fears are being triggered.

Instead of focusing on the fears, he shifts his attention to the stance of a neutral observer who can see the thoughts and habits that animate that fear. Because he has done much grieving for his childhood loss, the feelings have lost much of their intensity for him. He's able to stay clearer, more mindfully centered on the schema thoughts and feelings as they occur.

The chemistry is still there, but he's more cautious about it. Now when the old feelings emerge, he remembers the needs of that lonely little boy and takes the feelings as a warning. He's more free from the pull of the old self-defeating pattern.

He has reassessed his own situation and found that being on his own is not intolerable: he actually enjoys his solitude and the many dimensions of his life that give him a sense of well-being. Whether he is in a relationship or not, he loves hiking, his work in a hospital, reading.

When he starts to get that old feeling that his life will be worthless without the love of some woman who carries the subtle signs of rejection, he reminds himself, "She's a great woman—just not great for me."

From Emotional to Spiritual Alchemy ● There is an

ancient tale about a warrior in quest of a magical sword that will make him invincible. Along the way he meets by chance a wise old master who gives him a set of spiritual disciplines to follow. The warrior pursues them diligently for years. Then one day the magical sword finally appears to him, as promised. But as he grasps the hilt, he realizes that the spiritual practices have worked: he no longer cares about the powers the sword would give him.

So with schema work. As we recover from the spell of schemas, the old yearnings they created fall away. We no longer need what we had sought. Our perspective opens to wider possibilities.

For those whose focus is on changing emotional habits, the journey may end, or at least pause, at this point—this chapter completes our exploration of schema work. But for others, who feel drawn to spiritual dimensions, this journey is part of a larger odyssey.

Buddhism tells us that sometimes a deep insight into the nature of things can come from looking directly, with mindful awareness, at our suffering. In that sense, schema work marks the beginning of a deeper journey.

The work of emotional alchemy focuses on things as they appear in the relative dimension of our personal lives; spiritual alchemy moves in the direction of things as they are. This larger dimension is in touch with ways of seeing that go beyond our everyday understanding of things.

These two planes are, of course, both present in any moment. The transcendent perspective can be held in mind through every stage of this work. One way is in the compassionate insights we bring to bear as we challenge these personal myths that have controlled us, obscuring our authentic being.

When the light of clarity can penetrate the clouds of our delusion, when we sustain a mindful awareness of our emotional patterns, we can penetrate the confusion in our minds. This emotional work clears the way for plunging into the larger dimension. A client who went on a three-month mindfulness retreat sent me a note: "I feel the psychological work I've done is letting me sail right into the practice, settling into the retreat more easily. It's true that the clouds get lighter so I can get behind them into the clear sky of practice."

The alchemists sought to transform lead into gold, or denseness into subtle consciousness, and this work can follow that same pathway. Emotional alchemy can be a stage in the journey into spiritual alchemy.

As we will see in the next part of this book, the path we have trodden so far has remarkable parallels in the spiritual realm. Emotions offer an opportunity for inner transformation at each level in a single unified path of gradual awakening.

The Integration ● Becoming aware of our emotional patterns gives us an idea of where our attachments—and so our clinging and misperception—are especially thick. It can help with the main goal of spiritual work—to become free—to have a more precise awareness of the emotional patterns that motivate us.

Emotional suffering can be the motivator for our turning to the spiritual path. Our spiritual practices can profoundly affect how we perceive and relate to psychological dimensions, letting us see the transparency of our conditioning much more clearly and objectively, not reifying our emotional patterns or defining ourselves in terms of their limitations, but connecting more with an expanded sense of ourselves.

Yet even during our meditations and retreats our emotional patterns play themselves out as repetitive reactions that seem to have lives of their own. I have spent extensive periods practicing in intensive meditation retreats. In such retreats practice deepens, making it possible to experience very subtle states of awareness, so that the teachings come alive in our experience. This experience inspires us to try to cultivate this awareness in everyday life—to be able to live from this place, liberated from emotional habit.

And yet after these retreats, when I returned to my daily life, my habitual emotional patterns would be there waiting for me. I'd slip right back into these realities. They may have seemed a bit more transparent, but they were still there.

I was having a conversation with my friend Joseph Goldstein, a teacher in the mindfulness tradition, after he had come out of a two-month retreat. We were discussing this emotional work. He said, a bit ruefully, "These emotional patterns run deep, even in retreat."

For me, the integration of meditation practice—whether in daily life or on retreat—with this emotional work has been a powerful means of chipping away at my own maladaptive emotional patterns. Some patterns that once loomed large have become barely noticeable. I know this integration works because I've experienced it myself.

It's the Same Work ● Theorists like Ken Wilber point out that we move along many separate lines of development as we grow through life: spiritual, emotional, moral, cognitive, and so on. Each has its own lawful order and rate of growth, and so at any one point we can be quite uneven in how far we've come along these lines.

Someone might, for instance, be intellectually, spiritually, and morally advanced while being less than highly developed emotionally. That point is often lost, though, on people who assume that their spiritual development takes care of all the other lines of growth.

I was talking with my friend Erik Pema Kunsang, a highly respected translator of Tibetan Buddhism, who has sometimes been a skeptic about the need for emotional work among those doing spiritual practice. I pointed out to him how unconscious filters often operate in the choices we make in life and how knee-jerk emotional reactions can fill us with rage or fear in an instant, even in a meditation retreat.

Then I asked, "Don't you think some long-term practitioners have problems with emotional habits that can interfere with their ability to do spiritual work?"

"Definitely," he said, open to challenging his own assumptions.

"Then why not work directly with the emotional obstacles so they become easier to dissolve? Won't that help free attention for spiritual work?"

After a reflective pause, he replied, "It's the same work." Then he added, "The translation of *cho*, the Tibetan word for 'dharma,' or 'spiritual teaching,' is literally 'that which changes, cures, and remedies.' It has the same meaning as 'therapy,' which is from the Greek root meaning 'to heal.' In this sense Buddhism and psychological work share the same goal, freeing us from the hold of disturbing emotions."

The emotional and spiritual levels of this inner alchemy are a continuum; we work with the identical emotions at both levels. One major difference between these levels lies in the subtlety of the work we do. At the outset, our focus is on our obvious disturbing emotions. As we engage in the spiritual level, our inner work becomes more subtle, as do the emotions and assumptions we grapple with.

Gradually, if we choose to pursue intensive mindfulness practice, our awareness can become more refined, detecting more subtleties of our consciousness, greater nuances in our experience. A precision and clarity begins to illuminate our experience, as we continue to probe greater inner depths. Sustaining our attention refines our awareness to the point where we no longer are caught up in those initial emotional struggles, or even in the specifics of our thoughts or feelings, but rather in the nature of the mind itself—a shift in awareness akin to ice melting in warm water. Our solidified habits of mind dissolve into a greater awareness of our true nature.

Holding Both Perspectives ● I feel that each path, psychological and spiritual, has its own unique power to free the mind, whether it be a relative or ultimate freedom. While the first three sections of this book primarily take a mindfully enhanced psychological perspective on working with our emotions, the last section recasts that work from a spiritual vantage point.

In integrating these approaches I find the two perspectives of the seemingly real and the actual to be immensely clarifying. At the relative level, our lives are caught in the tides and eddies of a hundred competing thoughts and emotions, all seeming to define the truth of the moment for us. But behind it all lies our actual nature: a mind free of obscuring thoughts and troubling emotions—a possibility for each one of us.

As we investigate the nature of our minds, we can see it as a continuum of consciousness, from the relative realities of our concepts, through the subtler dimensions of more refined knowing and intuitive insight, and then to wisdom beyond concepts, our natural essence.

Holding these perspectives in mind allows us to accept our humanness without getting too trapped in our own emotional gravity, an especially crucial balance as we clarify our habitual emotional patterns on the way toward freeing ourselves from them.

These two views have been a way for me to understand the integration of the spiritual and psychological orientations and how they can work together. It reminds me of that old Judy Collins lyric, about looking at clouds "from both sides now." We can see the clouds of the mind from the vantage point of subjective truth, but also hold an awareness of a larger perspective, one that goes beyond the limited way we see things at the moment.

While there can be radical differences between spiritual perspectives and psychological views, they can also inform one another, enhancing the power of each. Both of these paths are complete on their own, with their own purposes and integrity. But drawing from the depth and breadth of both of these traditions allows us to build a new pathway to inner freedom.

Confusion can be transformed into wisdom. But what is wisdom? There can be revealing insights at the relative as well as at the ultimate level. Perceiving things through these two perspectives—the seeming and the real— allows us to use our everyday experiences as opportunities for wisdom.

New meanings, new realities, require their own alchemy. A wise reflection on such inner struggles and confusion allows us to be more accepting of the natural pace of emotional change.

Before we face difficult emotions, especially when we confront our deep patterns, it is important to understand how we experience and interpret our emotions, and to empathize with their symbolic meanings. Once that tender part of ourselves understands the hidden meanings behind these patterns, we can begin to open up to other perspectives and start to see more accurately how our interpretations may be distorting our perceptions and reactions.

Being attuned to the way our emotions can have an irrational logic of their own can bring more understanding and acceptance. This sensitivity can be extremely helpful when we are relating to these vulnerabilities in others, helping us understand them rather than staying stuck in these reactions. Our compassion can begin when we pause to reflect on our own emotional preoccupations, and as compassion releases us from the grip of self-preoccupation, we become more available to the needs of others.

If You Want to Blend Your Spiritual Practice with Emotional Work

You can use your daily meditation session as an opportunity to do reparative work on your main schema. At the end of your session, when you are feeling calm and clear, devote a few minutes to an explicit affirmation of a reparative wish, and reflect on its meaning.

The model for this prayer is the classic Buddhist meditation on loving-kindness described in Chapter 2: "May I be safe, happy, healthy, free from suffering. May I be liberated." You repeat the prayer in a series of versions, first bringing to mind those kind people who have helped you along the way in life, then yourself, then specific people you care about, then those you have trouble with, and finally all beings.

You repeat the prayer silently, expressing the wish first for each of that series of people. When you do it for your loved ones, for example, you bring to mind images of particular people as you repeat silently, "May all my loved ones be safe," and so on. You then repeat the prayer for the people in your life whom you are having the most trouble with. Finally you send it out in all directions, as a deep wish for all living beings: "May all beings be safe, happy . . ."

For a woman who was sexually abused in childhood and was plagued by perennial feelings of mistrust and insecurity, practicing loving-kindness meditation on a retreat was, as she put it, "the first time I felt safe in my skin." She now uses loving-kindness as a daily practice.

You can go another step and tailor the wording of the phrases of loving-kindness to send yourself a message that will be reparative for your schemas. You wish yourself and others the emotional antidotes to the schema. For the social exclusion schema, it might be the wish to be included; for the vulnerability schema, to be safe; for deprivation, to be cared for or nurtured. For abandonment, it might be "May I feel secure on my own."

One client, for example, has altered the practice to include an antidote for her perfectionism. At the end of her morning mindfulness session, she spends a few minutes with this wish:

> May I be accepted as I am.
> May I be free from judgments and self-criticism.
> May I be safe, happy, healthy, free from suffering.
> May I be liberated.

And, of course, she wishes the same for her benefactors, her loved ones, her problem people, and all beings in all directions.

This can be done for any schema. For example, for unlovability, the wish may be to "be known and loved as I am." For deprivation, to "be cared for and understood." The wish for subjugation might be to "express my genuine needs"; for vulnerability, to "feel safe and protected"; and for abandonment, to "feel strong and secure on my own."

Traditionally, the loving-kindness practice is a way of awakening compassion. A third step comes in tailoring the wishes to the schema needs of others, wishing for them to be free of their schema pain. If you are aware of their schemas, you can adapt this practice to wish them what they need that would be reparative. Bringing to mind their emotional vulnerabilities, you generate the sincere wish they be free of the suffering specific to the schema.

IV

Spiritual Alchemy

16

Perceptual Shifts

If you look at the turbulent waters of a brook, the frantic gyrations of storm clouds, or the jagged zigzag of a bolt of lightning, nature seems full of chaos. Yet chaos theorists find within the complexities of the natural world a hidden order, unseen patterns that reveal orderliness and symmetry underlying what seems like random confusion. ● These unnoticed patterns are repeated over and over from the smallest to largest levels—atoms to cells to organisms to ecosystems. The contours of a ragged riverbed may seem arbitrary, but its outlines will be echoed over and over in nature: in the forking branches of trees or the branches of nerves in the body. ● Geology tells us about the details that shape a landscape—the composition of soil and rock, the sculpting powers of wind and water, the collision points of tectonic plates as they cleave rifts or volcanic uplifts. But this close-up view leaves us mystified when it comes to explaining larger patterns, like the ways in which river systems seem to repeat the same branching patterns on every scale, from the grandest to the tiniest. ● Such answers take a new perspective—one made possible by the expanded view from laser-based zoom lenses, imaging devices that can map the earth from satellites with amazingly fine resolution. This expansive vista reveals the grand patterns hidden in the maze of a river basin or etched in the folds of a mountain range. ● A single guiding principle turns out to shape how electricity flows through complicated wiring and how water channels etch a landscape over the ages: nature takes the path of least resistance. The paths of the tiniest trickles of a rivulet and the meandering of a gigantic river delta both follow this law. This hidden order shapes an entire river network and so defines the etching in every fold of a mountain range. But that lawful pattern was invisible until the satellite's imaging device revealed it. ● When it comes to the turmoil within our own minds and hearts, a path to inner freedom can cultivate a wider perspective—mindfulness being like the imaging device that helps us refocus the way we perceive the seemingly chaotic forces of our own nature. This perceptual shift allows us to see a larger perspective—hidden patterns, the subtle causal relationships, that otherwise go undetected amid the confusion. And we can see how clinging to rigid emotional habits leads to suffering and narrows the scope of our choices in life.

A sudden glimpse of the hidden pattern in our inner chaos renders what was so bewildering into an unexpected orderliness. Being able to perceive such hidden patterns, writes Michael Barnsley, a mathematician studying chaos theory, means that "you risk the loss of your childhood sense of clouds, forests, galaxies, flowers, and torrents of water. Never will your interpretation of these things be quite the same."

The universe orders itself for its own purposes, not ours. Nature's hidden structures offer a healthy disorienting experience, with their constant shifts from moment to moment, or as we change our angle or means of perception. Perceiving these hidden realities can help shake us free from the limits of our conventional sense of the natural order and of ourselves.

While nature forms endless patterns, there may also be an element of surprise in these natural designs as they break down, transmute, change. It's the same with our own nature: we may have preconceptions and assumptions about how things are. But as mindfulness deepens into a careful, sustained attention, we can tune in to another level of the mind.

The Quantum Metaphor ● Our perceptual apparatus—the range of our vision, for instance—attunes us only to a certain scale. When we think of life in the sea, we bring along the assumptions built into our own range of vision and so think of fish or seals, missing the fact that more than 90 percent of the beings in the ocean are too small to see with human eyes. When we gaze at our face in the mirror, we are oblivious to the millions of microbes and mites that dangle from our hair or graze over the vast expanse of our skin—luckily perhaps!

What we find depends on how we look. "Zoom in smaller than life-size, and solid tables become airy expanses of space surrounded by furious clouds of electrons," writes K. C. Cole. "As you zoom in or out, the world looks simple, then complex, then simple again. Earth from far enough away would be a small blue dot; come in closer and you see weather patterns and ocean;

closer still and humanity comes into view; closer still and it all fades away, and you're back inside the landscape of matter—mostly empty space."

Mindfulness teacher Jack Kornfield describes the parallel insights that apply to our minds: "If you can make the mind very focused, as you can in meditation, you see that the whole world breaks down into small events of sight and the knowing, sound and the knowing, thought and the knowing. No longer are these houses, cars, bodies, or even oneself. All you see are particles of consciousness as experience."

Go deeper still, though, he says, and "consciousness is like waves, like a sea, an ocean. Now it is not particles but instead every sight and every sound is contained in this ocean of consciousness. From this perspective, there is no sense of particles at all."

Consider the possibility of order, of a hidden pattern, in the way things are in our own being, and that it is the way we are perceiving that obscures this concealed order. In investigating our emotional reactions, upon closer inspection we detected the patterns of schemas at work within our confusion. How we perceive the chaos makes all the difference.

Now, in the spiritual domain, we explore still deeper levels of pattern and purpose within our minds. From a Buddhist perspective, our notion of who we are shifts as we sense more subtle nuances. Everything changes; we see patterns within break down and alter rapidly. We find no one fixed pattern that we can call the self, but we do detect an ongoing series of patterns arising, changing, dissolving.

I don't pretend to be a teacher of Buddhism; I have been a student of these teachings since the mid-1970s, and I continue to study and practice. But my own understanding of Buddhist teachings and practice is that they can help us tremendously in our lives—in applying mindfulness not only to our emotional habits, but also to understanding the nature of the mind itself.

Emotional alchemy operates at the psychological level, but spiritual alchemy takes us to depths in the mind where we can begin to free ourselves from far more subtle afflictions. So I want to share here the insights I have been getting in the course of my own studies and discussions with Buddhist teachers, from the writings of Buddhist scholars, and from the teachings of the Dalai Lama and others. All of these sources have informed my own integration and understanding.

To put these teachings into practice, you will need to go beyond this book to other sources, to understand the context of the tradition from which they come. But I share these teachings here as inspiring possibilities.

A Gap in the Stream of Thought ● I remember a day many

years ago when I was learning to ride a horse. As I was riding along, my horse spooked at something, bucked, and threw me from her back. Time slowed down. With a strangely relaxed attitude, almost disembodied, I calmly watched my body fly from the saddle, arc through the air, and turn to the side as it approached the ground. My right hip hit first, then my head. I watched as my body, without missing a beat, lifted itself from the cold, hard ground, and jumped back on the horse.

In those few moments my mind stopped. It seemed free of thoughts *about* what I was experiencing—there was just the experience. It wasn't until my riding instructor asked, with great concern, "Are you okay?" that it occurred to me to think about whether I was hurt. Then came a rush of thoughts: My hip hurts. If I hadn't had my riding hat on, I might not be here. This is what they mean by getting back on your horse. . . .

My initial thought-free state of mind echoes accounts of a highly focused but calm and nonreactive clarity that I've heard about when people describe their experience during a sudden shock—an auto accident, say, or an account I remember reading by an explorer who survived being mauled by a lion. Biologists say it's the brain's automatic reaction to an extreme surprise, part of the organism's ability to adapt in the face of life-threatening circumstances. That response: a gap in the stream of thought.

While such gaps have their purpose at the psychological level, they serve us, too, in spiritual life. From a Buddhist perspective, the Tibetan Book of the Dead describes such a gap as part of what can happen in the *bardo,* the "in-between"—that is, the transition states after dying. The *bardo* offers a great opportunity to awaken spiritually, the text says, because the intensity of the experience overwhelms and breaks up our usual habits and patterns of perceiving and reacting. We have no ground to stand on.

But if we can open ourselves to the unknown, without resistance, if we can see our mental projections as such rather than reacting to them as though they were real, we have a chance to recognize a clear awareness that is distinct from the overlay of mental habit and conditioning. Many Tibetan Buddhist practices are said to prepare us for the moment of transition, teaching us how to stabilize or sustain that moment of pure awareness. Some Tibetan practices are intentionally designed to loosen up habitual patterns and attachments in order to help us stay more receptive to this natural, open awareness.

One interpretation of the *bardo* is as a metaphor for the opportunity in life offered up in disorienting moments of shock, rapid transition, loss—

times when we lose our bearings. Such opportunities, like that fall from my horse, shake us loose from the spell of habit; for a moment, we are free of the weightiness of the identities we cling to.

As James Gleick observes of the physical world, "Disequilibrium, too, has a purpose." If we can break out of these habits of the mind, we can connect with a quality of awareness free of our mental ruts—at least for a glimpse.

When we do so, we land in the present moment, but a moment undefined by our mental habits. In such an instant, when our ordinary coordinates evaporate, we can see such habits for what they are. Like inflated balloons, they have no solidity in themselves; without our investment in their reality, they go limp.

Those old habits will inevitably reassert themselves; they have vast momentum in the mind. But if we can stay mindful in that moment of openness, if we can relax into it—even rest our mind there a bit—then for that time those mental habits will lack the solidity and allure they typically have while we are under their full spell. We can see, at least for the moment, the ways they come and go, blown by the winds of cause and effect, like tumbleweeds of the mind.

A Shock Out of the Ordinary ● Certain spiritual practices facilitate recognizing that gap in our stream of thought. The Zen literature, for example, is replete with such moments of awakening. Some methods, like the koans of Zen, hurl the mind into that gap through grappling with questions that have no logical solution. When we attack such questions over and over, our habitual ways of thinking exhaust themselves. Suddenly the futility of applying ordinary logic sends the mind plummeting into satori, a momentary experience of the gap.

Such an awakening does not always come while the person engages in meditative practice. As the Buddhist monk Nyanaponika observes, "It often happens on quite different occasions—seeing a forest fire, stumbling and falling, a shock out of the ordinary."

That freedom from inertia can come in benign ways, too—through an exultant encounter with the beauty of nature or through genuine love and compassion. It can come through simply bringing full attention to the moment. This can happen during moments of high creativity. William Segal, a painter in his nineties, brings to his canvases a sense of the luminosity inherent in all things. Moments of perceiving this illumination, Segal says, shine through in the inspired work of great artists, composers, and poets. But achieving that illumination requires a shift in perception: escaping the hold of our usual way of seeing things.

"Ordinarily, we're asleep and we go along with the mechanical flow of things, and we can't experience very much outside of the ordinary," Segal explains. But painting this way requires seeing afresh, a keen focus on present experience. "The demand to be here, to maintain attention for a sustained period of time, kind of dispels the clouds which obscure the luminosity." In other words, the secret is "wholehearted application to the moment." And, Segal adds, "accumulations of moments of awakening begin to show you another world. . . . You know the way. It's a question of practicing."

Taming the Monkey Mind ● The classic Buddhist metaphor for

the ordinary state of our minds is a monkey jumping here and there, constantly distracted, restless, and on the move. That monkey mind always races on to the next thing before fully experiencing what's happening right now. The speedy mind continually closes the gap, filling it with a random scattering of half-thoughts, memories, reveries, daydreams—anything at all. In a sense, the simple act of pausing from the mind's murmuring to allow a gap is an initial awakening, a "small liberation."

Some methods of awareness training in Buddhist practice sustain this initial awakening, gradually cultivating the ability to sustain this open, non-clinging awareness. With such practice, we don't have to rely on serendipitous moments that shock us out of our rut so we can experience this open awareness.

Such mind training, if continued over time, can make us more receptive to such moments of attention cleared of the usual distractions that weave a spell in the mind. As we break free of the spell of mental habit, a more direct contact with reality becomes possible.

This insight leads me back to the psychology that lies within Buddhism. It's not only some shock out of the ordinary that can wake us up to larger insights. Buddhism offers a systematic path to discovering these truths in our own experience, through training the mind. Indeed, the sudden plunge into the gap brought on by a shock can be remarkably similar to the insights that can come naturally through deeper stages of meditation.

With the fruition of mindfulness, as the Buddhist scholar Steven Goodman says, "Increasingly one has moments—gaps in one's addiction to confusion and fascination with the stuff of experience—when there is an open, nonconceptual enjoyment, when one experiences a kind of interior luminosity that always seems to be there, beyond confusions and manipulations."

A glimpse of things as they are before the mind starts its elaborate constructions—a moment of experiencing the gap—is not the same as stabilizing that experience as an ongoing part of our existence. But with diligent practice, the stabilization of that luminous awareness can progress beyond temporary flashes of recognition, eventually to the stages of enlightenment. Full stabilization can bring true liberation; the glimpses simply show us what is possible if we continue on the path.

Constructing Things as They Seem ● Buddhism offers a

radical critique of our ordinary sense of reality. From the Buddhist view, what we think of as real is an illusion of sorts. Things as they seem to us exist relatively but not actually, at an ultimate level. Ordinarily, what arises in our minds—the thoughts and perceptions, hopes and fears, daydreams and memories—are just disjointed fragments, a fluid mosaic of constructs floating through the mind.

The mind caught up in things as they seem, rather than as they are, Buddhism observes, generates a sort of subconscious chatter, fascinated with our thoughts and emotions, whether lofty intellectual thoughts, domestic details, or random daydreams and memories. This mental background murmur creates the building blocks of things as they seem, distracting us from what actually is—that open, luminous awareness.

To understand how our minds construct things as they seem we need to go back to the Chain of Dependent Origination, which we spoke of earlier. This is the sequence, remember, that describes the most basic cause-and-effect links in the mind. It starts the moment the senses connect with a stimulus like a sight or sound. In broad strokes, the links run from sensing to perceiving, from thought and feeling to craving and clinging and then to intention and action.

In applying mindfulness to schemas, we focused on breaking the chain toward its end, between intention and action. Cutting those links offered us more freedom from the tyranny of emotional habits. But Buddhism proposes that cutting the links at an earlier point can yield an even greater liberation.

Grasping this deeper cut requires a more finely tuned analysis of the chain, one that focuses on the early link between our initial raw sensory input and the classification, naming, and reactions that immediately begin to form around it. In Buddhist psychology, perception is a receptive mode, taking things in as they are. Conception is reactive: it adds to how we perceive the biases of our memories, associations, and emotions, all products of our past conditioning.

Cognitive science tells us a similar story. When the brain first registers information from the senses—say the sight of a brilliantly colored parrot—that data enters the nervous system in the form of physical waves. Their first stop in the brain, the hippocampus, translates those waves into the language of neurons, the bursts of electrical activity they pass to and fro. The signals for that parrot disperse to a web of locations throughout the brain, where they are analyzed for pattern, color, shape, location, motion, and the like.

Within a matter of milliseconds these disparate elements come into coherent focus as a unified perception, and the brain then searches our memory and tags a label on it: "a brilliantly colored parrot." Once we register the sight, our old associations and emotional reactions to that idea come trailing along after, like the cars pulled along by a railroad engine, and the train of feelings and thoughts chugs merrily along its track. We are pleased, and creep closer for a better, more delightful look at the pretty parrot. All is well.

Buddhism, though, looks at this series of mental events very differently than does science. The Buddhist view sees that ordinary train of thought and feeling as leading us astray, away from things as they actually are, to a deluded universe of things as they seem. Concepts are creations of the mind, a mental generality that is built on preconceptions and that lacks the richness and detail of the original perception.

In this view, the moment a percept is tagged with a concept—the fluttering splotch of gaudy colors named a parrot—we lose contact with what actually is there. Instead, we become lured into a flimsy world of our thoughts *about* what is there: our ideas and feelings, our fantasies and illusions about those things.

"Whether we should react for or against or indifferently is automatically determined," says the Tibetan teacher Chogyam Trungpa, by what he calls a "bureaucracy of feeling and perception": the ruts of our associations and mental habits. That bureaucracy of the mind automatically spews out a label for what we perceive—"beautiful" or "ugly," "strange" or "familiar," "boring" or "fascinating," and on and on. This process builds up in a construction of reality that, from here on, becomes more intricate, with the mind speculating and interpreting, drawing on preconceptions and invoking labels that stand in for the direct experience itself. He adds that "you like it or you dislike it depending on your association of it with the past."

These mental habits, from the viewpoint of Buddhist psychology, are causes of the deluded world of disturbing thoughts and feelings that breeds our own suffering and our pleasures. Buddhism is blunt on this point. "Most of the time, our perception is illusory; we're not perceiving reality," says Lama Yeshe in *Becoming Your Own Therapist.* "Sure, we see the sense world—attractive shapes, beautiful colors, nice tastes, and so forth—but we don't actually perceive the real, true nature of the shapes, colors, and tastes we see. . . . So our mistaken perception processes the information supplied by our five senses and transmits incorrect information to our mind, which reacts under its influence." The result is that "most of the time we are hallucinating, not seeing the true nature of things."

From the ultimate perspective of Buddhist psychology, "in the minds of ordinary people," says Geshe Rabten, "the only true mental perceptions are those that occur for an extremely short moment immediately after a true sense perception and immediately prior to a conception"—in the gap of awareness.

Opening a Space in the Mind ●

In the movie *The Matrix,* humans are born into a world where their actual body lies in a cocoon pod, unmoving, while their brain is fed input that creates an entire world, a virtual reality of compelling resonance, though completely illusory. Although trapped in their cocoon pods, the people portrayed in *The Matrix* experience this collective dream as the reality of their daily lives. From the Buddhist perspective, that might be an intriguing metaphor to reflect on for our own situation: living in a dreamlike reality without realizing it.

Buddhism proposes a radical path to liberation from this illusory world we create with our habitual thoughts and emotions, a path that alters our ordinary way of taking in the world. To see clearly—to perceive things as they are—we break the chain between the percept and the concept. This break comes after the senses connect with the object of perception but before the great flywheel of mental habit boxes that perception in stale cubbyholes of thoughts and feelings.

Opening up a space in the mind at this critical point offers a fulcrum between our raw perceptions and the inexorable weightiness of our habitual thoughts and feelings. If we can suspend these mental and emotional habits for even a moment, that gap allows an insight into the mind at a new level. As we become aware of how our habitual mental responses rush in to fill that gap, creating their magical display yet again, we have a new opportunity to investigate the workings of the mind with a refined subtlety.

The ordinarily invisible mechanics of the mind that usually perceive reality are suddenly exposed to the light of awareness: instead of being terrified by the booming voice of the Great Oz, we suddenly see the little man behind the screen bellowing into a microphone. This revelation lays bare the magical hands that usually shape our world for us. And that gives us the chance to explore our emotional reactions, as well as the most basic elements of our thoughts, with fresh eyes.

We usually take our habitual thoughts and emotional reactions as a given, an inevitable part of our experience. But investigating the mind at the subtlest level lets us see how emotions and thoughts begin in our very first reaction to what we perceive.

If we are mindful during the gap in perception—the micro-moment between percept and concept—it becomes a choice point to see in the old habitual, distorted (or deluded) way, or to let things be as they are, free of imposed concepts and reactions. What Buddhism calls ultimate truth, in a key sense refers to direct perception, unclouded by concepts, that allows us access to this direct experience.

Breaking the chain at this more subtle level implies a radical shift in how we regard the mind. This shift reframes *all* habitual concepts, feelings, and reactions with the same regard as we had earlier for maladaptive schemas. In this sense even our benign ways of thinking and reacting are prisons in the mind when we let ourselves blindly and blithely fall under their spell—prisons with open doors. The opportunity is always there to see things as they actually are.

One of my teachers, Chokyi Nyima Rinpoche, explains this subtle spell of the mind: "In each moment of thought there is both habit and emotion: liking, or attachment, and disliking, or aversion. Even in our neutral thoughts: not wanting to investigate means close-mindedness or dullness. In each moment of thought, then, there are subtle forms of these three basic emotions. Karma is created because of these subtle habits of liking, disliking, and dullness. They are the seeds of the gross disturbing emotions."

The fundamental cause of our distress, from this perspective, is our very mental habits themselves. In an everyday sense, karma—the law of cause and effect—stems from what a Tibetan text refers to as "solidified patterns of grasping and fixation." These solidified patterns, or mental habits, are also known as "emotional and cognitive obscurations," the tendency of the mind to repeat patterns of thought and feeling over and over.

The more often we repeat a mental pattern, the more likely it becomes in the future; in this sense these mental patterns are the seeds of our karma. The path to liberation, to transcending our karma, then, begins with freeing our-selves from the most well-trodden paths—the deepest ruts—of our own mind.

Deconstructing the Self ● A cloud offers a prime example of what, in Buddhism, is known as an "illusory appearance." Clouds look solid and opaque. But in fact they are 99.9 percent empty. A low density of water droplets, each acting like a spherical mirror, is enough to bounce light about in a way that leads our eyes to see what appears as a dense mass, a "solid" cloud.

That same understanding applies to how Buddhism views the threads of cause and effect in the mind that are woven together to form what appears to be the self. The self, or the ego, has a firm place at the center of Western psychology but not in Buddhism.

As psychiatrist Mark Epstein observes, "There is no attainment of a higher self in Buddhist theory; instead only an exposure of what has always been true but unacknowledged: that self is a fiction." Under the close scrutiny of Buddhist practice, Epstein observes, the self breaks up; in its place there are seen to be only "thoughts without a thinker."

In the Buddhist view, what we take to be our "self" is actually, like every-thing else, an entity that deconstructs when viewed closely. "It all comes down to the fact that it's a *seeming* combination of factors that creates experi-ence," says Chokyi Nyima. The perceptual chain that culminates in the labels we apply to the entities we perceive *seems* substantial and real—so long as we don't investigate too closely the links that got us there.

That applies particularly to the sense of self. What we take as "self" rep-resents a collection of interdependent parts, none of which can function without the others. It's like growing a plant: it takes a seed with an intact genetic map, water, nutrients, sunlight—and when all those factors interact, we have what we call a plant. But the plant can be deconstructed into all these elements that gave rise to it.

So with the self, which is constructed, Buddhist psychology tells us, through the moment-to-moment working of the mind as it takes in the world and reacts to it. Our automatic habits of perceiving, feeling, and thinking are the building blocks of the most fundamental—but illusory—sense of self.

Another way of describing this illusion is in terms of identity. For ex-ample, when we look at a lawn, we actually see small individual blades of grass, which we identify as a lawn. It takes many individual blades for us to recognize the collection as "lawn," not just one blade, or a few blades, of grass. In the same way, the "self" is an identity we give to an aggregate of mental building blocks, none of which in itself is a "self." As Jon Kabat-Zinn notes, the sense of self amounts to "what is called in chaos theory a 'strange attractor,' a pattern which embodies order, yet is also unpredictably disordered. It never repeats itself. Whenever you look, it is slightly different."

No Self, No Problem ● The construction of self, in the Buddhist account, begins the moment we ignore the gap and its open awareness, and start to label and react to a bare perception. What we make of a perception— as cognitive science, too, tells us—amounts to a construction in the mind. But this mental creation fascinates us. We fail to realize not only that we ourselves are building it but also that our constructed conceptions draw us in further, to a predetermined set of reactions to our own creation. The mind reacts to our projections and constructions, not as such, seeing them for what they are, but rather as though they were substantial.

In the culmination of this emerging mental architecture, the mind constructs its most intricate creation: the concept "I"—the sense of a self. In this construction the mind ties together many strands: denying weaknesses, selecting self-referential memories to retrieve and others to forget, putting ourselves squarely at the center of events, and weaving a web of thoughts that reassure us by confirming our assumptions about the world.

Finally we make a mistake about identity: the mind takes the self to be like a solid entity, overlooking how it went about building the self up in the first place. In the Buddhist analysis, though, that constructed self is merely a collection of habits and tendencies, with no separate identity. Like a plant, the self arises from interdependent parts; like a cloud the self stands revealed as just another illusory appearance.

Without the intricate apparatus of the senses, of perception, of memory and thought that gives rise to interpretation and meaning, the edifice of self would crumble. While our mind views itself as a solid and ongoing thread in experience, a closer look—through the lens of a mindfulness at a subtle level—reveals the mind to be a rather disjointed collection of tendencies and events. Yet we continually fall under the spell of this illusion, as though hypnotized into ignoring how fragile and arbitrary is the stuff from which the sense of self is built.

Since, as Buddhism tells us, the root of suffering can be found in clinging to this sense of self, our habitual ways of perceiving the self are worth investigating. "The ego," says Lama Yeshe, is "the wrong conception that your self is independent, permanent, and inherently existent. In reality, what you believe to be 'I' doesn't exist. Ego is a mental concept, a construction."

That insight follows from observing our experience with a sustained, subtle mindfulness. Such keen observation eventually brings home the *autonomy* of the thoughts, images, memories, fantasies, emotions, sensations, and percepts that float by. It's as though these fragments of experience follow some plan of their own: the sense of self or "I" has little or no power to control them, but turns out itself to emerge from the innumerable thoughts flitting by.

From one perspective, schemas, emotional habits, or whatever other name we give them are simply one way to understand the habitual conditioning of our minds. From another perspective, we can see them as having no substance: they are as empty and illusory as a cloud that is formed, changes, and then evaporates into open sky.

If the root of suffering lies in clinging to ego, one meditation master offers a helpful reminder: "No self, no problem."

A client who was doing a three-month meditation retreat sent me a note: "The deep, tenacious conditioning is coming up—all that self-aversion stuff, and sometimes big globs of it stick to my mind. But there are those moments of letting go, and each time that happens, my wish to be free gets stronger. It's a wonderful gift to be able to clear the space in the mind so that all the thoughts can display their true nature. Then the trick is learning to keep letting go, accepting, softening."

We don't need to reify these patterns and think of them as defining who we are, identifying with them in a way that solidifies a sense of "myself" and the patterns as being "real." At the same time, it can be useful to understand these habits of the mind as ways we have learned to see the world and react to what we see.

The Positive Uses of the Self ● Still, the Dalai Lama points out that at the relative level a self as conventionally understood does exist, and that aspects of the self can be helpful in spiritual practice as a basis for self-confidence and motivation. He recommends that those on the Buddhist path hold the ultimate sense of emptiness of self, along with a relative sense of its existence.

In Western psychology it is often said that one needs a strong ego. But in the Buddhist view what we need is strong confidence. The Dalai Lama warns against "negative ego, the sense of self concerned only with the fulfillment of one's own selfish desires." This negative ego stems from the belief in self as an independent, solidified identity. But self-confidence can be constructive as a spiritual vehicle—for instance, combined with an altruistic motivation, to serve other people.

At a deeper level, understanding emptiness or selflessness in our own experience loosens the hold of our self-centered clinging, our tendency to view everything in terms of ourselves. As we let go of perceptions centered on our own concerns, we have more attention available for others; loosening the clutches of the self spontaneously allows greater empathy.

The young son of a friend fell from a height while playing and suffered a serious head injury. The boy was rushed to the hospital in a coma. The injury was so severe that my friend was unsure whether his son would live, or ever regain normal functioning. After a CAT scan, the boy's doctor reassured my friend that his son would have a chance eventually to recover his cognitive abilities. After hearing that news, my friend was deeply relieved.

Yet just afterward, when he tried to read his son a book, my friend was struck by how unresponsive the boy was, especially compared to the enthusiasm and interest he had once shown. "Comparing how he had been with how he was now, I saw him as deeply diminished," my friend said. "My mind raced to the future—how he might be indefinitely. I was petrified by fear, and then a deep sadness."

My friend said it was as if his mind started to close in on worries about how his son would be. For about ten minutes "It got very dark," said the boy's father. "It was as though I was going down this tunnel in my mind. I felt utterly hopeless. Rock bottom—I'd never been that depressed."

An experienced meditation practitioner, my friend became aware of the despair capturing his mind and "it shocked me into practice." He decided to do a loving-kindness practice: he began to repeat mentally the wish that every child in the hospital, not just his son, be well, be happy, be free from suffering. And not just the children, but everybody in the hospital, and not just the hospital, but throughout the city, throughout the entire world.

As he continued quietly with this practice, the darkness fell away and was replaced by a sense of lightness and by a radiating compassion, not only for his son but for all those suffering. He still wasn't sure how everything would turn out, he told me later, but he now felt a profound shift in his state of mind.

When I asked, "What do you think changed?" his immediate response was "My self got out of the way. It was no longer about 'my' pain, 'my' son, 'my' experience. Of course I wanted everything to be okay for my son. But from then on, I felt capable of dealing with whatever was going to happen."

As the self gives way to emptiness, compassion emerges. This does not mean we no longer have our personal views, needs, or feelings about things—but we need not be *driven* by them. We can look at life with more equanimity. In short, it's having a lightness of being—being empty behind our personal feelings, views, and desires.

The Dalai Lama exemplified that lightness of being during his press conference just after the announcement that he had received the Nobel Peace Prize. A huge pack of photographers jostled for the best camera position, TV crews were everywhere, and journalists were shouting to get their questions heard. This was, after all, a moment of crowning personal achievement in anyone's life. The very first question came: "So how do you feel about winning the Nobel Prize?"

To that the Dalai Lama said, "I feel happy," adding after a thoughtful pause, "for my friends who wanted me to receive it."

17

Investigating the Mind

In the Caribbean, dazzling colors play on the surface of the water: turquoise blues and lush greens, dappled with sparkles of silver. But if you dive into the water, a greater delight awaits: the rich rainbow of vibrant corals, spectacularly painted parrot fish and their neon-like brethren flitting about. And if you go deeper yet, there awaits you a vast, empty stillness that belies the welter of activity above and at the surface. ● So with our minds and the realm of emotion. If we dive in with an investigative awareness, we break through the assumptions and habits at the surface of our minds, and we find a rich stew of emotions beneath. The depths of the emotional mind can grip us with great turbulence, like the dangerous ebb tides in the sea. But if we plunge in deeper yet, a stillness awaits us, and a vast, open clarity. ● Mindfulness, in the form of an investigative awareness, equips us for this inner plunge to discover these worlds within. We found many uses in emotional alchemy for this investigative quality of mindfulness with our habitual emotional patterns. With ordinary investigation, we typically think about and analyze what we find. But even though this has been relatively helpful, from the Buddhist point of view such a conceptual effort gives us only part of the picture. ● Buddhist practice offers another mode of investigation, one beyond an inquiry still tied to concepts and limited by our thoughts. This nonconceptual investigation—a quality of awareness that simply knows—can allow us to plunge still deeper within, to realize our basic nature. ● Spiritual alchemy begins with bringing this mindful quality of investigation to bear on our habitual mental patterns. We can challenge assumptions more subtle than the distorted thinking behind our schemas: our very sense of self comes into question as we investigate the roots of our disturbing emotions. With emotional alchemy we were able to allay the more obvious, gross emotional obscurations in our minds, rendering them more transparent and less powerful. In this spiritual alchemy we go the next step, redirecting our inquiry toward the mind itself.

The Seemingly Real and the Real ● As the Buddha lay dying, his heartfelt advice to Ananda, his closest disciple, was, "Be a light unto yourself." That advice offers a guiding principle: we should find out what is true for ourselves, rather than just taking some authority's word for it. Instead of just blindly believing, we should use an investigative mode to discover our true nature: who we are apart from the constructed self and the fabrications of our ordinary perception.

This investigation takes us beyond the seeming, to explore the real. An ancient metaphor contrasts the seeming and the real in terms of someone who recoils from a snake, then looks more closely and discovers it was only a coiled rope. A modern metaphor: we watch a movie, completely lost in its story, like a sleeper absorbed in a dream. A precise investigation would dissolve the reality of the movie into light reflected through a lens, projecting onto the screen a series of twenty-four still images per second.

Buddhism distinguishes between two levels of relative truth: things as they seem when we are under the sway of distorted perception—for example, when we're in the grip of a schema—and things seen more correctly, as when we free ourselves from the schema's distortions. But this more correct perception is still only a relative truth from the Buddhist perspective. Knowing things as they are in an ultimate sense, Buddhism tells us, requires a more subtle understanding of how the mind creates our reality.

Within the relative sphere, an investigative attitude can make the difference between mistaking things as they seem—the snake, the movie, the schema—for a more accurate picture of things as they are. But other methods of investigation lead beyond this relative knowing to a connection with things as they actually are from an ultimate perspective. At this level, mindfulness broadens its focus beyond distorted perceptions and maladaptive habits, and explores the very workings of consciousness.

Buddhism offers many methods of investigation and analysis that help in this broader exploration. For instance, this investigation can take the form of a Tibetan method often translated as "logic" but closer to "science of truth" or simply "advanced common sense," as Tai Situ Rinpoche explains. In a sense, this approach is akin to the logical challenges we used with distorted schema beliefs, but instead applies them to our most basic assumptions, seeking to eliminate distortions that arise because of our less-than-perfect understanding and awareness.

At another level is what, in the Tibetan tradition of mind teachings, is known as the "cognizant quality" of awareness: the capacity of the mind simply to know. This knowing quality runs along the full continuum of consciousness, from its conceptual workings to a more subtle mode of inquiry without preconception—and finally to the empty, clear nature of mind beyond all concepts. This level of knowing the nature of mind can bring us beyond the turmoil of our thoughts and feelings to those vast, still depths within.

The Broken Cup ● A friend of mine confided to the Dalai Lama that she was chronically beset by worries about dying—particularly that someone she loved might die. It was more than a passing thought; for her the fear of death was nearly an obsession.

As the Dalai Lama listened carefully, nodding sympathetically, I could sense the rapport between them and feel his great empathy for her. She seemed comforted by his caring warmth.

Then, after listening with such care to my friend as she described her fear of dying, he said to her, "It's good to think about that a lot."

His reply may seem surprising, since typically—at least in American culture—the social instinct is to reassure people that they needn't worry so much. But the Dalai Lama was reflecting a perspective at the heart of Buddhism: that we *should* reflect on the impermanence of things, on the fleeting fragility of life. Such reflections can further our spiritual growth. Investigating our unquestioned assumptions about the permanence of things, for instance, can help us be better prepared for these inevitable changes in our lives. We do not want to part with what we cherish most—loved ones, personal possessions, treasured beliefs, or life itself.

Changes and losses are difficult, even painful, for all of us. They force us to adjust to our personal needs and to mourn our losses. But as things in life inevitably change, at one point or another we all encounter the suffering inherent in this change and loss. From the Buddhist perspective, reflecting on these circumstances can help us face difficult truths and adjust to hardships with more equanimity as we feel better prepared internally.

Of course sometimes change offers a welcome relief. Impermanence does not always mean the sorrow of loss; we can also find solace in realizing that, for instance, illness and suffering too are transitory. We can remind ourselves that this too shall pass.

But there is an old Zen saying: "This cup is already broken." It's a helpful perspective to keep in mind: these things change, they don't last. The cup is whole now, but someday it will break. We can extend this attitude to ourselves as well; someday, for each of us, this will be true for our body. We may live a long, full life, but when it ends, getting used to reflecting on the inevitability of change will allow us to prepare, to gradually adjust to life's inevitable closing. Keeping that in mind can inspire a sense of urgency to make good use of our lives.

This reflection on our own impermanence is one of the Tibetan Buddhists' "mind changings." Just as in working with our schemas we challenged the preconceived ideas that reinforced those patterns, so in the Buddhist path we bring a similar questioning attitude to some of our most hallowed and unquestioned assumptions.

That, in fact, is what the mind changings are designed to do: overturn the habitual assumptions that validate our ordinary ways of being. By abandoning old ways of seeing things, we make ourselves available to a new perspective. This radical questioning can motivate us for an equally radical reevaluation of our perception of reality and of the very workings of our mind.

The attitude that "I'm just fine the way I am" has a built-in limit: the assumption that we've faced the full scope of what's possible for us. So, for example, the first of the four mind changings reflects on the preciousness of a human birth, with the opportunity it offers for a spiritual journey of discovery that can infuse life with renewed meaning and purpose.

The cozy assumption that we may live into our eighties or nineties, leaving us plenty of time to do most of what we might want to in life, might be true—but not necessarily. The second mind changing challenges this false notion of permanence, the belief that things last.

The idea that "it doesn't matter what I do" is still another assumption that lulls us to sleep, from a spiritual vantage point. As we have seen, though, the actions or attitudes we repeat over and over become fixed habits, limiting our freedom, chaining us to repeating them.

The third mind changing acknowledges the power in our own lives of the laws of cause and effect. We need to take responsibility for our thoughts and actions: they have real consequences.

Finally, there is an attitude that refuses to believe that one day, inevitably, suffering will come our way, even if everything is just fine today. This fourth mind changing acknowledges the pain that life must bring at some point.

With these reflections, we see more clearly some universal facts of being: everything that comes, goes; what seems so solid and lasting breaks down on closer inspection into a flux. No lasting contentment can be found in grasping at any sensory experience, for they will all end. Greater contentment is to be found in letting go of our hopes and fears than in any clinging. These reflections on the natural laws that affect us can inspire us to turn toward spiritual practice as a refuge.

Subverting the Normal Order of Things ● These radical
shifts can open us to a revised perception of how things actually are. This revision came alive for me when I went to an art exhibit in which a great many of Claude Monet's impressionistic landscape paintings were gathered together for viewing in one place at one time. I saw Monet's paintings from a new perspective. I had been used to seeing a single rendition of Monet's haystacks in a meadow or of his lily pond—something like a still snapshot. But here were gathered all of the paintings he had done of each single subject, so that the eye read each series as a sequence, like a film.

He had depicted the same landscape at different times of the day, or in different seasons of the year. And while each painting in a series might on first glance seem just like the others, gazing from one to another revealed a subtle movement of light filtered through fluid templates of shifting color, as differing hues were accentuated from dawn to dusk. Crisply defined lines gradually faded as edges softened with the changing light. Monet captured the poignant aesthetic of the truth of impermanence. His paintings were contemplations of change.

Buddhism points out the continual flux in our mind. Whatever arises in our perception—our thoughts and feelings, whatever we see, hear, smell, taste—is the result of complex laws of cause and effect in a state of continual change.

This understanding of impermanence can lead to an opportunity for insight into the "empty" nature of all phenomena. All that we perceive is empty of an individual identity rather than being the fixed entities our minds tend to attribute to them.

From this perspective, the attribution of fixedness to any entity amounts to a perceptual assumption: we erroneously pin a label where in fact there is an ever-changing aggregate of cause-and-effect sequences arising and passing away. One reason this escapes our awareness is that we see ourselves, other people, and objects in a limited time span, as though the snapshot we hold now represents how they always will be and how they always were. If you look at the shape of a cloud, it doesn't seem to change. If you look back moments later, you see that the shape has shifted. So with a haystack, as Monet showed us, and with everything else, though that shift may occur so slowly as to be imperceptible to our eyes and minds.

Biology tells us a similar story about our own bodies. The typical cell in our body dies after one hundred days or so. Every second two-and-a-half million red blood cells are born, and in the same second a corresponding number die. The round of birth and death goes on every moment within the human body.

The taking of a form of any kind can be seen as an event, a cycle of birth and death, that lasts for but a moment. Of course, scales of time for that "moment" vary dramatically. A geological moment, like the birth and death of a mountain range, can take millions of years. For a giant redwood tree, that moment may be one or two thousand years. But if we assume the right time scale, all physical entities reveal themselves as impermanent. Change is ceaseless.

A similar insight into impermanence naturally arises from watching the mind at work, with an investigative awareness. A mindful insight lets us see a kind of birth and death in each moment. As Joseph Goldstein puts it, "We can see that all of the thoughts, feelings, emotions, and sensations in the body and mind are momentary, constantly in flux. . . . [W]e can see the changing nature of all the different parts. We can be with them without identification and see that they do not belong to anyone, that they are simply transient phenomena, arising and passing away."

Things Exist as Verbs ● Physicists know that every object can be

broken down into its constituent molecules, every molecule into atoms, every atom into still smaller particles of energy. But that just begins to get at the complexity of cause and effect.

"Chaos in the perspective of physics technically refers to unpredictability—the near-impossibility of predicting all the effects of a cause, or of deducing all the causes behind an effect," a physicist tells me.

"Every effect still has a cause," he adds, "but the causal relationships are so delicate and complex that it's nearly impossible for even the most powerful computer to understand them well enough to make predictions. Chaos theory extracts predictable (and often universal) patterns out of a physical system that is otherwise unpredictable, and gives the physicist some limited understanding of cause and effect in the physical world, without the enormous effort that would be required for a complete understanding."

All science is about understanding the laws of cause and effect that govern what happens in the physical universe. Buddhism takes that analysis in another direction in both the physical and the mental realm, acknowledging that all that arises comes from this complex web and has no existence apart from it.

"When you analyze things by mentally breaking them down into their constituent parts," the Dalai Lama explains, "you come to the understanding that it is simply in dependence on other factors that things come into being. Therefore nothing has any independent or intrinsic identity of its own."

When we see our lives as only a small part of a greater web, our perspective changes dramatically. It's like the image my brother once used of "a few grains of sand swirling around in the dust storm of time."

If everything that seems to exist as an independent entity actually takes shape as part of a great web of cause and effect, then, as Buddhism tells us, it is "empty" of any independent nature. It's like a reflection of a face in a mirror: it *seems* to exist, but appears there only because of how our eyes receive the play of light on the glass.

Of course things do exist, relatively speaking, from the conventional point of view. But from an ultimate perspective they are part of the great fullness of the weaving of cause and effect that creates apparitions out of emptiness. Things exist as verbs, as process—not as nouns, as fixed entities.

A Bubble on the Water ● Everything that arises, whether a drop of dew or a mountain range, will eventually change and pass away. Nothing lasts. The Tibetan word for "impermanence," says Chokyi Nyima Rinpoche, implies being "perishable, fleeting, passing, like a bubble on the water. The Buddha said that when we look at a bubble in the water it looks like it is there, like it exists, but then the next moment it is gone. Everything is like that; every single moment is changing."

On a very subtle level, Chokyi Nyima offers the example of a vase: "For a person who does not really think about it, it seems the vase is permanent from the moment it was made until it breaks. But someone who really examines this vase will find that it changes at every single moment. The vase discolors; it becomes antique—not all of a sudden, but moment by moment."

Buddhist teachers urge us to investigate this for ourselves. An intellectual inquiry is a beginning, but if this understanding remains solely on the intellectual level, it may make little real difference. For that reason, the Dalai Lama observes that greater conviction of the truth of impermanence requires direct insight into our own experience, not just hearing about the idea. That direct understanding "needs to be further perfected," he adds, "since our grasping at impermanence is so deeply embedded in our consciousness." For such a strong habit of mind, "just one single insight is not enough to dispel it. It requires a long process of deepening our insight."

The truth of impermanence is symbolized powerfully in some Tibetan rituals in which an exquisite and intricate mandala is constructed from colored sand. After days or weeks in which the mandala finds uses in extensive rituals, there is a closing ceremony where the bright colors are summarily swept into a muddy brown heap, taken to a river, and thrown away. The discarding of what had been so beautiful reminds us that because every experience passes, to the extent we cling to them we will inevitably be disappointed.

From Relative to Ultimate Compassion ● Changing our

mind in these profound ways leads us to a greater openness to challenge the mental habits that underlie our ordinary confusion. In Tibetan Buddhism, this challenge takes the form of a special mind training.

The Tibetan tradition of mind training speaks of two complementary modes of practice: method and wisdom. In this context, method refers to a gamut of practices designed to help us become more open, honest, confident, and compassionate. Loosely interpreted, any practice that helps us get closer to perceiving things as they are—whether through therapy or spiritual practice—comes under the heading of method.

Similarly, "relative compassion" refers to practices that reduce disturbing emotions and shift our attitude away from a self-centered stance and toward the aspiration to help others. The loving-kindness meditation described in Chapter 2 is just such a practice in relative compassion. Concentration meditations, such as focusing on the breath, are also in this category, since they tend to calm the mind and so suppress disturbing emotions, leaving us more open, less reactive, and more responsive to the needs of others.

Many practices in Tibetan Buddhism cultivate relative compassion.

There is, for instance, the intentional cultivation of the wish to benefit others; the dedication of whatever merit our practice yields to the well-being of others; seeking to use every opportunity to increase virtues like applied compassion; and rejoicing in other people's happiness—to name but a few.

These practices provide an important foundation for exploring deeper truths: the cultivation of what is called ultimate compassion, where method gives way to the wisdom practices. While meditations that concentrate the mind or that cultivate a compassionate attitude are all to the good, being calm and altruistic is not enough if the same habitual patterns still play themselves out in the mind. So long as those habits prevail, we are stuck with seeing things as they seem, not as they are.

Seeing things with the greatest clarity requires that we somehow clear the mind of whatever may be obscuring our view. The main goal of mind training is to remove the two main kinds of obscurations: cognitive obscurations—subtle thoughts and their underlying assumptions—and emotional obscurations, our automatic reactions for or against whatever comes to mind. While the method and compassion practices, like concentration and cultivating loving-kindness, clear away emotional obscurations, the wisdom practices do the same for the subtler cognitive obscurations.

Any training that dissolves emotional and cognitive obscurations, says Chokyi Nyima, "is a true mind training."

When Confusion Dawns as Wisdom ● A famous verse by the great Tibetan sage Gampopa encapsulates this path of mind training:

May my mind turn toward the dharma.
May my dharma practice become the path.
May the path clarify confusion.
May confusion dawn as wisdom.

That first line refers to the mind changings mentioned earlier, and their power to shift our personal priorities, so that practice—the dharma, or spiritual teachings—is a source of inspiration and guidance in our lives. The second recognizes that it's not enough just to have these insights into what matters; we need to walk the path through spiritual practices. And the third line offers the wish that our practice will be free of the perpetuation of the mental and emotional habits from which we seek liberation.

At a practical level, these lines refer to practices that help clear away emotional obscurations. Our disturbing emotions—at least the obvious ones, those we immediately recognize as such—are reduced or made more subdued by methods like calming meditations. These quiet the mind and focus us outward with a positive attitude, away from our personal preoccupations. Their effects include making us more emotionally stable, confident, and compassionate.

But the crucial step in mind training comes with the shift mentioned in the fourth line, when "confusion dawns as wisdom." This refers to practices that remove the more elusive cognitive obscurations, which are seen as the very basis of the mind's delusion. Cognitive obscurations include any unfounded concepts or assumptions about reality or distorted ways of perceiving. Dissolving these obscurations allows us to perceive things clearly, revealing the nature of the mind itself.

The practices that have this effect come under the category of wisdom, and include in particular insight, or *vipassana,* a Pali word widely used in the West (the Tibetan form is *vipashyana*). The specifics of these insight practices vary somewhat in the various schools of Buddhism. Training the mind in this sense means freeing ourselves from the grip of our ordinary mental and emotional habits, finally stabilizing in the wisdom of a wakeful awareness.

The two levels of training the mind are reflected in the underlying motivation for pursuing each. The motive for cultivating compassion at the relative level finds expression in the wish to relieve one's own suffering and that of others. The motive for cultivating the ultimate level of compassion is the desire to see reality clearly and to help awaken this same potential in others.

Some texts use the metaphor of ice and water in speaking of this shift from relative to ultimate, and the parallel shift in the quality of compassion. The ordinary mind is likened to ice: the rigidity of our thoughts and assumptions centered around our clinging to the ego, the "I." As this spiritual alchemy has its effects, the ice gradually melts until finally there is no hardness of conceptual habits left, just crystal-clear water. From one point of view, the ice is transformed into water, but from another, it is still the same mind-stream. It just unfreezes as it gets less and less fixed and closed in around itself.

The warmth of relative compassion can melt the ice of mental rigidity. The more selfless we are, either through compassionate actions that benefit others, or in compassionate wishes and thoughts within our own mind, the more we are able to realize the empty nature of mind. As the notion of separateness dissolves, ego-centered clinging is released.

Clearing Away Confusion ● There is a direct link between our ability to be compassionate, Buddhism holds, and the clarity of our own

mind. If our own mind is troubled, we are that much less able to be skillful when it comes to helping to ease someone else's pain. For that reason the wish to alleviate the suffering of others leads to the wish to cultivate our own wisdom and to replace confusion with clarity.

The clouds of confusion in our mind dissolve the moment we interrupt our habitual ways of perceiving. The Tibetan word *sherab* denotes the inquiring intelligence that clears away this confusion.

This faculty of mind might be called an inner teacher, the ability to use life experiences to wake up to things as they are rather than as they seem. This inquiring intelligence uses the conceptual mind—the mind that thinks, labels, and reasons—to transcend itself. The experience of our true nature, Buddhism teaches, lies beyond the realm of ordinary thinking and feeling. The leap from conceptual to nonconceptual marks a key transition in mindfulness practice.

This inquiring intelligence is not satisfied with merely filtering our perceptions through the distorting lenses of thought and emotions, nor will it allow the assumptions implicit in those lenses to define our reality. It seeks to know the very nature of *what thinks, what feels,* rather than staying satisfied with seeing life through the haze of habitual thought and feeling.

As such, this mindful investigation offers a direct way to break our deepest habits and tendencies of thought and emotion, including the false certainty that comes from assuming that things as they seem to us ordinarily reflect things as they are in actuality. The quality of investigation works in direct opposition to habit. When things go unchallenged, we go on automatic, letting habits play themselves out, with our conditioning dictating how we see, interpret, feel, and react. But the investigative frame of mind lets us wake up and see afresh by shaking us loose from our habitual ruts.

Just as at a gross level an investigative inquiry can yield insights into our emotional habits, at a more refined level the inquiring intelligence allows insights that transcend the more subtle cognitive and emotional obscurations. This natural knowing quality of the mind is like a spotlight illuminating whatever we perceive, giving the mind the power to know and understand. It gives us the ability to follow a map to our destination as well as to clarify the inner map of consciousness, knowing the nature of mind itself. *Yeshe,* or wisdom—knowing things as they actually are—is the truth that remains after the flood of thoughts and feelings and erroneous assumptions subsides. *Yeshe* is like the open sky; *sherab,* or inquiring intelligence, is like the wind that clears away the mental clouds obscuring the sky.

The Thickest Clouds ● Of all our mental clouds, some of the thickest swirl around our emotions, becoming storms in the vicinity of our schemas. Tibetan Buddhism tells us that these distressing emotions can sometimes offer an opportunity to gain spiritual insight. That, of course, requires applying the right methods.

The process can begin with a psychological investigation. "When your negative mind arises," advises Lama Yeshe, "you should examine it more closely," with a questioning attitude that challenges your assumptions. The method he recommends parallels applying mindfulness to a schema attack: "Instead of busily doing something to distract yourself, relax and try to become aware of what you're doing. Ask yourself, Why am I doing this? How am I doing it? What's the cause?"

The answers he proposes are at a more subtle level than we have applied in working with schemas, however. If our understanding floats on the surface of things as they seem, we'll fail to penetrate to things as they are. Lama Yeshe gives this analysis of our condition when we are caught by habits of mind: When we understand our mind's perception of the world, we may realize that we are clinging to the sense world. As he puts it, we're "too concerned with what's going to happen in a nonexistent future and totally unconscious of the present moment." In short, we are "living for a mere projection."

A mindful stance counters the strengthening of emotional habit by bringing an investigative awareness to bear each time a negative emotion arises in our mind. This strategy, from the Buddhist perspective, is far preferable to our ordinary habit of letting our emotions blindly drive our actions—doing that leaves a strong impression in the mind, a deepening of the rut of habit for doing the same thing in the future. These lasting mental tendencies to enact yet again an emotional pattern we've engaged in many times before have a subtle power.

Chokyi Nyima Rinpoche likens this subtle trace of a habitual tendency to the lingering fragrance in an empty perfume bottle. The traces of these mental tracks may be hard to discern, but their power remains great. "Habitual tendency," as Chokyi Nyima puts it, "implies a kind of automatic power or energy. Quite often irritation and anger do not require much effort on our part. Due to habitual tendency, they seem very spontaneous, and can blossom into full-fledged anger when the right object presents itself."

From the ultimate perspective, positive as well as negative emotions harbor the "seeds of karma"—the propensity to deepen emotional ruts and so strengthen a habit. In this view, *all* our emotions might come under the scrutiny of mindfulness, just as do all our thoughts and other reactions. And so the inquiry expands to include the workings of the mind itself.

A Subtle Investigation: The Three Poisons ● To understand this level of inquiry, it helps to trace back to their root how emotions begin. After the senses make contact with an object and register that contact as a perception, the next step includes a reaction: how we feel about that object. Do we like it, dislike it, or feel indifferent about it?

From this judgment arises the full-blown emotion, from craving and clinging, to disgust or hostility, to coolness or apathy. Because these three reactions are the ultimate source of destructive emotions that arise in our minds, Buddhism refers to them as the Three Poisons.

Emotions do not, strictly speaking, arise in the mind because of the things we perceive. Whatever appears to us, "it is liking or disliking these appearances that creates the emotion," says Chokyi Nyima. As Tilopa said, "You are not bound by the thing perceived, you are bound by the clinging. To like is a subtle form of attachment; when it grows it becomes grasping or craving. To dislike is a subtle form of what can grow into anger"—still a kind of clinging.

We are typically far more aware of emotions at the gross level than we are of the more elusive and subtle ones of liking, disliking, or indifference that give rise to them. If allowed free rein, a minor disturbance can bloom in the mind into anger. But the investigative power of mindfulness can detect the more subtle level, tracing the roots of a strong emotion like anger back to its source in the mind. We get to that critical moment when the mind reacted to the initial perception with dislike. With a schema reaction, for instance, we might be able, with the right investigative awareness, to trace its source back to an initial moment when the mind registered "dislike" at what became the trigger.

If we let our reactions play out unnoticed, they will manifest themselves as gross emotions, the specifics of which depend on our habitual patterns. But no matter the final form the emotion takes, at its root lies one of the three primary reactions. These are the seeds for all our intense emotions—if a mindful awareness does not intervene.

According to the Chain of Dependent Origination, the birth of attachment starts with the moment of contact, when the eye or ear first begins to be aware of the thing being sensed, which leads to feeling or perception. In

Buddhist thought, this sequence can offer an analysis of both the second and third Noble Truths: the causes of suffering and the key to its cessation.

Not being mindful of that first moment of contact quickly leads through a few more stages to craving, or attachment to the thing perceived. But classical Buddhist thought proposes an alternative to forming an instantaneous attachment to what we perceive by reacting to it with one emotion or another. Instead we can simply be aware of it with equanimity. Then no attachment is formed; the chain of conditioning is broken.

As the chain breaks, we are free from the automatic liking, disliking, or indifference that ordinarily plants the seeds of afflictive emotions. This allows us just to have equanimity with how things are naturally, not wanting them to be any different. In short, not clinging to our liking or disliking.

If You Are Interested in Using Investigative Awareness as a Practice

You can apply mindfulness to the link of grasping. This more subtle level of mindfulness can be done more easily on retreat, where you have the opportunity to intensify the steadiness of your mindfulness and refine qualities like precise investigation. This allows you to strengthen your awareness while also building the equanimity that allows a greater freedom from grasping.

In your mindfulness practice, try simply being with, and closely observing, the sequence that occurs when you sense something. When you see, hear, or feel a sensation, what are the immediate next steps in the mind? Can you detect the tendency to grasp—to have a preference, liking or disliking what is sensed?

This is a crucial link in the Chain of Dependent Origination, the mind's point of choice between habitual ruts and nonclinging. Observing this allows a direct insight into how clinging to hope or fear, to the pleasantness or unpleasantness of experience, obscures the mind.

18

Reframing Suffering

During the darkest days of the Nazi regime, Viktor Frankl, a teacher, was incarcerated in a concentration camp. The inmates of that camp had virtually no control over their fate, but they might still control their state of mind. Writing about that desperate time, Frankl recounts how most of the prisoners eventually lost all hope. But Frankl did not. He stayed occupied, thinking through how he might someday draw on his nightmarish experiences in lectures and writing. ● Finding meaning in that horrible situation had several effects: it kept Frankl motivated to survive, it kept his mind lively, and it kept his spirit intact. He survived to write and lecture about his experiences for almost forty years. And he founded a school of psychotherapy based on the premise that a sense of meaning can transform suffering. ● In reframing his own suffering, Frankl offers an inspiring perspective for seeing the possibility of dealing with our misery from a more expansive awareness. We each have our unique ways of responding to life's challenges, and we need to respect our own needs, temperament, and timing. I offer my reflections as an exploration rather than as a recipe for dealing with suffering. I'm not presuming to know what's right for anyone else in confronting the struggles that are part of our lives. ● In my own inquiry, I've been intrigued by the enduring courage that allows some people to triumph in adversity, to gain access to inner sources of insight and compassion even in the most trying circumstances. People seem to draw on certain natural human qualities to get through difficult times. But doing so requires that we trust in our natural intelligence, in the inner compass that helps us find our way through our pain and our grief. ● This perspective is not meant to deny or to minimize the harsh realities that people endure. Some struggles are so hard to bear that we just want them to go away. But this perspective allows—indeed, encourages—us to trust our ability to know when to act and when to be still, to understand our unique reality, and to respond in the wisest, most sensitive and informed way.

Sometimes we need time to ourselves; sometimes we need the support and caring love of those we trust. Sometimes we need time to express our pain to ourselves or to others; sometimes we need to turn to perspectives and practices that can help us heal. We all have our own ways of naturally responding to the difficulties we face in life.

At times this means being open to *not* knowing how to respond, allowing ourselves just to accept the mystery of why this is happening. If we accept these needs and respond to them by taking care of ourselves, being fully present to our experience as it is, without rushing to change it, an understanding can develop in its own time.

Whether a person is a practitioner of meditation or not, the qualities of courage, resilience, and patience—to name a few—are the same ones that mindfulness enhances. The practice of mindfulness cultivates and deepens these natural qualities. As the Tibetan teacher Tulku Thondup has said, "The greatest source of strength and help is our own minds—by opening our minds, we may be surprised at our inner strength."

What Turns Us to the Spiritual Path ● Some years ago I

worked with a wonderful therapist for a while. She didn't have much knowledge of Buddhism, but she respected my interest and commitment to practice as a way of getting clarity about emotionally confusing issues. One day I was telling her about some early losses in my childhood and how I adapted to them. She looked at me, and with her natural insight said, "It was as though you already understood impermanence."

Her words went straight into my heart. She was acknowledging how those early childhood losses had been more than just a cause of grief and suffering for me, that they had also yielded a deeper insight and helped lead me toward the spiritual path.

I've heard this from many people who have been drawn to Buddhist practice. Turning to a spiritual path, in a sense, can be an adaptive response to suffering, whether from emotional confusion, physical pain, or loss.

I remember facing fears of abandonment when my dear cat, whom I had for twenty years, was passing away. It's amazing how bonded we can become to our pets. In some ways I expected that it would be difficult to let go of her—given my pattern of abandonment fears, personal losses can have an intensified impact.

At the time, I was struggling with my fear of losing any being whom I cherished, and at times the unsettling abandonment fears made it even harder. So after twenty years of raising my cat from when she was a kitten, I had assumed that losing her would be too much to bear. The part of me that can tend to detach when I detect a sign of abandonment was about to kick in after the vet said, "She only has a few more weeks of life." I felt a very strong urge to distance myself from her emotionally, one of the classic ways those of us with the abandonment pattern try to avoid the pain of an expected loss.

Then I remember intentionally choosing not to give in to those fears and not to distance myself, but rather to stay very close to my cat while she was dying. For weeks I spent every spare moment by her side.

Staying so close to her even while I was afraid of losing her altered something. It challenged my assumption that losing someone was always going to be too painful to bear, the feelings of abandonment too intense.

Finally she became so helpless that she could not move much more than her head. In these, our final hours together, I told her how much she meant to me, how I would miss her, and how deeply I loved her. By now she hadn't moved at all for a couple of days, but seemed to express her love through a steady, engaged gaze.

Then it was getting late and I got up to get ready for bed. I came back to say good night to her. She was facing away from me as I stroked her back. For the first time in days she moved her body to roll over, facing me. She meowed a few times, and I knew immediately that she was asking me to hold her.

I lifted her on the pillow she was lying on, and held her close to me. She immediately exhaled three times in a row—and passed away.

It was almost as if I was watching her consciousness move through her body in a wave-like pattern and be ejected out of her on that final breath. I was awed to witness that transition from the cuddly long-haired cat whom I had held all those years, to the hollow body, empty of life force, that she left behind.

I sat silently with this wonder. Impermanence was no lofty, abstract concept, but a real experience. The teachings of Buddhism came alive for me in that moment. There is no fixed, solid, permanent self—just a series of changing patterns of experience.

Feeling so deeply connected to her while I was losing her made it more possible to feel a bond that went beyond physical forms. Even while feeling the fear and sadness, I found myself connecting to love itself.

Transforming Adversity ● The Dalai Lama points out there are two basic ways to respond to suffering: "one is to ignore it and the other is to look right into it and penetrate it" with awareness. The recommended response for a spiritual practitioner, he adds, "is to go into it, not simply to avoid it." If we can change our relationship to our unpleasant experiences, if we can resist them less and observe them more clearly, we may be more able to diminish the added layer of suffering that comes from our resistance and reactions.

That, of course, is not always so easy. I remember the Dalai Lama being asked if going through deep suffering could be beneficial, helping people become more compassionate themselves.

His answer: "Yes, it certainly does happen." But he went on to caution that suffering can also simply lead to despair or depression: "If we become obsessed with our suffering and become depressed and overwhelmed by it, that will further increase the suffering." Yet when suffering joins with what he called "skillful means," in the sense of helpful inner circumstances, it can lend itself to greater courage.

The notion of "helpful inner circumstances" deserves our attention. Included in that phrase are abilities of mind that we can cultivate. One such is the power of a focused attention itself, a sharpened concentration that calms the mind, making it less reactive. Another is adaptability, a resiliency that lets us respond with more openness and creativity instead of being confined by the limits of constricted lines of thought. Others are patience and trust, the ability to accept those things over which we have no control. Then there is equanimity, which is not the same as insensitivity or apathy, but rather a mind that rests in an attitude of balance, not pushed or pulled by likes or dislikes.

An old Tibetan lama who endured seventeen terrible years in a Chinese concentration camp after his country was occupied was telling the story of his imprisonment. He talked about how difficult it was, at times so hard to bear. But, he said, even though he was in prison, he still had his inner freedom. They could control his body, but, as with Frankl, they couldn't control his mind.

How we relate to adverse conditions is our choice. No one else has that power over us. This resiliency of mind is also a powerful tool in unraveling our schema conditioning. Other people's actions are one thing, but how we respond and are affected by those actions is within our power to change. This flexible, resilient quality of mind—all the "helpful inner circumstances"—can be cultivated through mindfulness practice.

One of the great gifts of the human spirit is the ability to transform suffering so that adversity becomes a force that awakens us. Rather than being overpowered by forces of confusion or despair, we can begin to see that we have a choice in how we let ourselves be affected, that we're not entirely helpless in the face of adversity.

Of course, that's not to say it's easy; when in the midst of suffering, we may not know how to use it as an opportunity for transformation. There can be some wisdom in *not* knowing for a while, just letting us loosen habitual ways of relating to our problems and the limited ways we define ourselves. We cannot always change the perplexing conditions of our lives—but we can change how our minds relate to them.

Then there are the inner challenges of facing our own schemas and afflictive emotions, when the chaos of our minds seems out of control, hard to make sense of. But even if we are utterly confused, if we can remember to rest in mindfulness within that confusion, it's like finding a calm sea beneath turbulent waves. We still may not know what to do, but at least we have this inner haven.

One of my therapist friends was telling me about a client who finds refuge in meditation. Her outer life is so chaotic, filled with problems with her health, her relationship, her children, that she finds a quiet haven to turn to which is unaffected by the outer turmoil. It's reassuring to her to realize that this haven exists within her own mind.

Sometimes life presents us with such tragic experiences that it can take us some time to recover. It's not that we always can use such difficulties in this way. We need to accept our feelings without rushing through them—to go through feelings of sorrow, for instance, or to express our grief. When we're ready, at the right time there's an opportunity, a doorway to greater freedom. If we choose to use it that way, mindfulness allows a way to be with our suffering that can open us to painful experiences with equanimity and a courageous heart.

What makes the crucial difference is how we *relate* to the suffering. If we only resist and try to escape, we can never relax into it, see it from a new perspective and perhaps find a way to make some sense out of the chaos. In any turmoil or with any problem, as Tulku Thondup says, "The greatest source of help and strength is our minds."

A Glimpse of What's Possible ● Life itself can be a teacher, presenting us with chances to transmute the emotions brought up in us. When life disappoints us, it offers an opportunity to reach beyond ordinary conven-

tions and understandings toward a greater perspective: to consider that there must be more to this than there appears to be. This inquiry just might propel us to new possibilities and the opportunity for new depths of understanding.

Sometimes those painful experiences are a hidden door to freeing ourselves from the limited ways we may be perceiving the suffering we experience. The Chinese character for "crisis" has two parts: one means "threat" and the other means "opportunity." If we can seek greater meaning in our distress instead of simply resisting or resenting it, that very effort has the power to reframe our suffering, at least a bit.

My friend Ram Dass, an inveterate explorer of the inner realms, had a stroke some time ago and, as I write this, has gradually recovered. His spiritual orientation has always emphasized seeing the predicaments of life as teachings, and so an opportunity for spiritual learning. Ram Dass seems able to use his stroke for his spiritual growth—"stroke yoga," as he calls it— rather than simply letting himself be defined by the new, stark limitations on his body and his mind.

A short while after his stroke, as he was regaining the ability to speak, he told me, with some difficulty, "I feel this illness has been a blessing, because it has erased my superficiality—my sports car, golf, all that." Later he wrote, "From the ego perspective the stroke is no fun—but from a soul perspective, it's been a great learning opportunity."

That the root of liberation from suffering ultimately lies in the mental realm rather than the physical was brought home starkly by a halting comment by Ram Dass. While he was still in the hospital a month or two after the stroke, I asked if he was suffering. Struggling to find words, he told me, "When I think of who I was, there can be suffering. Or if I think about the future. But when I'm in the present there's no suffering."

He added, "The doctors here think that consciousness is in the brain— but my consciousness isn't affected by this illness."

Ram Dass used to tell an ancient tale about a poor farmer who had just one horse and one son. One day the horse ran off, and a neighbor was commiserating with him about how tragic that was. "We shall see," said the farmer.

The next day the horse returned, with a wild mare. Now the farmer could breed them, and raise more horses—a great addition to his wealth. Now the neighbor was happy for the farmer. But all the farmer said was, "We shall see."

Then when the son was trying to break in the mare, he was thrown and broke a leg. Now he couldn't help his father in the fields. Again, the neighbor said how tragic it was. "We shall see," said the farmer.

The next week, a cruel warlord captured the village, and all the able-bodied young men were forced to join his troops. But the son was left behind. And all the farmer said was, "We shall see."

Of course, it's not always so easy to stay open to whatever will be, especially when we just can't seem to find a way to change how we relate to our suffering. But still, such a change can occur, given the right circumstances and approach.

"Strong positive energy can prevent or ease suffering," says Tulku Thondup. "But the most significant result of a positive attitude is not necessarily to keep suffering from happening but to keep it from becoming a negative force when it does come."

Two Perspectives ● Buddhism teaches us there are two perspectives that apply to any situation or experience: the perspectives of relative and ultimate truth. The ultimate view can be particularly powerful when it comes to reframing suffering.

The realm of cause and effect operates at the level of relative truth. The truth of what goes on at this level fits conventional understanding. How schemas work—or habits in general, or the mind, or our sense of self—can all be understood at this relative level. In the relative view, the theories offered by psychology or cognitive science are valid.

But from the ultimate perspective, our schemas, our habits, our very selves, do not exist with any independent, intrinsic reality. They are no more real than the reflection of a face in a mirror.

The ultimate level goes beyond our ordinary understanding. While the relative truth makes sense to us ordinarily, insights at the ultimate level begin with the radical rethinking of our most basic assumptions that is embodied in the Chain of Dependent Origination.

One of these cherished assumptions is that we exist as discrete, separate entities. From the Buddhist perspective, everything owes its seeming existence to something else, as multiple causes and conditions interact. In other words, the apparent existence of *everything*—you, me, our galaxy—depends on multiple factors. If any one of them did not play its right role at the right time, no you, no me, no galaxy.

"This absence of some kind of independent, autonomous reality is said to be ultimate truth," the Dalai Lama says. But this example of an ultimate truth, he observes, "is not obvious to us at the level of our ordinary perception and understanding of the world."

To get to this level of reality takes deep probing. Yet relative and ultimate truths are two perspectives on the same world: our very experience. An investigative awareness can hold both in mind. As Tai Situ explains, "The relative principlc allows an individual to relate to the variables of the situation, but it is all the while backed up by the perspective of ultimate truth, which allows us to avoid getting carried away by changing interrelationships."

Of course, the ultimate view may seem rarefied, even inaccessible to us, in our day-to-day lives, especially in those moments when things appear serious, perhaps dire, and we lose all perspective in the pulls of gravity and urgency. But allowing the possibility of a larger perspective can help us perceive anew the relative reality of our lives.

Reflecting at the relative level helps us understand the repercussions of personal history and the resulting emotional and perceptual habits that obscure our perception of the ultimate reality, our true nature. But when we hold these perspectives in mind at the same time, we can be more compassionate, less judgmental about or bound by our emotional blind spots and self-defeating habits. We can also make the leap to the ultimate view, even as we grapple with a relative understanding.

Holding this larger perspective can bring an expanded awareness to emotional wounds. One client, who became a dedicated meditator, shared a journal entry with me. While on a meditation retreat she had a powerful dream that someone she was involved with told her he was going to leave her. She awoke feeling a pervasive sadness—her abandonment schema, she recognized, had been triggered by the dream.

"On a personal level," she wrote in her journal, "one could interpret someone not really being there as a lonely experience—especially when there have been so many losses, and silent wonderings if anyone was ever really there. But without needing to distract myself from the personal realm, I find it possible to hold my attention there, just being with a sadness, with a sense of these personal losses, appreciating the relative nature of this reality. A wholehearted attention feels like the nurturing presence that I always wished I had in a parent. Now I am free to be there for myself in a way that I assumed I needed from someone else. The sadness dissolves as a new realization dawns: people come and go. Awareness is unchanging."

Four Noble Truths ● The relative and ultimate views on our experience can help us understand the Four Noble Truths—the Buddha's famous analysis of the causes of human suffering and the path to liberation from that suffering—in a profound way.

At the relative level there are countless causes and varieties of suffering: physical, social, economic, political, and on and on. If due to human cruelty, poverty, disease, or other such remediable reasons, then of course everything possible should be done to change the conditions that cause the suffering. But there is another level of suffering—the pain created by our own mind.

This variety of suffering results from how we react to our experiences. For example, those who treat people who suffer chronic pain from medical conditions know that the mental suffering such pain brings heightens to the degree that people fear and resist the sensations, adding another layer of emotional anguish atop the raw sensations. So with the rest of our lives: whatever the objective reality, our emotional reactions to it add another layer to the suffering.

In Buddhism, there is a more subtle understanding of the cause of suffering, as we've seen: clinging—the initial liking, disliking, or indifference—which in turn gives rise to our disturbing emotions. There is a radical response to suffering: if we can investigate the mind at a more subtle level, then the workings that produce that sense of mental suffering can become more transparent. We see the links in the mind's chain of cause and effect laid bare.

Buddhism offers a fine-grained analysis of the varieties of suffering, all grounded in our state of mind. The most subtle suffering—the "suffering of conditioning"—stems from the basic flaws in the workings of the mind, the deep habits and misperceptions that stain our ordinary experience. From this perspective, the Four Noble Truths offer a remarkable analysis of the root causes of suffering and its cure, all in terms of the primary role played by the mind.

The first two truths can be understood to describe cause and effect at the relative level: the conditioning in our minds causes our suffering. Experience that is defined by conditioning of any kind—every mental and emotional habit, for instance—limits our freedom. This conditioning manifests itself at one level as disturbing emotions and at a more subtle level as a latent vulnerability to such reactions, whether in our thoughts and feelings, our words, or our deeds.

The third and fourth Noble Truths describe cause and effect at the ultimate level: we can bring an end to suffering by stopping the cause—our initial grasping. The path of practice offers the real remedy for the problem, and its result is freedom.

Inner Freedom ● Liberation from suffering can go beyond the relative to the ultimate. In our quest for relief from our suffering, Buddhism

teaches, the most insidious enemies are internal—our afflictive states of mind. The Sanskrit term for these internal saboteurs means literally, "that which afflicts from within." Most often it is translated as "afflictive emotions," but its broader meaning refers to our negative patterns of thinking and feeling—and the actions that result. Freedom from suffering, Buddhism teaches, comes with the cessation of these afflictions.

At the subtle level, suffering is created by the instantaneous liking, disliking, or indifference woven into each moment of our experience. This represents a radical shift in awareness. While before we looked at our maladaptive emotional patterns as the source of suffering, the Buddhist view widens the scope of how we see the root causes of that suffering. Buddhist psychology emphasizes subtle mental dimensions of suffering more than the obvious, gross ones.

The Dissatisfied Mind ● Consider one symptom of the malady of modern life: people who live the most privileged lives, who have abundant wealth, good health, loving family and friends, can be prey nonetheless to a chronic low-grade dissatisfaction in the midst of this abundance. The richest banquet, the most exotic travel, the most interesting, attractive lover, the finest home—all of these experiences can seem somehow unrewarding and empty if we don't really attend to them fully—if our minds are elsewhere, preoccupied with disturbing thoughts.

By the same token, the simplest of life's pleasures—eating a piece of fresh-baked bread, seeing a work of art, spending moments with a loved one—can be amply rich if we bring a full attention to them. The remedy to dissatisfaction is inside us, in our minds, not in groping for new and different outer sources of satisfaction.

If while eating an apple we're thinking of something else, we don't really notice the apple, so it's not all that satisfying. As meditation teacher Sharon Salzberg noted in a talk, at such moments "it's very rare that we say, I should have been paying more careful attention. . . . Mostly we think that the fault is with the apple. So then we say, If I only had an orange, then I would be happy. So we get an orange. But if we eat it in the same way, it's still not a very satisfying experience. So we say, the trouble with my life is that it is so mundane— I need something special. So we get an exotic fruit, like a mango. And if we eat it in the same mindless way, it's the same kind of experience, the same search for a more intense sense of stimulation to feel an aliveness or sense of fulfillment."

But what if we let things be as they are and instead change our reactions to them? What if we turn our attention to the dissatisfied mind itself?

Mindfulness can have this effect when we use our practice to look into painful feelings, with a penetrating, investigative awareness, experiencing the mind just as it is.

Buddhism points to a contentment beyond our usual cycle of pursuing desires and fleeing unhappiness: the ultimate equanimity comes from a mind free from wanting. True freedom goes beyond the ordinary concept of happiness; with such liberation comes the capacity to let things be just as they are, without wishing they were different.

But the Buddha always said people need to find out the truth of these notions themselves, through their own experience. His last words, as he lay dying, were to his main disciple: "Be a light unto yourself."

The Reality of the Relative ● Much of this book has focused on acknowledging, empathizing, and working toward healing deep emotional wounds, mainly from a psychological perspective. This personal work on our emotional healing weaves into the tapestry of inner work, where psychological and spiritual threads intertwine, as each dimension seeks our attention. Emotions are opportunities for insight, at any level.

Sometimes insight can emerge spontaneously when we are present to a painful experience with a mindful awareness. The practice of mindfulness meditation allows us to cultivate an outlook that can use life situations, including suffering, as an opportunity to take a second look, to frame our understanding in a new way.

A word of caution, though. As we open to the larger dimensions of our being, we need to be careful not to ignore our personal needs, the reality of the relative. Along the way, as we shift perspectives, exploring adversities to see if they can connect us with an expanded view, we need also to stay connected to our own emotional requirements and those of others.

From the relative perspective of our personalities, egos, or personal stories, we need a tender empathy when experiencing painful feelings. But from an ultimate perspective, that expansive view allows a broader definition of ourselves. I sometimes experience these two levels shifting back and forth during conversations with people who are telling me about a difficult time. Their personal story looms in the foreground as they describe their pain, and there's a sense of sharing their trouble, connecting in the parts of ourselves where we all resonate with the suffering of others. Then their voices may deepen, their eyes become clearer, and I watch as they go through a shift where their usual sense of themselves seems to dissolve into a larger dimension of their being.

They begin discussing something they hadn't realized before, or they speak of how their suffering gave them a greater sense of themselves or of what they felt capable of facing or doing. One of my clients, for example, was struggling with the end of her marriage. Facing divorce, with three very young children, she was worried about how she would take care of her family on her own. Her life was going to change drastically, and the prospect triggered many of her schema fears.

Lost in confusion while on a plane flight one day, she reflected on how her mind felt like the dense clouds she was flying through as the plane found its way through a storm. Exhausted, she fell asleep for a few minutes and had a dream in which a close friend appeared to her and said, "Don't worry; the sky is clear just beyond these clouds." In this dream she felt a great sense of relief to be reminded of another perspective rising above the turbulent clouds of her mind. She woke up and saw the plane had leveled off and was flying smoothly above a thick layer of clouds.

She felt lighter inside, and thought that maybe something positive would come out of that tumultuous time—something she couldn't see yet.

Several months later, as she reflected back on that dream, she realized that her life definitely had improved. By now divorced, she found herself unexpectedly content rather than frightened and desperate, as she had feared. Of course she struggled with the transition, but then she discovered that she was capable of caring for her children on her own. And now she felt more able to live a life she found meaningful.

It's hard to see clearly when you're in the thick of the clouds. But that metaphor had been a helpful reminder that a clear sky sparkled beyond the temporary confusion.

If You Want to Work with This Expanded Way of Seeing Things

Try using the metaphor of clouds and sky as a visualization. Imagine dark and stormy clouds, representing your own stormy emotions, obscuring the clear openness of the sky—your own clear awareness.

As a practice to help you remember your own ability to bring mindfulness to your beclouded moments, you can bring the image of cloud and sky to mind as a way to shift your perspective when you are caught up in an emotional storm. It can help you take the emotions less seriously, and you may realize that, like clouds, they will pass.

Just as the warming sunlight and the changes brought by winds will dissolve clouds, our own intense reactions are temporary—they don't determine who we are.

Trusting that there's a clear, open sky—our true nature—behind the clouds will inspire a confidence in a larger perspective and grant us the patience to let the clouds dissolve in their own time.

19

May Confusion Dawn as Wisdom

Over many years of practice at a retreat center, I have become fond of the friendly chipmunks that live there. These chipmunks are so trusting they will eat sunflower seeds out of your hand. Sometimes a chipmunk will scamper up to you, put its delicate paw over its heart in a begging gesture, and gaze innocently into your eyes. I got used to having sunflower seeds spilling out of my pockets in case one of my affectionate friends crossed my path. ● One day I had been doing walking meditation outside. I've valued walking meditation, applying mindfulness to a simple activity, because as awareness becomes very precise and strong, you can learn a lot from the unfolding of your experience, and you have a wider range of experiences when you're out walking than while you sit inside on your cushion. ● This particular day I had an unexpected encounter with the nature of suffering. As I was absorbed in the changing patterns of experience amid the movements of walking, I suddenly saw a cat run by with one of the chipmunks in its mouth. I was devastated. ● I made a futile demand that the cat let the chipmunk go, but it was gone in a flash. I was in despair, left feeling helpless.

A Mindful Investigation ● Ordinarily I would have been very, very sad over the tragedy I had just witnessed. When another being—especially one you're fond of—suffers, you naturally feel sad. But on that day, after several weeks of practice, the intensity of awareness I brought to that moment took me to a different place. I found my mind penetrating deeper, investigating the nature of suffering. ● "There's no way around it—*this* is suffering," my mind observed. I became aware of feeling helpless because I hadn't been able to relieve the chipmunk's suffering. I saw how my mind

wanted to be angry at the cat, blaming it for inflicting pain on this helpless creature. ● But as I continued to investigate this wanting to blame and the stirring of anger toward the cat, I realized that the cat was, in a sense, following its habitual impulse, acting from its cat instincts. I may not like it, but that seems to be something cats feel compelled to do.

The blame couldn't be placed on my inability to save the chipmunk. It seemed futile to continue to blame the cat or even the "faulty" design of cats. It was the nature of suffering itself, and my reactions to it, that needed investigation. The strong emotions that I felt as my mind was searching for some way to understand this pain propelled my awareness to new depths. As the Dalai Lama has said, "The moment you think of the well-being of others, your mind widens."

I felt a very strong desire to be free from suffering, which in some way seemed to include the chipmunk's suffering, the cat's suffering, and the suffering of all beings as well as my own. Unseen forces are at work that keep us bound to seeing and reacting only to the pain in suffering. But I realized that *how* I was seeing this suffering made a crucial difference. Was it the situation that made me suffer, or was it how I was *perceiving* the suffering itself?

Part of me still assumed that when a chipmunk died in the mouth of a cat it was definitely suffering. But there is a more complete view of suffering and its nature. On the relative level, of course, this qualifies as suffering. But from an ultimate perspective, I began to open to a larger understanding.

I realized that part of my struggle was in wishing things were different: that the cat would ignore its hunting impulses or not have them at all, that it would be afraid of me and drop the chipmunk, that it might have preferred its cat food to hunting chipmunks . . . or that I could have been somewhere else so I wouldn't have had to witness such pain and suffering.

It was humbling to realize that I don't necessarily have control over the suffering that happens in my world. Of course there *are* times when we can do something to prevent suffering for someone, and we should do so without hesitation. But in this case I had no choice but to accept the suffering as part of life's package—the impermanence of life—or to resist it. The choice we do have is in how we relate to the suffering: we can choose to see it with aversion or with equanimity and compassion.

Being free from suffering in that moment with the chipmunk meant not resisting the inevitable pain but to relate to it with a compassionate equanimity. Imagining myself as the chipmunk, I would want someone to protect me, of course. But if that wasn't possible, if it was my time to die, I think I would want someone who tried to protect me to let her sadness be transformed into a compassionate wish for me to be peaceful—to be able to face with equanimity an experience that would otherwise have been terrifying. This shift to equanimity and compassion in the face of the inevitable can help us endure suffering with greater courage.

The Compassionate Deity ● Tara, the Tibetan deity of compassion, comes to mind when I think of such equanimity in the midst of suffering. Sometimes her very posture expresses a wise compassion: she is half in an active, caring pose, ready to protect and care for beings, and half in a meditative position, symbolizing the lightness of being behind her compassion. Her emotions are in the service of wisdom. Tara's compassionate wish is to appear to billions of beings in whatever way they need and in whatever form they can relate to, in order to release them from their suffering.

How can we embody this mix of lightness and inner freedom with the loving warmth of caring? How can we preserve our tenderness while not being overwhelmed by the obstructive forces of our negative emotions?

The poignancy of the compassion that I felt for the chipmunk, and the yearning for freedom from suffering—that of other beings, as well as my own—brought a renewing fire of intensity to my practice. In this way, as Nyanaponika says, "adversity was transformed into the teachers of the Four Noble Truths" that analyze the cause of suffering and the path to liberation.

The experiences of life can become our teachers; the accidental predicaments of our lives are, in this sense, spiritual opportunities. In this instance, on retreat, these teachers included qualities of awareness themselves, one being an inquiry that penetrated the layers of conceptions I had about suffering. This passionate inquiry, fueled by the mixture of sadness and compassion, inspired a fresh way of perceiving and understanding—and challenging—my assumptions, an opportunity I might ordinarily have missed.

I remember the Dalai Lama telling an audience, "Before cultivating compassion, first cultivate impartiality." On that retreat, tempered by the equanimity of mindful awareness, I watched the waves of emotions refining themselves. And these emotions helped me to open to a penetrative insight: I experienced a deep yearning to be free from suffering—a yearning that pierced the layers of my mind from my emotional reactions and concepts to an intuitive experience and understanding that are beyond thought.

Within the Tibetan Vajrayana tradition, in some methods feelings are not discouraged but rather utilized as a part of the path to free the mind. It is understood that emotions, even when intense, can be a fuel for insight—if we have the right preparation and training. In this sense, a passionate inquiry can help crystallize the understanding of our experience.

The image of Tara, the compassionate goddess, is a reminder that when equanimity is balanced in the right way with the energy of love, the combination can allow an awareness to pierce through obscuring veils and through our dense habitual patterns. The image of Tara offers an ideal we can aspire to, the integration in ourselves of a warm and caring heart with a mind that clings to nothing. The goddess Tara has been an inspiration to me, a reminder of an inner balance between feeling and equanimity. When this passionate energy is directed toward the wish for liberation, inner gateways fly open.

Spiritual Alchemy ● Alchemy, in its classic form, concerns a hidden reality, the order of truth beyond the everyday reality. "Alchemy pertains to the hidden reality which constitutes the underlying essence—the absolute," as one alchemical writer puts it. Its essence lies in the goal of a transmutation of consciousness from our ordinary, lead-like perception to a more subtle, gold-like mode of perceiving.

To the alchemist this transformation is both spiritual and material, both an ideal and yet highly practical. The grand goal of escaping our inner prison can be seen as requiring something quite concrete, freeing ourselves from the grip of our own conditioning and habits. The question for the alchemist is how this can be accomplished.

"I think 'alchemy' is the perfect word for this process," a client told me recently, referring to the work we were doing together. "Sometimes I think of this process as all kinds of experiences in my life being put together in a big pot—my anger at my ex-husband, at my friend, at my ex-boyfriend, at my boss—and it all gets stirred together and reaches a boiling point. This emotional brew offers me an opportunity to transform how I've been reacting. It's the intensity of the heat from all this that makes the change possible. If things were lukewarm all the time, they would slip by me unnoticed. But once I can see all these patterns of reactivity together, catch them as they are occurring, I can start to change them."

The intensification of emotions, then, can be an opportunity both for emotional work and for spiritual growth—if we know how to use it that way.

As my teacher, Tulku Urgyen, said, "Wisdom can arise with greater intensity when emotions are more intense."

One key to going from the level of emotional alchemy to that of spiritual alchemy has to do both with our aspirations and with the inner tools we apply. As another of my teachers, Nyoshul Khen, said: "Often we find ourselves involved in strife with family, friends, and so forth . . . yet it does not need to be seen as a big problem." The key is in cultivating positive intention, he added, "For everything depends on our intention. We can work with anything and integrate it into the path, our spiritual practice, through pure mind and good heart, always from the point of view of benefiting others." And, he says, cultivating "good heart"—an altruistic attitude—naturally transforms strife and struggle.

Two Paths in the Mind ● What happens when we sit in practice
with an obstacle in our life—something that, whether or not it is driven by a schema, we find deeply troubling? If we sit quietly, our awareness will be drawn to the agitation in the mind. We can see how our identifications, resentments, fears, and hopes all percolate within, a cauldron of thoughts appearing, and reactions to those thoughts, where one leads inexorably to the next.

One path in the mind leads to the ordinary way of grappling with an issue: trying to figure it all out but staying within the limiting perspectives of our ordinary thoughts and reactions. Down this path, the one our minds follow so much of the time, we're so focused on reacting, and reacting to our reactions, that we don't realize what's really happening: that we're reacting at all.

The other path, the path of spiritual practice, leads us to a broader perspective, not caught up in the reactive mind. We simply sit with all of it, without fueling the chain of thought and reactions with even more reactions, neither pushing it away nor further identifying with it. Then we can see clearly that this is the stuff of confusion, of the deluded mind caught in things as they seem. There's no judgment about it—just a clear understanding.

That choice point marks where practice makes such a difference: it's knowing when the mind runs along its usual ruts of habit and when it rests in a clarity free from those ruts. And it's knowing the difference between the two—that there even *is* a difference.

Here can begin the alchemical process of transformation. As we allow the mind to settle down and see itself, our perspective broadens. We can connect with a sensibility *behind* the reactions and thoughts, with what lies in that gap between percept and concept. In that gap we catch a glimpse of a bigger sense of things, one not limited by the narrowing definitions imposed by the rut of mental habits.

In that larger sensibility, we may find an opportunity for our limited sense of self to dissolve. The troubles that we were so preoccupied with just moments ago begin to feel more workable, less claustrophobic, less daunting. They loomed large partly because of the limited ways we were seeing them. But that narrow attitude shifts as we develop a more expansive sense of things.

That more expansive quality of mind drops the tight bundle of our small self, the entrenched habits accumulated throughout our life. As we let go of that burden, a sense of interconnection with all beings emerges, which lies at the heart of a compassionate attitude. When we let go of our absorption in the small stuff of our lives, as the usual sense of ourselves constructed from the countless habits of emotion and thought dissolves, we connect with a greater vision.

This process of connecting with deeper truths opens a gateway to insight. On one level, more options are now available to us, new perspectives that emerge as we let go of our habitual mind-sets and allow the potential of the flexible, creative mind to illumine our understanding.

As we drop the seemingly fixed and permanent, limited sense of self, we can see in a way that is free of our usual lenses on reality, free from our blind spots, from whatever obstructions are built into our ordinary lens on life.

This unobstructed view of life, Buddhism tells us, is available to us all: it is the natural quality of our minds freed from habit. Turning to this source of awareness is itself a practice—a habit of freedom that can gradually replace the inertia of our ordinary mental ruts. Of course at first we get only glimpses that fade; until we strengthen that free awareness, our minds will be swept down those old ruts of thought and feeling over and over again. But even a glimpse can remind us what's possible.

Beyond the Spell of Habit ● I heard the Dalai Lama say in a talk that if we don't bring a higher purpose to our lives, then we only live an ordinary life. It's a sentiment that many wisdom traditions have expressed in their own way. Likewise, my teacher Tulku Urgyen spoke about ordinary beings and extraordinary beings. The difference, as I understood it, has to do with the process of transformation that culminates when someone

recognizes and rests in her own true nature, free of the gravitational pull of mental habits. At that point, she does not just know about wisdom; she is *being* wisdom—and so has a greater ability to be of benefit to others. Compassion is a natural expression of wisdom, arising out of its selfless nature.

Of course, from the relative level our ordinary thoughts and perceptions, our mental habits, are essential; we need them to make our way through life. But Buddhism points out the sense in which our usual thoughts and feelings limit and imprison us, cutting us off from a larger—and freer—perspective. We do not need to abandon those thoughts, but only to step beyond the circle of their spell.

Nyoshul Khen sometimes used the metaphor of the philosopher's stone, which transforms whatever it touches into a more refined element. The philosopher's stone as he meant it refers to our own awareness. When awareness penetrates disturbing emotions, the alchemy begins.

In the Buddhist tradition, transmutation—an inner alchemy—does not mean suppressing or rejecting our ordinary habits of mind, but freeing ourselves from their gravitational pull. In the alchemical metaphor the metallic quality of lead is not rejected, but rather transformed into gold. So with our ego-centered emotions. Gold can be covered in mud for thousands of years, but still retain its natural essence—just as with awareness, when the sediment of habit is cleared away.

But the need for a teacher who knows the byways of this less trodden path is clear: we can't do this work without a well-qualified teacher. The dangers of self-deception are too great; someone might believe he is freed from clinging, when in fact he is not. If one goes astray this way, the warning holds, the energies of hatred, passion, and pride can run amok.

Tibetan Buddhism uses the energy of emotions as part of spiritual work. One of the Vajrayana scriptures describes primal energy as "the driving force of emotion and thought in the confused state, and of compassion and wisdom in the enlightened state."

Harnessing Negative Emotions to Positive Ends •

The essence of mindfulness practice is to make use of "all experiences as aids on the Path," in the words of the Buddhist monk Nyanaponika. "In that way enemies are turned into friends, because all these disturbances and antagonistic forces have become our teachers."

I thought of this passage as I listened to a young African-American man living in an urban ghetto, who was part of a dialogue on peacemaking at a conference with the Dalai Lama. The young man was complaining about the slow response time of ambulances to emergencies in his neighborhood. With a fiery intensity he told how one day he had called an ambulance in a panic, to rescue a friend who had just been stabbed by a robber. The minutes ticked on as he tried to stanch the bleeding from his friend's wound, praying the ambulance would come. After what seemed an interminable wait, there was still no sign of an ambulance. By the time it arrived, his friend was close to death from bleeding. He died on the way to the hospital.

"Those ambulance drivers always take their own sweet time when they have to make a call in the 'hood, but they're really quick if the call comes from a better neighborhood," the young man complained. "It's outrageous. I get mad just thinking about it. After my friend died, I tried to figure out how I could get revenge—maybe I'd burn down the fire station, I thought."

Even though I didn't agree, I could understand how his frustration could lead him to contemplate such an action.

"So you know what I'm going to do?" he went on.

During a pregnant pause, my mind raced with thoughts of the revenge he might seek, of what desperate acts his still-seething anger might drive him to.

Then, in his confidently streetwise manner, the young man calmly said, "I realized that more violence wasn't a solution—it wouldn't help anybody. So I enrolled in a training course for ambulance drivers. And once I get the job, you can be damn sure we'll get to the 'hood as soon as we can, every time."

In our day-to-day lives the world confronts us with countless challenges and predicaments that arouse the energies of our emotions. If we can direct those energies to a positive end, as the young man did his anger, we are transmuting our emotions.

In Vajrayana Buddhism, where the teaching is not to suppress or oppose these energies but to transform them, there is a useful model and system for doing this. Known as the Five Buddha Families, this system describes the transmutation for each of five major energies and their emotional tendencies: anger, pride, passion, jealousy, and apathy.

This method uses emotions themselves as a spiritual vehicle by transforming their energies from a deluded, neurotic mode to a wise, enlightened mode. In this sense, the Buddha Families approach is akin to emotional alchemy in transforming our emotional habits, but it takes them to the next level, in a spiritual alchemy.

While the actual practice requires the instructions of an adept Vajrayana teacher, it offers a clarifying and inspiring model for what is possible in working with emotions at a profound level: using these emotional energies themselves as part of the spiritual path.

The Buddha Families ● Each of the five energies has an aspect that represents its manifestation as the familiar negative emotion, on the one hand, and as a wisdom representing that same energy when liberated, on the other. The basic energy does not change; only the way it manifests itself will change. Each of us, Vajrayana holds, has a fundamental personal style—tendencies to experience a particular emotional energy, and so a characteristic way of perceiving and operating in the world. In a sense—and with the right alchemy—that neurotic energy can be transmuted into wisdom.

These energies have been richly described by Chogyam Trungpa. At the neurotic level, for instance, the energy of anger is all too familiar: an aggressive fixation on one way of seeing things, hostility, and a prickly defensiveness. Angry people are closed to other points of view, quick to object or take offense—in short, uptight. In this Tibetan system, anger is also associated with a sharpness of intellect, which flowers as the energy of aggression is transmuted to a more liberated form. It then becomes a discerning and mirror-like awareness, flexible and able to see things from multiple perspectives, to evaluate with precision and to perceive with a crystalline clarity.

The energy of pride, at the neurotic level, looks like narcissistic self-absorption. The narcissist applies no limits or self-discipline, seeing himself as special, wallowing in the admiration of others, in ostentation, and in frivolous pursuits. Beneath the facade of pride lurks a sense of underlying shame or defeat. When transformed, this same energy transforms these fears into equanimity. This security allows an openness, an expansive feeling of plenitude, that encourages extending oneself generously to others, whether physically, emotionally, or spiritually.

Passion, in the sense of neurotic clinging, grasping, and craving, can manifest itself as a hysteric's shallow seductiveness, or as the hypnotic charisma of a manipulative con artist. It manifests as an alluring, pleasing, and always seductive pursuit of objects of desire. When transmuted, this energy takes the form of discriminating awareness—taking a precise interest in, and paying keen attention to, whatever presents itself. This ever-inquisitive awareness opens up communication: other people are seen and understood in their full distinctiveness, and related to with empathy and a warm compassion.

Jealousy and envy revolve around comparing oneself to others and judging them. At an extreme, this becomes resentment of the accomplishments of others and a paranoid fear that others will outdo one. This judgmental attitude breeds condescension and a flurry of activity around setting things right—that is, in accord with one's own view of how things should be—and so imposing one's own order. When transformed, this busy energy becomes competence, allowing activities to flourish effectively. Action becomes well aimed, opportunities are seized, and the possibilities inherent in a moment become actualized.

Finally, there is the energy, or lack of energy, embodied in slothfulness. In its worst form, this takes the form of dullness, indifference, and sheer laziness. Such people take the path of least resistance in life, doing whatever is easiest rather than what is needed, appropriate, or effective. When transmuted, this energy becomes a spacious awareness, the basis for a deeply contemplative experience. This energy, in its enlightened form, is said to suffuse the other emotions, bringing a lightness, an accommodating spaciousness and wisdom, to the ways in which they are manifest.

Utilizing Emotion ● The perspective of the Buddha Families recognizes the positive potential within our feelings. "There's a positive side to the energy of every emotion," Tsoknyi Rinpoche, one of my teachers, explains. "Within attachment and clinging, there's a discriminating wisdom—if you don't want anything or care about anything, then you don't discriminate. Without the energy of jealousy, nothing matters; then there's no progress—it gives you the energy to get things done. The same with anger—its energy can lend a sharpness and clarity to what you do."

Among the broad range of Buddhist approaches to strong disturbing emotions, there are three main stances. Which one we choose will depend on our abilities, our inclinations, and the methods we are drawn to.

In the first approach, we try to abandon disturbing emotions: whenever they arise, we attempt to drop them or to be continually on guard against their arising in the mind. A goal of this kind of mindfulness practice is the cessation of disturbing emotions entirely.

In another approach the practitioner tries to transform disturbing emotions into more positive ones. This strategy opposes each negative state with an antidote: loving-kindness for aggression, say, or equanimity for clinging. A goal of this practice is to replace a negative emotion with its more wholesome opposite.

In the third, the Vajrayana approach, disturbing emotions themselves become part of the spiritual path. Instead of eliminating them, this approach utilizes the disturbing emotions at a subtle level. This path poses perhaps the toughest challenge, and so is known as the "steep path." The easiest path is "simply [to] give up negative actions and emotions," says Chokyi Nyima. "It is easier to give them up than to transform them, and easier to transform them than to utilize them, to take them as a path." Taking emotions as a path, he adds, is "risky but also very advantageous."

It is because of this risk that using strong emotions as a path requires the help and guidance of a qualified Vajrayana teacher. But simply understanding a bit about this steep approach can help us relate to our emotions as friends rather than enemies. We can see them as opportunities for wisdom.

The Vajrayana path has several specific practices designed to work with these energies, such as meditations on a mandala designed to evoke and transmute one of the five emotional energies. The specific methods are individualized, given by a Vajrayana teacher to a student to suit her particular temperament and tendencies. But at a more general level, there are principles involved that are instructive to anyone interested in understanding the path of inner alchemy.

Paradoxically, the stronger an emotion, the more useful it can be as a vehicle for awakening—though only if one knows how to use it that way. One reason, as Tsoknyi Rinpoche explains it, is that "coarser thoughts and strong emotions are more readily noticeable" than are the subtle undercurrents of background thought and feeling or the daydreams and fantasies that can seduce and lull us during our waking hours or during our sessions of meditation. Strong emotions are like a jolt in awareness; they arouse and energize our attention. For that reason, he adds, every emotion gives us the opportunity to awaken.

How does this transformation of emotion begin? An ancient Tibetan text, "The Aspiration of Samantabhadra," gives some guidance. The opportunity for a confused, distressing emotion to be transformed into its enlightened aspect comes when we can be with the energy of the emotion without clinging or rejecting—with equanimity, resting unperturbed in clear awareness.

The key is in the quality of awareness within the emotion. Ordinarily, we try to escape a disturbing emotion because it is so unpleasant. In this approach, however, those emotions are approached, not avoided. "The Vajrayana," says Trungpa, "speaks of looking properly, directly at the emotion and feeling, its naked quality," without preconceptions attached.

As Tsoknyi Rinpoche explains, "If ego-oriented clinging is removed, then wisdom can emerge with more intensity from strong emotions." He gives the example of two ways of being angry. "Ego anger"—our usual kind—is selfish, heavy, rigid. But the wisdom energy of anger comes and goes lightly, dissolving easily.

Ordinarily when we are angry, he points out, the anger and our ego-centered clinging are mixed together. "When angry, investigate the clinging," Tsoknyi Rinpoche advises. "The feeling itself is no problem—it's the clinging that's a problem. If we retain the rigid selfishness, then we will do something that hurts others. When angry, the selfishness, the ego-clinging, needs to be released. What we need is to do away with the ego: energy comes, ego gone." While that may sound easy, he adds, the danger here is in thinking we know how to "dissolve ego" when we are actually reinforcing a subtle sense of ego through clinging.

Those who have mastered this path have typically put years of diligent practice into the effort. As that practice comes to fruition, Tsoknyi Rinpoche says, "If there's no owner or director of the emotion, just its potency remains." In other words, as clinging wanes, the aggression of anger dissolves, leaving the raw forcefulness of the emotional energy itself.

The way to this release of clinging is through a heightened awareness. As Lama Gendun says, "The only difference between an emotion and its corresponding wisdom is the presence or absence of awareness. When we are aware of the true nature of things, we see the Five Wisdoms. From this perspective, no emotions are inherently bad, impure, or undesirable. It is simply that we are not seeing the emotion for what it really is." In other words, we can perceive an emotion as one of the Five Wisdoms—if we have mastered methods for being free of ego.

Self-Liberating Emotions ● Ordinary anger is akin to ice: a frozen set of mind, a fixed stance of irritable hostility; the pure energy before it has frozen into anger is akin to water. When an emotion like anger arises in our minds, advises Tsoknyi Rinpoche, "The energy behind the anger doesn't have to be rejected, just the concepts and thoughts that fuel it. They can be released while the energy is still present. Then the anger turns into mirror-like wisdom, a clear precision."

Likewise, with desire, the moment "attention becomes interested in ego-oriented desires, then it's, How do I get it?" says Tsoknyi. "But if it's egoless energy, then it's only seeing clearly what is being desired."

From the Vajrayana perspective, then, the point is not to discard emotions but rather to liberate them. There is a danger here, however: if we lack the basic tool for liberating our emotions—if we are unable to let go of the subtle clinging and aversion at their root—then, says Tsoknyi, "you just have another emotion—you're not free."

Ideally, emotions become self-liberated, or freed of the overlay of our habitual reactions, the moment they arise in the mind. "An emotion arises, and then there's an instant attempt to cling. If that is released, the emotion is freed by itself," says Tsoknyi Rinpoche. The key to such self-liberation, he adds, is to drop the clinging. If so, "the moment the thought is released, the emotion dissolves," leaving its pure energy.

A text by the Buddhist master Longchen Rabjam puts this level of accomplishment quite beautifully:

> Whatever appears and whatever arises,
> All things that proliferate and abide
> As dynamic expressions of awareness
> Such as the five emotional poisons
> No matter how they arise, even as they do,
> There is recognition, perfection of their dynamic energy,
> And their natural fading, leaving no trace.

From the perspective of using disturbing emotions as a path, Tulku Urgyen has said that, "in essence, the three poisons are the three wisdoms." No one doubts, he explains, that if one ate real poison, one could die. However, in Tibet there were herbal medicines that included minute amounts of poison, and these medicines could cure diseases. In the same way, he says, "the suffering of beings can be transformed into wisdom."

Tsoknyi Rinpoche comments, "It is very important for people to know that it is possible to transform emotion, to feel confident that this is possible." This very transformation is emotional alchemy, according to Tsoknyi: "If you follow what is being said, and apply yourself to it, that *is* therapy."

The Levels of Alchemy ● This alchemy—transmuting emotions —can occur at many levels. When this transmutation takes the form of spiritual practices like the Buddha Families method, the requirements for skillful execution are quite steep: being free from even the most subtle level of clinging to the mental habits that make up the edifice of ego. Freedom of that sort is in itself spiritual liberation.

These are rarefied attainments and practices. But for those who simply aspire to some inner freedom, the model of the Buddha Families can be an inspiration for how we relate to our own emotions, if only in leading us to see them as opportunities rather than as threats. Instead of seeking to suppress or abandon our emotions, we can open to them with mindfulness.

And in terms of working with our own emotional patterns, even at the relative level we can recognize adaptive qualities. The judgmental inner voice of the perfectionism schema represents a negative twist on an underlying ability to make sharp distinctions. The arrogant conceit of the entitlement schema harbors a confidence that could be harnessed in positive directions. The neediness and hurt of the deprivation schema can give rise to an empathic and caring awareness.

In this sense, when we bring a mindful awareness to our ordinary experiences of negative emotions, it represents a gradual approach, a progression from rigidity to openness. That nonreactive awareness, if focused on the sensations in the body, can feel the energy of the emotion, letting it relax from constriction to a freer flow and release. If we bring that investigative quality to our thoughts, it can sometimes yield a spontaneous insight. In short, when we relax in a mindful presence with our emotional patterns, through the natural qualities of awareness, they alchemize.

The equanimity that allows us just to be with a strong emotion can offer a new perspective, letting us relate differently to the experience. If we are not under the spell of the emotions' story line, instead of assuming that we have to react or act from them, we can shift our focus to learning from them. We can invite them into our awareness and spend time just being with them, not thinking that they define us, but listening attentively to any insights they have for us, taking these to heart, and then letting the feelings pass in their own time.

In this way even disturbing emotions can be like visiting friends, enriching our lives—if we use them that way. Aung Sang Sui Kyi, the courageous leader of the opposition to Burma's military dictatorship is also a longtime student of Sayadaw U Pandita, a mindfulness master and one of my own teachers. Sui Kyi once said that she was not angry with her oppressors, the military dictators of Burma, because she had no fear of them—she had equanimity. She has used her years of house arrest in part as a chance to pursue her meditation practice, even as she kept alive the spark of political resistance among her countrymen.

Her composure and serenity, even after years of threats and bullying, bears witness to one of the greatest gifts of the human spirit: the ability to transform adversity by awakening to a greater potential within. Her equanimity allowed her to send a message of hope and solidarity against political tyranny. Aung Sang Sui Kyi found an opportunity to transform fear and anger into compassionate action.

Of course, compassion is a natural quality of being, one that spiritual practice can enhance, but that stems from our basic human essence.

Hearing the Truth ● One of the things I love about being a therapist is the opportunity to see how honest people can be with themselves, how much trust and openness comes out of that honesty, and the power of truth. The truth of someone else's personal story resonates with your own experience—it's one way to get a clear sense of the interconnectedness among us all.

"What is so profoundly transformative," says Pema Chodron, an American Buddhist nun, "is the courage to look at yourself and not to give up on yourself when you see negative qualities. In facing these things we develop a compassion for our shared humanity. When we are willing to expose our defects, we expose some kind of heart to other people."

She adds, "Curiously enough, people respond more to our honesty about our imperfections. People resonate with the bravery of someone who is courageous enough to express their pain." At the relative level, we are connected through our shared personal stories just as, at an ultimate level, we're connected through our shared human essence.

Touching one another's truthfulness reminds me of how the immune system operates to keep us healthy. Cells of the immune system flow throughout the entire body in the bloodstream, contacting every other kind of cell and momentarily linking with them through lock-and-key receptors that establish their shared identity within the greater whole, then moving on. It's as though the immune cells are circulating through the community of the body, asking every other cell along the way, "How are we alike?" And then on to the next: "How are we alike?"

Through this mutual recognition, the immune cells establish a solidarity within the vast and diverse array of cells that make up the body. And when a virus or bacteria enters that threatens disease, the immune cells rush to the site, selflessly sacrificing themselves to protect the whole. In a similar way, when we hear someone else's story, it naturally draws a compassionate response from us.

A Wise Love ● When we cultivate mindfulness as a practice, we train our mind in the continuity of this awareness, bringing it to whatever we encounter. Much of this book has focused on how we can enhance mindfulness in our lives. But what mindfulness ultimately trains us in is already a natural quality of our minds—it's simply the full presence of awareness, which ordinarily gets covered over by habits of inattention.

This awareness can occur quite spontaneously in our lives—when we are in the stillness of nature, for instance, watching a brilliant sunset, in a moment of genuine love, or a creative project that absorbs and focuses our attention. Sometimes the qualities of full awareness can become spontaneously present through acts of compassion or through genuinely honest and skillful communication.

When we can be open to feelings we've been avoiding, perhaps for years, we find that we no longer have to be afraid of them. To be able to look honestly at our own minds, our emotional reactions and patterns, takes courage. To look uncompromisingly at our fears and our attachments and not run away, blunt our feelings, or hide behind pretense takes a strength of heart. Such honesty demands that we empathize with ourselves, staying connected to our experience no matter what unpleasantness, pain, or discomfort that brings us. It amounts to an act of kindness toward ourselves.

But a great sense of compassion for others can naturally grow out of facing our own suffering, our own imperfections. From that acknowledgment can grow a profound acceptance of, and empathy for, others. There is not only the opportunity for a deepening of insight through being with the truth of suffering, but a deepening of compassion. Our sense of separateness can dissolve. Less absorbed in our own suffering, we can be more open to that of others.

Freeing our minds can result in having more compassion for others. The ultimate freedom means letting go of our habitual patterns completely—a level of freedom, of course, that comes only with extensive spiritual practice. This path finally leads to a freedom from clinging that lets us avoid starting those habits up all over again. Instead, we can experience a new kind of psychological health—liberation from the pull of emotional habit itself offers a freshness and flexibility of mind, a lightness of being.

Buddhist scriptures refer to liberation as freedom from both fears and hopes—beyond recoiling from, or grasping at, life. That freedom from inner preoccupations allows one to be more aware of others, more responsive to even subtle needs in the moment.

That lightness makes possible a genuine empathy toward others. Once we are freed from the pull of our schemas—of our habitual ways of defending, reassuring, and protecting the self—we are more available to see to the needs of others. Not needing something for ourselves from them, we are free to be attentive and available, generous and kind. That is why Buddhist teachings say that from egolessness comes genuine compassion.

The Zen master Ryokan, expressing this compassionate spirit, said, "If only my robes were wide enough to hold all the suffering people of the world."

In the end, emotional alchemy boils down to wisdom and compassion. The meltdown of our habits of clinging and pushing away, and of centering everything on ourselves, reveals a wise compassion. There emerges a sense of interconnectedness and a deep wish for everyone, all of us, to experience that freedom.

Bearing Witness ● Bernie Glassman, a Zen teacher of Jewish origins, was telling me about a meditation retreat he led at the site of the Auschwitz concentration camp. Hundreds of thousands of Jews, Gypsies, Polish resistance fighters, and other "enemies of the Nazi state" had passed through this concentration camp in Poland on their journey to death. Now, more than five decades later, people from several countries had gathered together at this grim memorial to inhumanity, to bear witness on retreat.

Bernie's stance at the retreat was that of mindfulness: neither resisting nor judging, just accepting the realities, the feelings and thoughts, as they came and went. He simply watched and listened to people's reactions. He saw that the Germans felt guilty and the Poles felt helpless in the face of this monument to human cruelty, and he felt compassion for their historic legacies.

"What was it like to hear their stories?" I asked.

"At the beginning you're very aware of everyone's differences," Bernie said. "Some very raw and painful words were said. But you just sit with it and listen to it all. Eventually everyone feels heard. They start to lighten up, once they feel heard and cared about. Then, after a while, you feel that you're just bearing witness to all of it: the pain and sorrow, the joys and triumphs. As we all settled into this attitude of just bearing witness, a feeling emerged of a connection between everyone, even through all the differences."

Just as Bernie brought a neutral, witnessing awareness to the turbulent emotions of his fellow retreatants, we can do the same with the feelings that come and go within our own hearts. Emotions run amok "are responsible for all the conflict in the world," says Lama Yeshe, "from two small children fighting over a piece of candy to two huge nations fighting over their very existence."

Likewise, schemas can be seen as operating globally, on a collective level. Sometimes I look at the world as one big dysfunctional family, different nations acting out their entitled, controlling, subjugated, needy, or rebellious modes. Yet there are those moments of gaining a transcendent perspective, such as when the astronauts who first circled the globe described our verdant planet from space, a unity with national boundaries dissolved.

Our emotional patterns can be a force that separates people or, if we free ourselves from them, that connects us all. It's up to us. When we can respect others' differences without having to agree with them, we can listen to one another's perspectives and hear one another's stories. Bearing witness to our collective schemas, we can walk one another home.

The work of making these clouds in the mind more transparent helps shrink them as obstructions. It all depends on how we use our emotional experience, whether in life or in practice.

The road forks. One path leads to further entanglement, reactivity, and a thickening of the fog of confusion, the other toward the refinement of awareness and the unfolding of compassionate wisdom. The choice is ours, in every moment.

Guide to Resources

For mindfulness meditation   Many approaches to the practice of mindfulness can be found within the various schools of Buddhism, each emphasizing differing aspects of the basic practice. I have studied several and found that each can be useful in its own way. Here is information about where to learn some of the mindfulness methods I've found particularly helpful in working with emotions.

If you want to learn mindfulness, there are many excellent centers for training in mindfulness meditation worldwide. The Insight Meditation Society schedule is at www.dharma.org. For information on Jon Kabat-Zinn's mindfulness programs, go to www.umass.edu/cfm.

One of the best sources for the many courses offered in the United States and abroad, most of them suitable for beginners, is the *Inquiring Mind*, a newsletter available from Inquiring Mind, P.O. Box 9999, North Berkeley Station, Berkeley, California 94709. If you can't get to a mindfulness retreat, a correspondence course is available through www.soundstrue.com.

Finding a schema therapist and learning more about schema therapy   If you want to understand schemas in more detail and to explore specific strategies for dealing with a given schema, I recommend *Reinventing Your Life* by Jeffrey Young and Janet Klosko (Plume, 1993).

Those therapists who have been trained by Dr. Jeffrey Young and his associates are most experienced in schema therapy. The pool of those who practice schema therapy is becoming quite extensive as well as international. To find out if there is a schema therapist in your area, you can go to www.schematherapy.com or call the Cognitive Therapy Center of New York, 212-588-8880, and ask for a referral.

For information on emotional alchemy   For more about my workshops or related information, please visit my Web site at www.emotional-insight.com.

Notes

page 7 "**In almost every bad situation**": Nyanaponika Thera, *The Power of Mindfulness* (Kandy, Sri Lanka: Buddhist Publication Society, 1971), p. 24.

page 30 "**Our most dangerous enemies**": Nyanaponika Thera, *The Power of Mindfulness* (Kandy, Sri Lanka: Buddhist Publication Society, 1971), p. 26.

page 31 **Zen and the orienting response:** See Daniel Goleman, *The Meditative Mind* (New York: Jeremy Tarcher, 1988).

page 34 **Mindfulness strengthens ability to tone down disturbing emotions:** Richard Davidson, Jon Kabat-Zinn, et al., "Alterations in brain and immune function produced by mindfulness meditation." Working paper, Laboratory for Affective Neuroscience, University of Wisconsin at Madison, 1999.

page 37 "**The opposite of investigation is assuming**": Narayan and Michael Liebenson Grady, "Investigation," *Insight,* Fall 1996, p. 36.

page 39 "**Without the eyeglasses of concentration**": Sayadaw U Pandita, *In This Very Life* (Boston: Wisdom Publications, 1992), p. 53.

page 40 "**The steadying of the mind**": Tulku Thondup, *The Healing Power of Mind* (Boston: Shambhala, 1996), p. 32.

page 40 "**The ability to let go**": Ajahn Nyanadhammo, interviewed in the *Forest Sangha Newsletter,* Summer 1998, p. 4.

page 56 **The basketball video:** Ulric Neisser, *Cognition and Reality* (San Francisco: Freeman, 1976).

page 56 **Anxiety and selective perception:** Lester Luborsky, Barton Blinder, and Jean Schimek, "Looking, recalling, and GSR as a function of defense," *Journal of Abnormal Psychology* 70, 1965, pp. 270–280.

page 58 "**A momentary impulse**": Nyanaponika Thera, *The Power of Mindfulness* (Kandy, Sri Lanka: Buddhist Publication Society, 1971), p. 50.

page 59 **Neuroscience view of habit:** Gerald Edelman, *Neural Darwinism* (New York: Basic Books, 1987).

page 60 **"The momentum of habit"** Amaro Bhikku, *Silent Rain* (Redwood Valley, California: Abhayagiri Buddhist Monastery, 1994), p. 125.

page 71 **Maladaptive interpersonal patterns:** Mardi Horowitz, *Maladaptive Interpersonal Schemas* (New York: Guilford Press, 1989).

page 71 **"Core conflicts":** Lester Luborsky et al., *Who Will Benefit from Psychotherapy?* (New York: Basic Books, 1988).

page 73 **Dr. Jeffrey Young's model of maladaptive schemas:** See Jeffrey Young and Janet Klosko, *Reinventing Your Life* (New York: Plume, 1993).

page 90 **Janet Jackson:** Steve Pond interviewed Janet Jackson in *US,* January 1988.

page 107 **The amygdala as an emotional storehouse:** Daniel Goleman, *Emotional Intelligence* (New York: Bantam, 1995).

page 110 **A hot amygdala:** Richard Davidson, "Affective Neuroscience," *Psychology Bulletin,* August 2000.

page 119 **"Wisdom, free from the clouds":** Prayer to Manjushri, translator unknown, unpublished.

page 144 **The magic quarter-second:** Benjamin Libet, "Unconscious cerebral initiative and the role of conscious will in voluntary action," *Behavioral and Brain Sciences,* volume 8, 1985, pp. 529–566.

page 155 **"Everyone knows how panic":** William James, *Psychology: Briefer Course* (Cambridge: Harvard University Press, 1890/1984), p. 42.

page 159 **Changing negative stereotypes:** Peter M. Gollwitzer, "Implementation intentions: Strong effects of simple plans," *American Psychologist,* July 1999, pp. 493–503.

page 160 **"Mr. Howard":** Lester Luborsky et al., *Who Will Benefit from Psychotherapy?* (New York: Basic Books, 1988).

page 185 **Breast cancer support groups:** David Spiegel, *Living Beyond Limits* (New York: Fawcett, 1993).

page 186 **Healing effect of private journals:** James Pennebaker, *Opening Up: The Healing Power of Expressing Emotions* (New York: Guilford Press, 1997).

page 193 **"That closely interwoven tissue of our habits":** Nyanaponika Thera, *The Power of Mindfulness* (Kandy, Sri Lanka: Buddhist Publication Society, 1971), p. 52.

page 193 **"When you are practicing Zazen":** Suzuki Roshi, *Zen Mind, Beginner's Mind* (New York: Weatherhill, 1971), p. 40.

page 197 **"Step back *within* yourself":** Marsha Linehan, *Skills Training Manual for Treating Borderline Personality Disorder* (New York: Guilford, 1993), p. 63.

page 200 **Mindfulness and depression:** John Teasdale et al., "How does cognitive therapy prevent depressive relapse and why should attentional control (mindfulness) training help?" *Behavioral Research and Therapy*, vol. 33, 1995, pp. 25–39.

page 213 **It's much like those experiments:** Robert Anton Wilson, *Quantum Psychology* (Phoenix: New Falcon, 1993).

page 262 **"You risk the loss of your childhood sense"**: Michael Barnsley, quoted in James Gleick and Eliot Porter, *Nature's Chaos* (New York: Viking, 1990), p. 16.

page 262 **"Zoom in smaller than life-size"**: K. C. Cole, *The Universe and the Teacup* (New York: Harcourt, Brace, and Co., 1997), p. 59.

page 263 **"If you can make the mind very focused"**: Jack Kornfield, quoted in Mu Soeng Sunim, *Heart Sutra* (Cumberland, Rhode Island: Primary Point Press, 1996), p. 20.

page 266 William Segal, interviewed in Tracy Cochran and Jeff Zaleski, *Transformations: Awakening to the Sacred in Ourselves* (New York: Bell Tower, 1995).

page 266 **"Increasingly one has moments"**: Steven Goodman, interviewed in *Inquiring Mind*, Winter 1999.

page 268 **"Bureaucracy of feeling and perception"**: Chogyam Trungpa, *Cutting Through Spiritual Materialism* (Berkeley: Shambala, 1973), p. 126.

page 269 **"Most of the time, our perception is illusory"**: Lama Yeshe, *Becoming Your Own Therapist* (Boston: Lama Yeshe Wisdom Archive, 1999), p. 29.

page 269 **"In the minds of ordinary people"**: Geshe Rabten (translated by Stephen Batchelor), *The Mind and Its Functions* (Mt. Pelerin, Switzerland: Tharpa Choeling, 1979), p. 42.

page 271 **"There is no attainment of a higher self"**: Mark Epstein, *Thoughts Without a Thinker* (New York: Basic Books, 1995), p. 154.

page 272 **"What is called in chaos theory"**: Jon Kabat-Zinn, *Wherever You Go, There You Are* (New York: Hyperion, 1994), p. 240.

page 273 **"The ego is the wrong conception"**: Lama Yeshe, *Becoming Your Own Therapist* (Boston: Lama Yeshe Wisdom Archive, 1999), p. 26.

page 277 **"A Tibetan method"**: Tai Situpa Rinpoche, *Relative World, Ultimate Mind* (Boston: Shambala, 1992).

page 282 **"Perishable, fleeting, passing"**: Chokyi Nyima Rinpoche, *Indisputable Truth* (Boudhanath, Nepal: Rangjung Yeshe Publications, 1996), p. 23.

page 284 **"May my mind"**: Gampopa, traditional Tibetan chant.

page 287 **"When your negative mind arises"**: Lama Yeshe, *Becoming Your Own Therapist* (Boston: Lama Yeshe Wisdom Archive, 1999), pp. 27, 12.

page 287 **"Too concerned with what's going to happen"**: Lama Yeshe, *Becoming Your Own Therapist* (Boston: Lama Yeshe Wisdom Archive, 1999), p. 13.

page 287 **"Habitual tendency"**: Chokyi Nyima Rinpoche, *Indisputable Truth* (Boudhanath, Nepal: Rangjung Yeshe Publications, 1996), p. 49.

page 294 **"One is to ignore it"** and **"If we become obsessed"**: His Holiness the Dalai Lama, *Worlds in Harmony* (Berkeley: Parallax Press, 1998), pp. 27, 37.

page 297 **"The absence of some kind of independent"**: His Holiness the Dalai Lama, "Basically Good," *Shambala Sun*, May 1999, p. 57.

page 298 **"The relative principle"**: Tai Situpa Rinpoche, *Relative World, Ultimate Mind* (Boston: Shambala, 1992), p. 118.

page 312 **The five energies of the Buddha families**: Chogyam Trungpa explains these in his books *Cutting Through Spiritual Materialism* (Berkeley: Shambala, 1973) and *Journey Without Goal* (Boston: Shambala, 1994).

page 314 **"It is easier"**: Chokyi Nyima Rinpoche, *Indisputable Truth* (Boudhanath, Nepal: Rangjung Yeshe Publications, 1996), p. 50.

page 314 **"The Vajrayana"**: Chogyam Trungpa, *Cutting Through Spiritual Materialism* (Berkeley: Shambala, 1973), p. 239.

page 315 **"The only difference"**: Lama Gendun, *Working with Emotions* (Boston: Wisdom Publications, 1993), p. 39.

page 316 **"Whatever appears"**: Longchen Rabjam (translated under the direction of Chagdud Tulku by Richard Barron), *The Precious Treasury of the Way of Abiding* (Junction City, California: Padma Publishing, 1998), p. 15.

page 318 **"What is so profoundly transformative"**: Pema Chodron, "It starts with uncertainty," *Shambala Sun*, November 1999, p. 58.

Acknowledgments

I gratefully acknowledge the help of many beings in creating this book:

All of my teachers, who have shared with me a treasury of wisdom through their skillful and compassionate guidance: His Holiness the Dalai Lama, Nyoshul Khen Rinpoche, and Tulku Urgyen Rinpoche and his four sons who carry on the practice lineage—Chokyi Nyima Rinpoche, Chokling Rinpoche, Tsoknyi Rinpoche, Mingyur Rinpoche, Sayadaw U Pandita, and Neemkaroli Baba.

My husband, Daniel Goleman, who has lived and breathed this work with me, and selflessly contributed his editing skills and enriched this work with his knowledge of cognitive and brain science—and for his great love and loyal companionship, and being great to talk and laugh with.

My clients and those who participated in workshops, for their courageous honesty and trust and for making this work come alive.

My family, for their great hearts, wise perspectives, and enduring love, including Julie Bennett-Blue, Bill Bennett, Diana Broderick, Gilda Barracano, Jack Blue, Hanuman, Gov and Hazel Goleman.

Erik Hein Schmidt—though he insists he was "just pontificating"—he has been an endless source of knowledge, wisdom, and refreshingly witty perspectives. He wishes to pass this acknowledgment on to his teachers, Tulku Urgyen Rinpoche, Chokyi Nyima Rinpoche, and Tulku Pema Wangyal.

Jeffrey Young, for his ingenious guidance in schema therapy and for wonderfully combining a sensitive perceptiveness with greatness of vision.

Jon Kabat-Zinn, for his inspiring guidance during my internship in the University of Massachusetts mindfulness-based stress reduction clinic, for his pioneering, streetwise wisdom, and for preserving the integrity of the tradition of mindfulness while making this practice accessible to the greater population.

Jessica Brackman, for her insightful editorial suggestions and her stead-fast support at every stage.

Cathy Flannigan, for her generous and brilliant consultations on the details of schema therapy, her encouragement in branching out into new territory with this work, and her delightful Irish laugh.

My readers: Lynn Schroeder, Sunanda Marcus, Lila Anderson, Zuleikha, and Deborah Klimburg, for their incisive comments and enthusiasm—and to Naomi Wolf, for her exceptional editorial suggestions. Susan Griffin, for her valuable guidance on writing.

Sharon Salzberg, for her kind supportiveness, clear advice, and magnanimous spirit at every stage of this book project. Diana Rogers, for her discerning comments and loving support. Ram Dass, for his inspiring conversations about our work and for his unconventional wisdom.

Richard Gere, for inspired artistic vision and creative advice. Jonathan Cott, for his astute comments and illuminating sources on alchemy.

Josh Baran, for his enthusiasm in trying to find the right subtitle and to others who joined in: Amy Gross, Mark Epstein, Helen Tworkov, Mark Matousek, and Carey Lowell.

Anne Milliken and Jane Wright, for their healing wisdom. David Berman, for helping me develop a healthy relationship with my computer.

Joseph Goldstein and Sharon Salzberg, for our many years of traveling together to remote Asian lands to study with our meditation masters, receiving many of the teachings that inform this work. And for others who helped me make connections with my teachers: Francisco Varela, Erik Pema Kunsang, Surya Das, Alan Clements, and Robert Thurman. Marcia Schmidt, for her selfless dedication to making dharma teachings available. Achan Amaro and Tulku Thondup, for their wise counsel.

John Erskine, Mads Julius Neilsen, and Al Shapere, for consultations on physics. And to my friends on the retreat land in Denmark, for discussing the connections between physics and dharma late into the night under the Nordic twilight—moments like that make me miss working on this book.

My editor Linda Loewenthal, for her precise, brilliant editorial suggestions and for sharing my vision; for taking this book project seriously, yet always being ready to laugh; and for making the world of publishing feel like home. And to everyone at Harmony Books for their dedicated support and heartfelt enthusiasm.

My agent Eileen Cope, for her amazing skill at what she does, her invaluable guidance, enthusiastic support, and for making it possible for this book to find the right home.

For a plentitude of different kinds of help: Amy Fox, Iris Marchai, Beth Ellen Rosenbaum, Rowan Foster, Buzz Bussewitz, Jami Fisher, Catherine Ingram, Kate Wheeler, Jocelyn Sylvester, Steve Armstrong, Deborah Wolf, Stephan Rechtstaffan, Gretchen Hayden, Bodhi, and Yeshe.

And to the many beings who have inspired me without ever knowing it, through the gifts of their wise hearts.

Index

abandonment schema, 68, 69, 75–77, 168
  emotional trade-off for, 175
  examples of, 95, 143–44, 147–48, 169, 179–80
  inappropriateness of, 110
  memory and, 179
  mind reading and, 105
  naming of, 125
  in relationships, 208–9, 216, 219–20
  wise reflection with, 175–77
  withdrawal and, 142
acceptance, 35–36
  equanimity and, 21, 24
  of inner turmoil, 23
  of unlovability, 84
Achan Cha, 273
actions
  automatic, 157–58
  emotion linked to, 143
  impulses to, 145, 149
  intentional, 155–56
  magic quarter-second before, 144
  physical movement, 156–57
  power to avoid, 145–46
  and schema therapy, 120
adaptability, 70, 294
adaptive mind states, 66, 68–69
addictions, 243–44
adversity, transforming, 294–95
afflictive emotions, 154–56, 192, 227, 300
Ajahn Nyanadhammo, 40
Alchemist, The (Coelho), 6
alchemy
  inner, 3–15, 253, 314
  levels of, 316–18
  metaphor of, 6–7
  transformation via, 6, 252, 307–18, 320
Alcoholics Anonymous, 159

Allen, Woody, 195
altruistic attitude, 308
Amaro, Achan, 60, 127, 140, 149, 176
amygdala, 34, 178
  emotions and, 108–9
  negative thoughts and, 110, 141
  perception in, 190
  schema reality in, 182
  schema triggers and, 107–8, 141–42
anger
  avoiding action in, 145–46
  dissolving, 37
  experiencing, 130, 137, 226, 246
  giving way to, 155
  loving-kindness vs., 154
  making use of, 172, 226, 234
  mindful alchemy of, 137–38
  mindfulness of, 123
  mistrust schema and, 168
  subjugation schema and, 79, 81, 168
  transmutation of, 311–12, 313, 315
antarayame (knower of the heart), 185
antidotes, 154–56, 163, 170–71, 201–2
anusayas (dormant tendencies), 69
apathy, transmutation of, 311–12
approach avoidance, 110
Aristotle, 130
arrested development, 228
assumptions, 37
  challenge to, 194–95, 199
  distortion of, 42, 285
  emotions and, 192
  perceptual, 280–81
attention, 8, 35, 198, 201, 203
  and avoidance, 171
  boredom vs., 32
  continuation of, 44
  distraction vs., 30, 56, 124, 294

About the Author

TARA BENNETT-GOLEMAN, M.A., is a psychotherapist and teacher who has developed emotional alchemy, an innovative integration of mindfulness meditation and Buddhist psychology with a new dimension in cognitive therapy. For the last decade she has taught workshops on this approach with her husband Daniel Goleman, author of *Emotional Intelligence*. Bennett-Goleman has studied for more than two decades with Buddhist masters from Tibet, Nepal, and Burma. Her postgraduate training, at the Cognitive Therapy Center of New York, was in schema therapy, which focuses on changing self-defeating emotional patterns. Her humanitarian projects have included working for Tibetan causes and counseling the elderly and terminally ill. She is a longtime student of Japanese flower arranging and tea ceremony, as well as Kathak Indian dance. She lives in Massachusetts, where she affectionately spoils her two horses.